HOLLY KING

EDGING TOWARDS THE MYSTERIOUS

LINDA JANSMA | FRANCINE PAUL

The Robert McLaughlin Gallery
Thames Art Gallery
Musée des beaux-arts de Sherbrooke
Art Mûr
Musée du Bas-Saint-Laurent

Éditeurs / Publishers

The Robert McLaughlin Gallery
72 Queen Street., Civic Centre
Oshawa, ON L1H 3Z3
www.rmg.on.ca

Éditions Art Mûr
5826, rue St-Hubert
Montréal, QC H2S 2L7
T. 514.933.0711 • F. 514.933.0721
www.artmur.com

Thames Art Gallery
75 William St. N.
Chatham, ON N7M 4L4
www.chatham-kent.ca/ThamesArtGallery

Musée des beaux-arts de Sherbooke
241, rue Dufferin
Sherbrooke, QC J1H 4M3
www.mbas.qc.ca

Musée du Bas-Saint-Laurent
300, rue Saint-Pierre
Rivière-du-Loup, QC G5R 3V3
www.mbsl.qc.ca

Catalogue d'une exposition tenue à la /
Catalogue of exhibitions held at :

The Robert McLaughlin Gallery, January 9 – April 17, 2016; Thames Art Gallery, May 13 – July 10, 2016; Musée des beaux-arts de Sherbrooke, October 1, 2016 - January 22, 2017; Galerie Art Mûr, March 5 – April 23, 2016; Musée du Bas-Saint-Laurent, June 8 - October 9, 2017

Couverture / cover

Holly King, *Chalk Shoreline*, 2013
épreuve à développement chromogène / chromogenic print
122 x 152 cm

Publication

Direction de la publication / Publication Director : Art Mûr
Graphic Design / conception graphique : Mike Patten
Photo Credits / crédits photographiques : Don Corman,
Guy l'Heureux, Brian Merrett, Mike Patten
Révision française / French Revision : Jennifer Couëlle, Anaïs Castro
Révision anglaise / English Revision : Edwin Janzen, Anaïs Castro
Traduction / Translation : Colette Tougas, James Rae, Anaïs Castro
Impression / Printing : Deschamps

Library and Archives Canada Cataloguing in Publication

Holly King : edging towards the mysterious / curated by Linda Jansma.
Catalogue of a traveling exhibition held at the Robert McLaughlin Gallery, Oshawa, Ontario, January 9 to April 17, 2016 and at four additional venues thereafter.
Co-published by: Thames Art Gallery, Chatham,
Musée des beaux-arts de Sherbooke, Sherbrooke and
Musée du Bas-Saint-Laurent, Rivière-du-Loup, Art Mûr, Montréal
Text in English and French.
ISBN 978-1-926589-89-3 (hardcover)

1. King, Holly, 1957- --Exhibitions. 2. Photography, Artistic--Exhibitions.
I. Jansma, Linda, writer of added text II. Paul, Francine, writer of added text III. King, Holly, 1957- . Photographs. Selections. IV. Musée des beaux-arts de Sherbrooke, issuing body, host institution V. Musée du Bas-St-Laurent, issuing body, host institution VI. Robert McLaughlin Gallery, issuing body, host institution VII. Thames Art Gallery, issuing body, host institution VIII. Art Mûr (Art gallery), host institution IX. Title: Holly King. X. Title: Holly King. French.

TR647.K59358 2016 779.092 C2015-906931-9E

Distribution

ABC: Art Books Canada
327 Ste. Catherine W., Suite 229
Montréal, Québec H3B 1A2
www.abcartbookscanada.com

TABLE DES MATIÈRES | TABLE OF CONTENTS

2 Introduction
Donna Raetsen-Kemp, Carl Lavoy, Cécile Gélinas,
Rhéal Olivier Lanthier & Françcois St-Jacques, Mélanie Girard

7 *L'invention des paysages, théâtralité et photographie mise en scène chez holly king*
Francine Paul

21 *Invented Landscapes*
Theatricality and the Staged Photography of Holly King
Francine Paul, translation by James Rae

PORTFOLIO I

33 *The Realms of Night*
36 *The Gardens*
40 *Mining Project*
42 *The Viewless Winds*
46 *Forest of Enchantment*
50 *Mirages*
54 *Coming Into View*
58 *The Transcendent Sublime*

61 *The Sublime and Beautiful in the Work of Holly King*
Linda Jansma

73 *Le sublime et le beau dans l'œuvre de Holly King*
Linda Jansma, traduction par Colette Tougas

PORTFOLIO II

84 *Twisted Roots*
88 *Mangroves : Floating Between Two Worlds*
94 *Grand Canyon : Unseen*
100 *English Cliff series*

106 *Edging Towards The Mysterious,* Liste des œuvres / List of works
107 Curriculum vitæ
114 Biographies
116 Remerciements / Acknowledgements

INTRODUCTION

La présente publication est le résultat d'une collaboration entre plusieurs institutions. Deux projets se sont amalgamés afin de créer ce livre qui est la fois un catalogue d'exposition et une monographie. C'est avec enthousiasme que nous avons uni nos ressources pour ce projet. Le dernier ouvrage dédié exclusivement à la production de Holly King a été publié par le Musée canadien de la photographie contemporaine en 1998. Vingt ans plus tard, il semblait important de proposer une nouvelle publication qui engloberait les productions récentes et les œuvres plus anciennes qui sont à l'origine de la recherche artistique de Holly King.

Holly King est connue pour ses photographies, or l'acte photographique lui-même ne représente qu'une parcelle de sa production. Elle est avant tout une artiste multidisciplinaire. Elle peint, sculpte, réalise des performances et photographie. Son travail est précurseur des univers photographiques fictifs créés par une nouvelle génération d'artistes travaillant avec des programmes informatiques tels Photoshop. La plupart de ses œuvres précèdent la manipulation informatique qui prévaut aujourd'hui, et ses univers sont créés de toutes pièces. Holly King réalise des installations composées de tableaux peints, de branches, de cailloux, de sculptures, de papiers et d'un ensemble d'éléments qui s'unissent dans la photographie pour composer un paysage à la fois sublime et mystérieux. Le travail de Holly King a été présenté au Centre George Pompidou à Paris, au Musée d'art contemporain de Mexico, au Museum of Contemporary Canadian Art à Toronto, au Musée d'art contemporain de Macédoine, au Vancouver Contemporary Art Gallery, au Musée national des beaux-arts de Taïwan, au Musée des beaux-arts de Montréal, au Musée national des beaux-arts du Québec, au Musée des beaux-arts du Canada à Ottawa et dans plusieurs centres d'art à travers le monde. Elle compte à son actif plus d'une quarantaine d'expositions individuelles et plus de soixante-dix expositions de groupe.

Cette publication accompagne une série d'expositions qui sera présentée dans plusieurs musées et galeries à travers le Québec et l'Ontario. C'est donc avec beaucoup de plaisir que nos institutions s'unissent afin de vous présenter *Holly King: Edging Towards The Mysterious*. Entrer en contact avec le travail d'Holly King, c'est vivre un sentiment qui a partie liée à la mémoire – un souvenir évasif de ce qui est réel. Afin de rejoindre le monde merveilleux que King met à notre portée, il faut de prime abord admettre que la mémoire ne puisse être fidèle à un récit authentique des faits, qu'elle livre un compte-rendu construit en partie par la réalité qui se modifie, par l'ajout de données fictives et par des distorsions. Nos félicitations, ainsi que toute notre gratitude vont à Holly King.

Nous remercions également Linda Jansma pour sa vision de commissaire qui a permis de créer le concept de l'exposition, ainsi que pour son dévouement et son enthousiasme dans la réalisation de ce projet. Nous sommes ravis de présenter cette publication et remercions Francine Paul et Linda Jansma pour leurs textes réfléchis qui enrichissent le dialogue sur l'ensemble des œuvres mises de l'avant dans cette exposition.

Image : p.3 Atelier de l'artiste / Artist's Studio, 2014

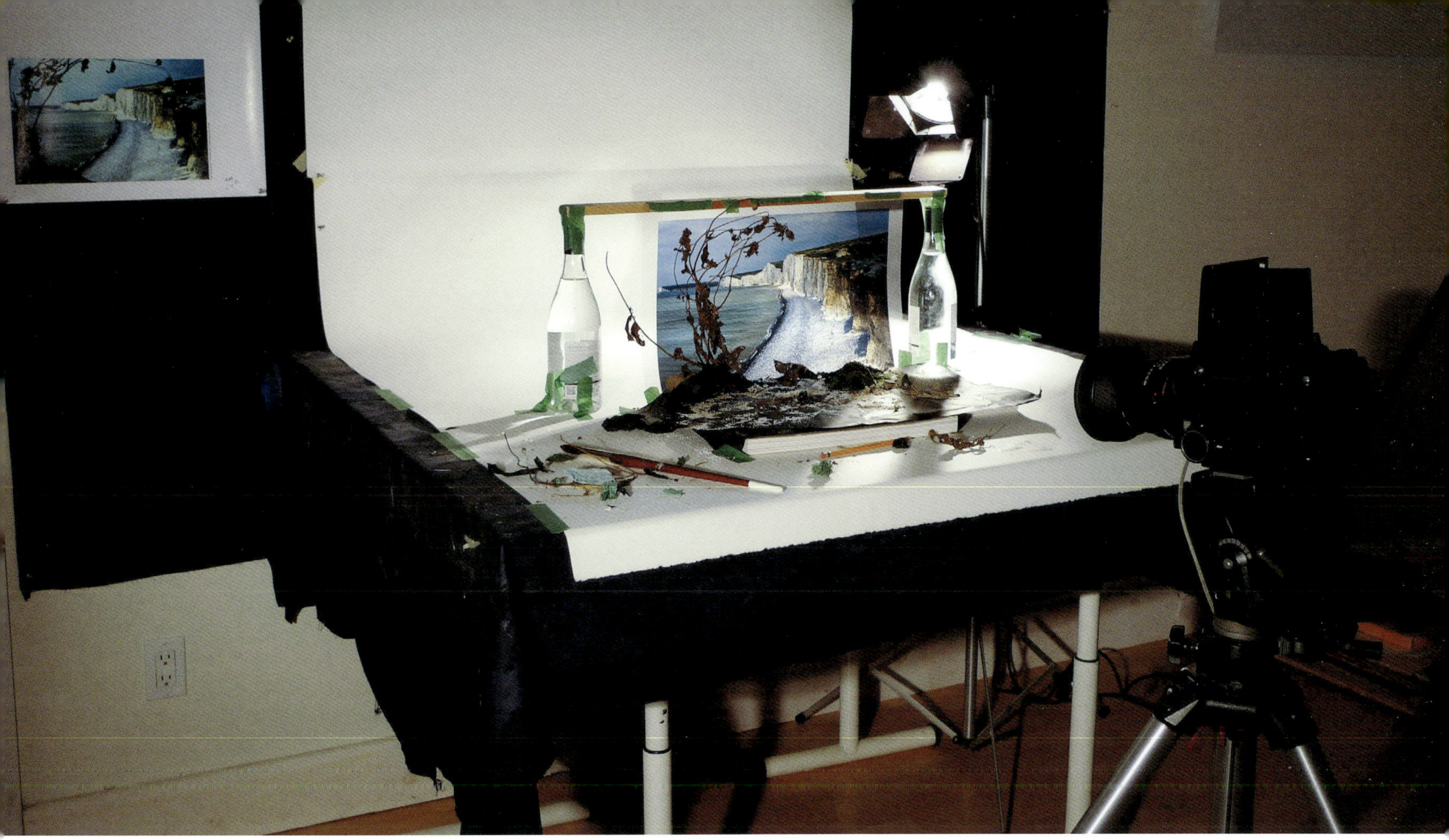

Collaborer augmente notre capacité à présenter des expositions. Comme partenaires institutionnels, nous souhaitons remercier la générosité des organismes de financement qui donnent de l'ampleur à nos programmes respectifs : Le Conseil des arts du Canada, Le Conseil des arts de l'Ontario, le Ministère de la Culture et des Communications du Québec, la Société de développement des entreprises culturelles du Québec, la ville d'Oshawa, la ville de Sherbrooke, la ville de Rivière-du-loup et la Municipalité de Chatham-Kent.

Donna Raetsen-Kemp, Chief Executive Officer, The Robert McLaughlin Gallery
Carl Lavoy, Director/Curator, Thames Art Gallery
Cécile Gélinas, Directrice, Musée des beaux-arts de Sherbrooke
Rheal Olivier Lanthier, François St-Jacques, Directeurs, Art Mûr
Mélanie Girard, Directrice générale, Musée du Bas-Saint-Laurent

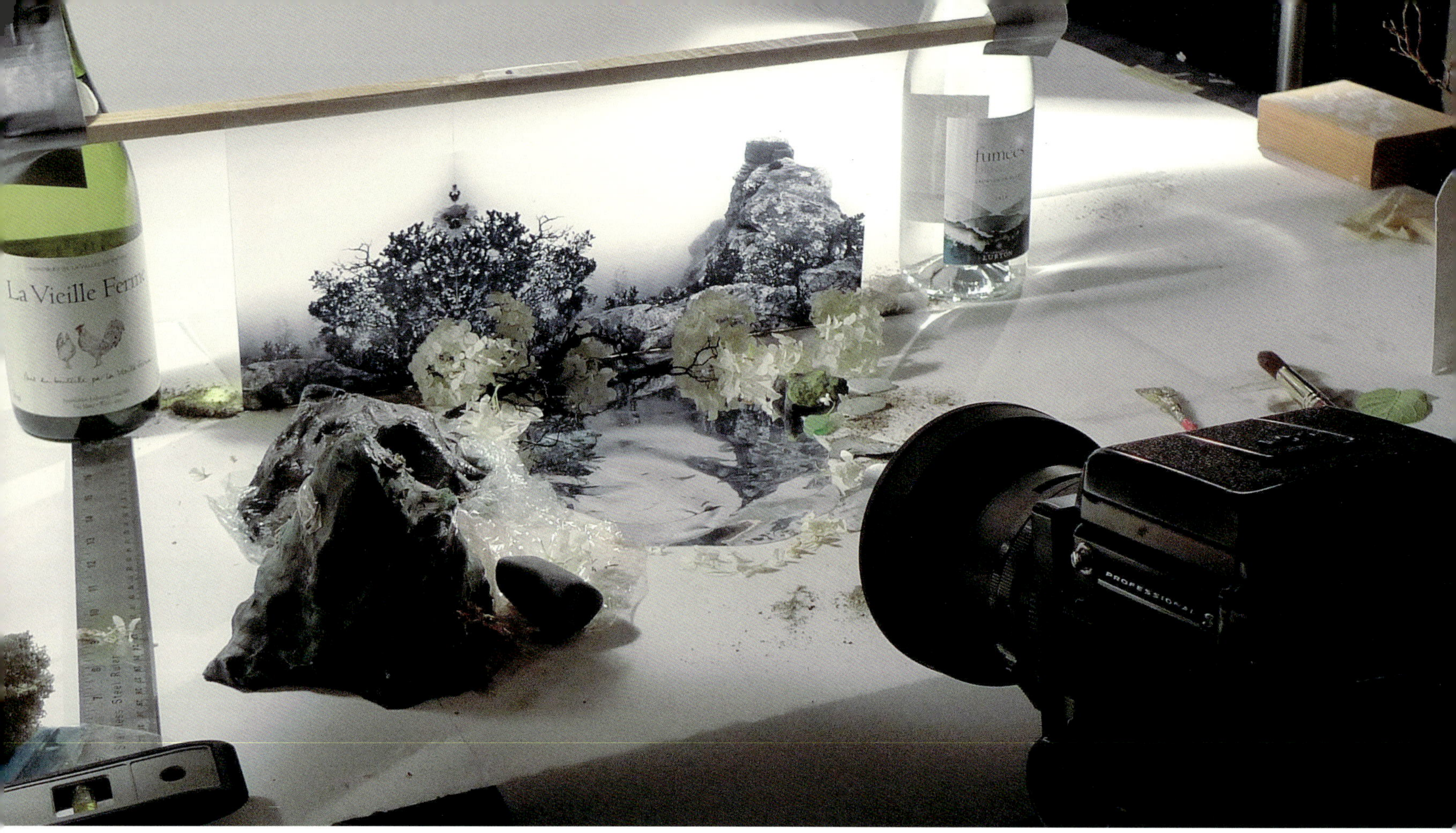

Image : Atelier de l'artiste / Artist's Studio, 2014

INTRODUCTION

This publication is the result of a collaboration between our institutions that has spanned over two years. It is with enthusiasm that we united our resources in the combination of two projects: an exhibition catalogue and a monograph. Holly King's previous publication, produced by the Canadian Museum of Contemporary Photography, was published in 1998; we thought it was important that this book be published to highlight her more recent work. It accompanies the exhibition *Edging Towards the Myserious* that will be presented in various museums and galleries across Quebec and Ontario.

Holly King is best known as a photographer, but photography only constitutes a fraction of her artistic production. She is a multidisciplinary artist who paints, sculpts, performs and photographs. While computer programs such as Photoshop allow a new generation of artists to create fictional worlds, King's manipulations occur before the photograph is taken. Her universe is created from maquettes with painted backgrounds, branches, rocks, sculptures, papers and other items that come together in her photographs to create landscapes that are both sublime and uncanny. Holly King's work has been shown at the Centre George Pompidou in Paris, the Museum of Contemporary Art in Mexico, the Museum of Contemporary Canadian Art in Toronto, the Macedonian Museum of Contemporary Art, the Vancouver Contemporary Art Gallery, the National Taiwan Museum of Fine Arts, the Montreal Museum of Fine Arts, the Musée national des beaux-arts du Québec, the National Gallery of Canada in Ottawa among other art galleries and centres both nationally and internationally. She has had over forty solo exhibitions and participated in over seventy group exhibitions.

It is with great pleasure that our galleries present the exhibition *Holly King: Edging Towards the Mysterious* to our respective audiences. To view King's work is to experience a sense of memory—an elusive recollection of what is "real." If we understand that memory is never a true account of past experiences but rather a reconstructed story built in part from reality and modified with fictional additions and distortions, we can step, without hesitation or question, into the wonderful world that King lays out before us. We extend our congratulations, together with our thanks, to Holly King.

Thank you to Linda Jansma for her curatorial vision, which yielded the exhibition concept, and for her dedication and enthusiasm to the realization and completion of this project. We are pleased to present this publication, and to thank Francine Paul and Linda Jansma for their thoughtful essays, which advance the dialogue on the body of work brought forward in this exhibition. Collaborations enhance our ability to present exhibitions, and as partnering institutions we would like to acknowledge the generosity of the funding agencies that make our programming possible: the Canada Council for the Arts, the Ontario Arts Council, Ministère de la Culture et des Communications du Québec, the city of Oshawa, Ville de Sherbrooke, Ville de Rivière-du-Loup and the Municipality of Chatham-Kent.

Donna Raetsen-Kemp, Chief Executive Officer, The Robert McLaughlin Gallery
Carl Lavoy, Director/Curator, Thames Art Gallery
Cécile Gélinas, Director, Musée des beaux-arts de Sherbrooke
Rheal Olivier Lanthier, François St-Jacques, Directors, Art Mûr
Mélanie Girard, Chief Executive Director, Musée du Bas-Saint-Laurent

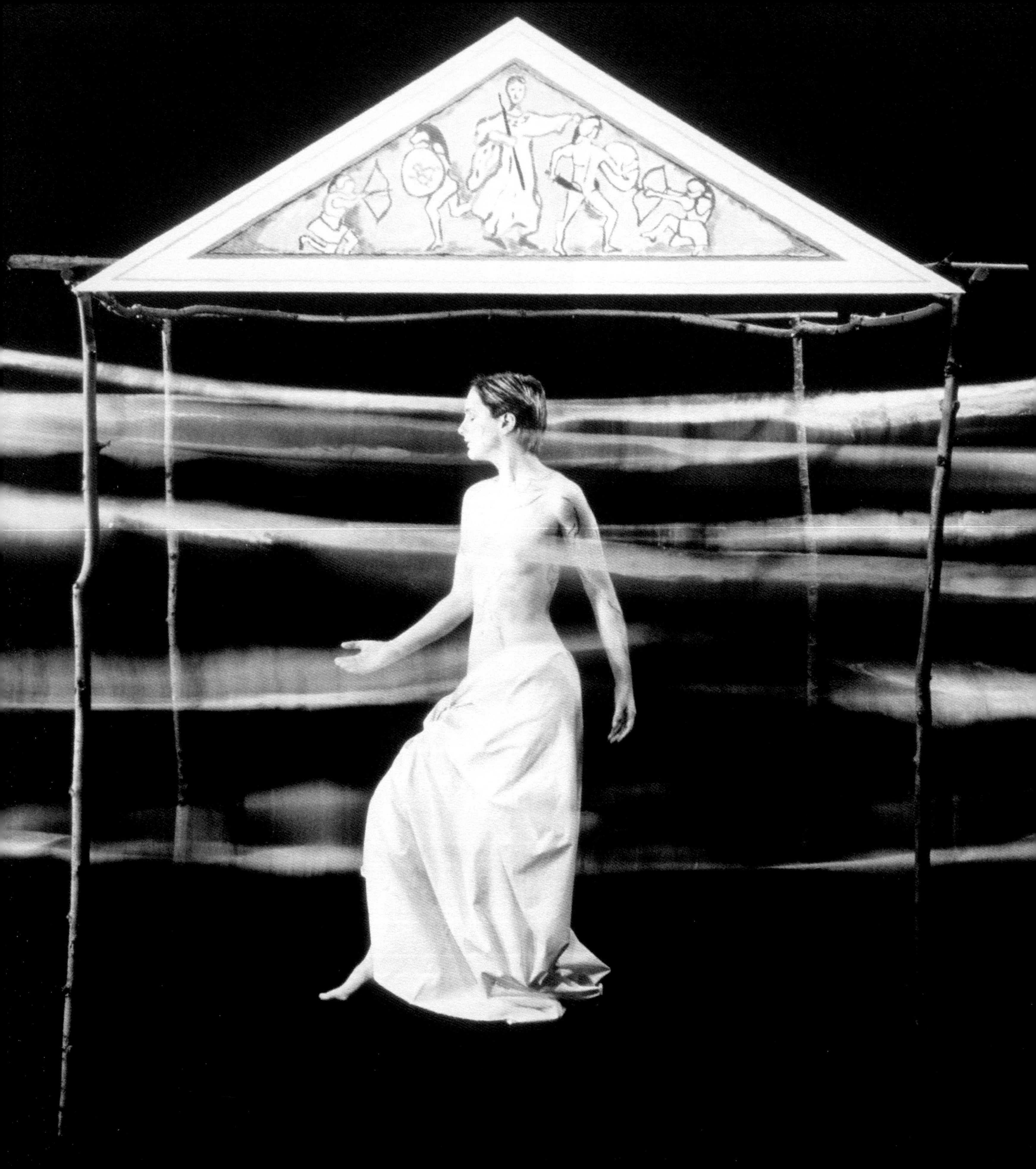

L'INVENTION DES PAYSAGES THÉÂTRALITÉ ET PHOTOGRAPHIE MISE EN SCÈNE CHEZ HOLLY KING

FRANCINE PAUL

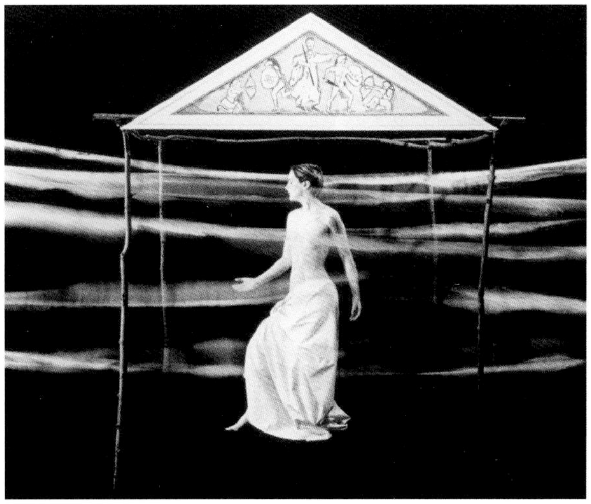

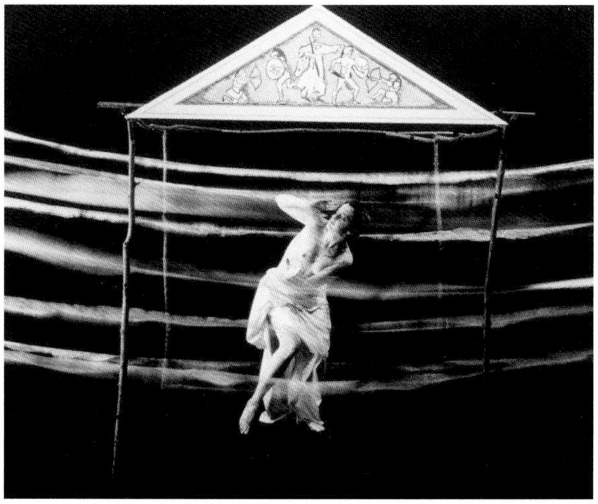

Images : p. 7, 8-9
Hellenic Winds, 1982
épreuves argentiques sur gélatine
/ silver gelatin prints
102 x 559 cm (ensemble)

L'invention des paysages[1]
Théâtralité et photographie mise en scène chez Holly King

Francine Paul Faire la traversée d'une carrière artistique aussi longue et soutenue[2] que celle de Holly King peut prendre l'allure d'une odyssée tranquille tant les œuvres aperçues ont une forte cohérence. Plastique d'abord, avec le paysage comme pivot. D'autres récurrences font surface : la photographie, le dispositif scénographique, le regroupement en série d'œuvres de grand format dont les assises esthétiques reposent sur une connaissance et une pratique de la peinture et du dessin, puis des titres qui invitent aux errances métaphoriques et dont les accents de théâtralité laissent sourdre des voix intérieures qui sous-tendent l'image.

Le temps long, tranquille de ce qui dure, se densifie et prend de l'ampleur tandis que les œuvres se font écho. Des figures végétales, minérales, aquatiques les traversent et dévoilent leurs attraits. Sont-elles réelles ou artificielles ? Les approchons-nous ou s'éloignent-elles ? Tels des archipels, elles forment une longue suite de variations, de transformations, comme si le cours de la vie n'épuisait pas la vie elle-même et que le monde se révélait.

Pour moi, d'entre toutes ses œuvres, il en émerge une, toujours la même, qui me fascine depuis que je l'ai vue il y a trente ans. Cette œuvre, *Hellenic Winds* (1982), est l'une des toute

1. Titre inspiré de cet ouvrage d'Anne Cauquelin : L'invention des paysages, Paris, Plon, 1989, 181 p.
2. Depuis 1979, Holly King a exposé son travail plus d'une centaine de fois, dont cinquante fois dans le cadre d'expositions personnelles. Elle a aussi présenté sept performances. Parallèlement à sa pratique artistique, elle enseigne le dessin et la peinture à l'Université Concordia.

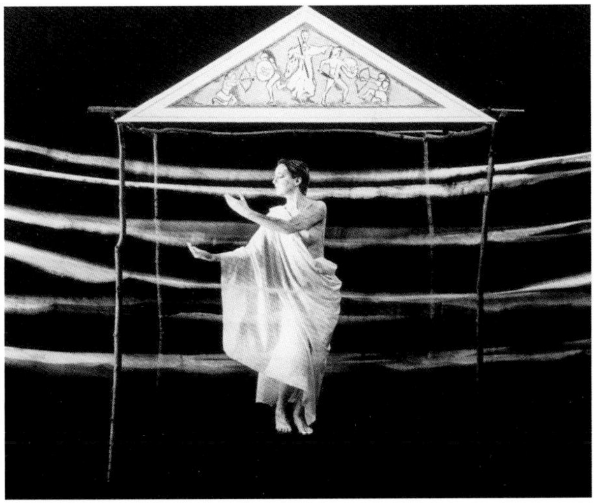 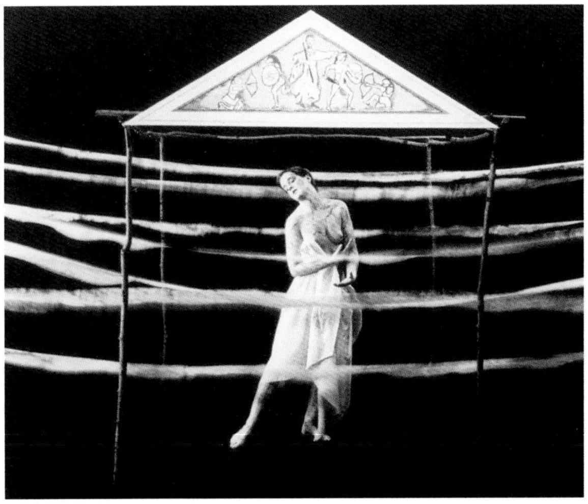

premières photographies de Holly King. Il s'agit d'une suite photographique où l'artiste prend des poses inspirées de la statuaire grecque tout comme de l'architecture devant laquelle elle se met en scène. Dans cette chorégraphie, elle se fait aède, actrice et artiste. Un drame en quatre actes aux apparences de tragédie, où l'intensité émotionnelle répond au classicisme du décor, des gestes et de la composition. Cette pièce emblématique présente la performance comme premier mode d'expression, la mythologie comme inspiration, et l'atelier, lieu de tous les espaces, où elle théâtralise de fabuleuses rencontres entre la peinture et arrêt sur image.

Telle une démiurge, elle s'invente, elle invente.

Ier acte : Performance et théâtralité
Au début de sa vie professionnelle, à la fin des années 1970, alors qu'elle est encore étudiante en arts visuels à l'Université Laval, Holly King explore les toutes nouvelles avenues de la performance, qui définissent cet art comme un processus de dématérialisation de l'objet au profit de l'action, où le corps, les sons et les gestes de l'artiste modulent l'interaction avec le public[3]. Elle présente dès 1978 ses premières performances, d'abord en duo avec Cyril Reade, ensuite seule devant l'auditoire de La Chambre Blanche à Québec, puis en 1981 au Musée d'art contemporain de Montréal et à Toronto.

3. J'emprunte ces éléments de définition à Guy Sioui Durand, « Notes critiques sur l'ambiguïté des performances au Québec », *Inter, art actuel*, no 58, automne 1993, p. 5.

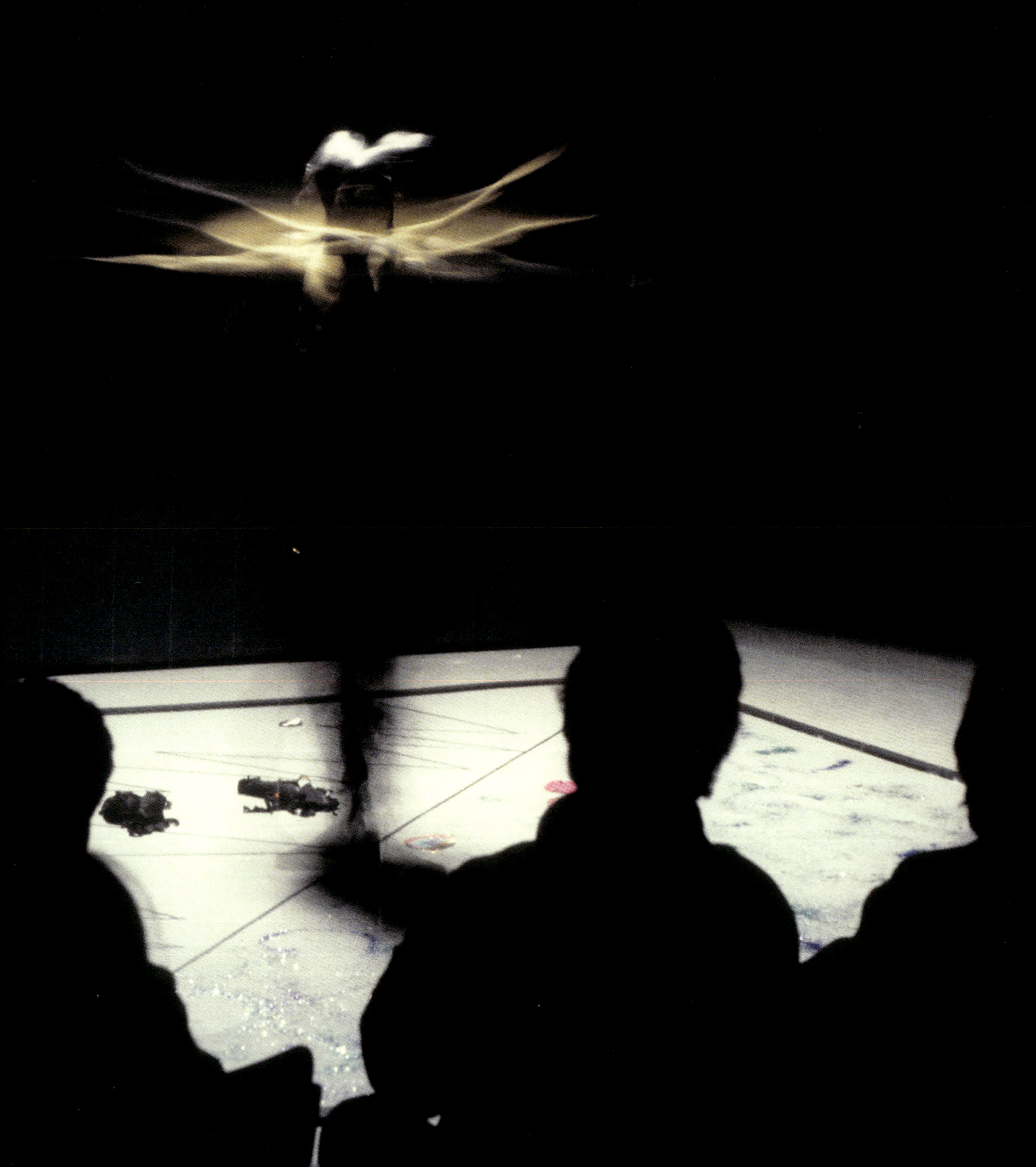

En solo, elle s'inspire des textes de Freud et de Jung sur la psychologie et sur les symboles pour scénariser l'action et nourrir le contenu de ses représentations. Elle circonscrit sommairement l'espace à l'aide d'accessoires simples, conçoit les costumes et la gestuelle. Elle module également la durée, les effets sonores, les éclairages, les projections de diapositives que commande une partition corporelle attentive aux limites spatiales et aux effets de la lumière. Ce sont toutes ces stratégies d'un corps en action dans un volume qui constituent les fondements de sa démarche, comme ce fut le cas par exemple pour *Two Characters* (1980).

Image : p. 10
Two Characters, 1980
performance
The GAP, Toronto (ON)

En effet, lorsqu'elle se met en scène dans son atelier en 1982 pour *Hellenic Winds*, Holly King a l'habitude de tenir compte du point de vue des spectateurs et sait l'intégrer pour une prise de vue frontale. Elle découvre également quelles sont les poses les plus efficaces, les plus expressives et comment traduire l'émotion dans ses gestes, dans son visage. Elle saisit aussi comment créer illusoirement un mouvement, planifier une séquence et proposer un rapport de proportions adéquat pour l'architecture de la composition. Ainsi, lorsqu'elle plante son appareil photo dans l'atelier, qu'elle se fait à la fois actrice, artiste et conteuse d'un jeu théâtral devant l'objectif de l'appareil, elle a déjà compris et assimilé, grâce à son expérience de la performance, tout ce qui participe de la *photographie mise en scène.*

La photographie mise en scène, comme nous l'apprend la publication dirigée par *Lori Pauli Acting the Part: Photography as Theatre*[4], peut faire la part belle, par l'intermédiaire des acteurs et des modèles, à la narration et à la théâtralité, comme le firent antérieurement la peinture et la sculpture. Ce type de photographie, semblable à l'image fixe d'un film, a connu une nouvelle impulsion depuis les années 1960, entre autres raisons parce que les photographes contemporains se plaisent à laisser au spectateur la possibilité de compléter l'histoire de ces instants dramatiques figés dans le temps. Quant aux apports de la théâtralité dans la photographie actuelle, la commissaire indépendante Karen Henry en explique ainsi la complexité conceptuelle :

> Le caractère théâtral de la photographie du début du vingt-et-unième siècle ne fait aucun effort afin de rejeter son public ou nier ses propres fictions. Au contraire, celle-ci invite le spectateur à participer dans un rapport imaginatif avec l'idée même de la représentation et avec l'état des choses dans la société en général. [...] Ils révèlent les techniques d'illusion tout en réaffirmant

4. *Acting the Part: Photography as Theatre*, sous la direction de Lori Pauli, London, National Gallery of Canada, Merrell Publishers, 2006, 176 p.

5. Lori Pauli, « Setting the Scene » dans *Acting the Part: Photography as Theatre*, op. cit., p. 13.

6. *Ibid..*, p. 18 : « the way that staged photography, like painting – or probably more accurately, like the film still – leaves the completion of the narrative up to the viewer. The staged photograph has become once again a dramatic moment frozen in time. »

7. Karen Henry, « The Artful Disposition: Theatricality, Cinema, and Social Context in Contemporary Photography », dans *Acting the Part: Photography as Theatre*, op. cit., p. 154. Voir citation originale p. 25

> la possibilité d'une représentation significative. Comme des tableaux classiques, ils suggèrent le projet continu de la transformation éminente.[7]

Comme nous le verrons, Holly King apporte dès le milieu des années 1980 une contribution originale et soutenue à la photographie mise en scène non pas par sa direction d'acteurs ou de modèles, mais par la construction de créations dramatiques dans lesquelles elle accorde le premier rôle au paysage et invite les spectateurs à participer, avec leur imagination, à la représentation elle-même.

IIe acte : Paysage et mythologie

C'est à partir de 1985-1986 que l'atelier de Holly King devient le lieu de ses explorations picturales et photographiques qui, à l'époque, se résolvent principalement par la pratique du dessin et de la peinture sur papier. L'artiste y fait entrer les grands récits de la mythologie grecque, y introduisant dieux et déesses qui font et défont le monde et les héros qui l'habitent.

Tantôt terribles, souvent excessifs, ils se faufilent dans les œuvres, et quelques-unes de leurs fantastiques histoires induisent la trame narrative. Les grands moteurs de la tragédie humaine – terreurs, pulsions, rêves et aspirations – prennent place dans les paysages, y trouvant là des espaces que rendent féconds les inextricables paradoxes entre mobilité et stabilité.

Il nous semble alors que Holly King trouve dans la tradition expressionniste de la peinture de paysage le style le plus apte à esquisser ses partitions dramatiques. Ainsi, des gestes déliés aux couleurs souvent vives et contrastées représentent sommairement des référents naturalistes qui appuient l'apparente subjectivité de l'artiste plutôt que de répondre aux canons objectifs d'un mimétisme appliqué. Ces élans lyriques éloignés d'une description aliénée autorisent l'expressivité par la couleur, la forme, le mouvement et la lumière, pour mieux libérer un vaste registre d'émotions et de tensions intérieures.

Le plus souvent dans les tableaux de l'artiste, notamment dans *River on Fire* (1986) de la série *Rivers of Hades*, la partie centrale est clairement cernée alors que des diagonales conduisent notre regard jusqu'au fond de la scène ou sur la ligne d'horizon. Le point de vue en plongée, privilégié pour les premiers plans, favorise notre incursion dans le paysage dont les plans successifs créent une profondeur limitée. Les figures aquatiques, végétales et minérales abondent, sont mises en valeur par un superbe

Image : p. 13
River of Fire, 1986
huile sur papier / oil on paper
105 x 85 cm

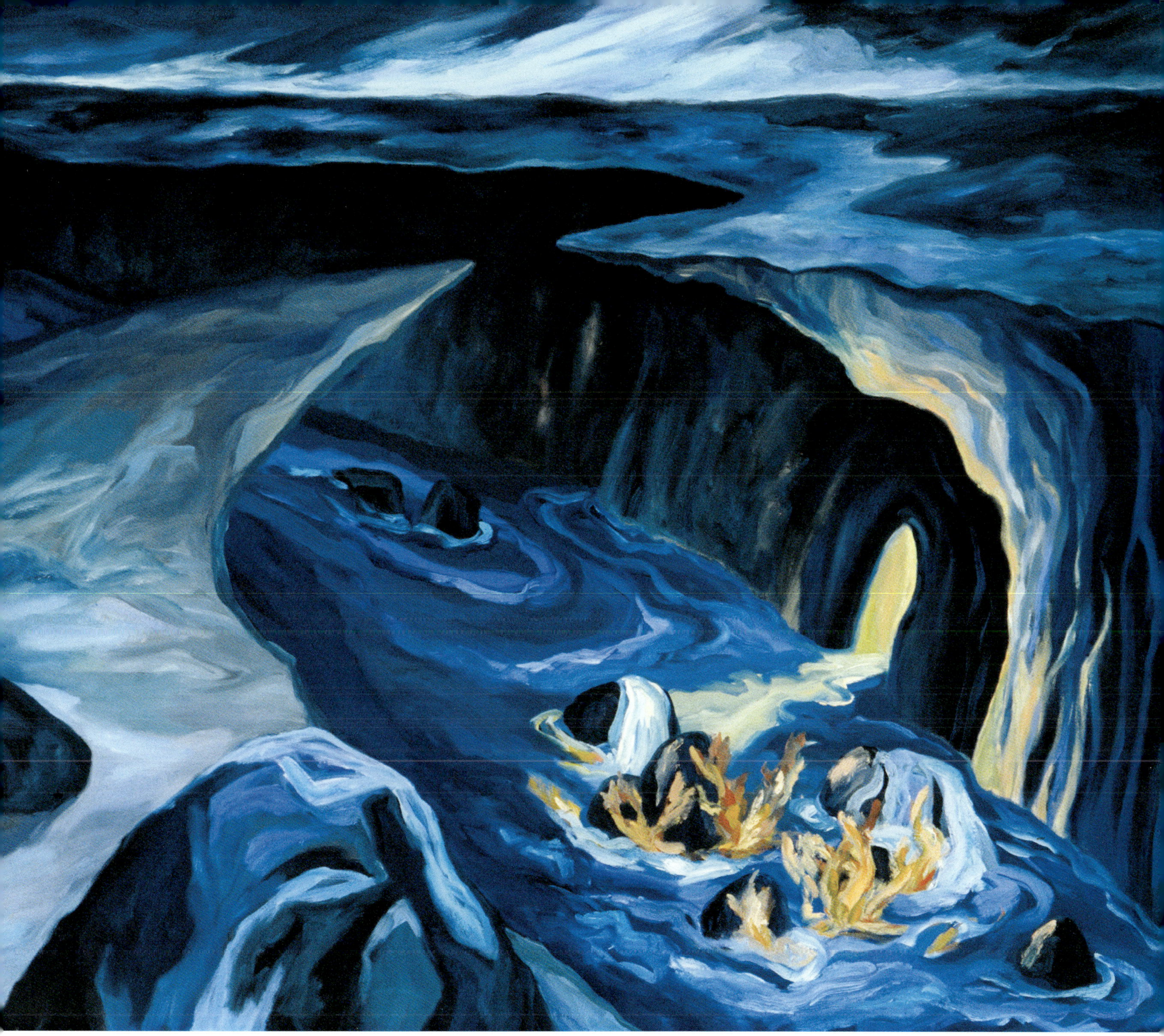

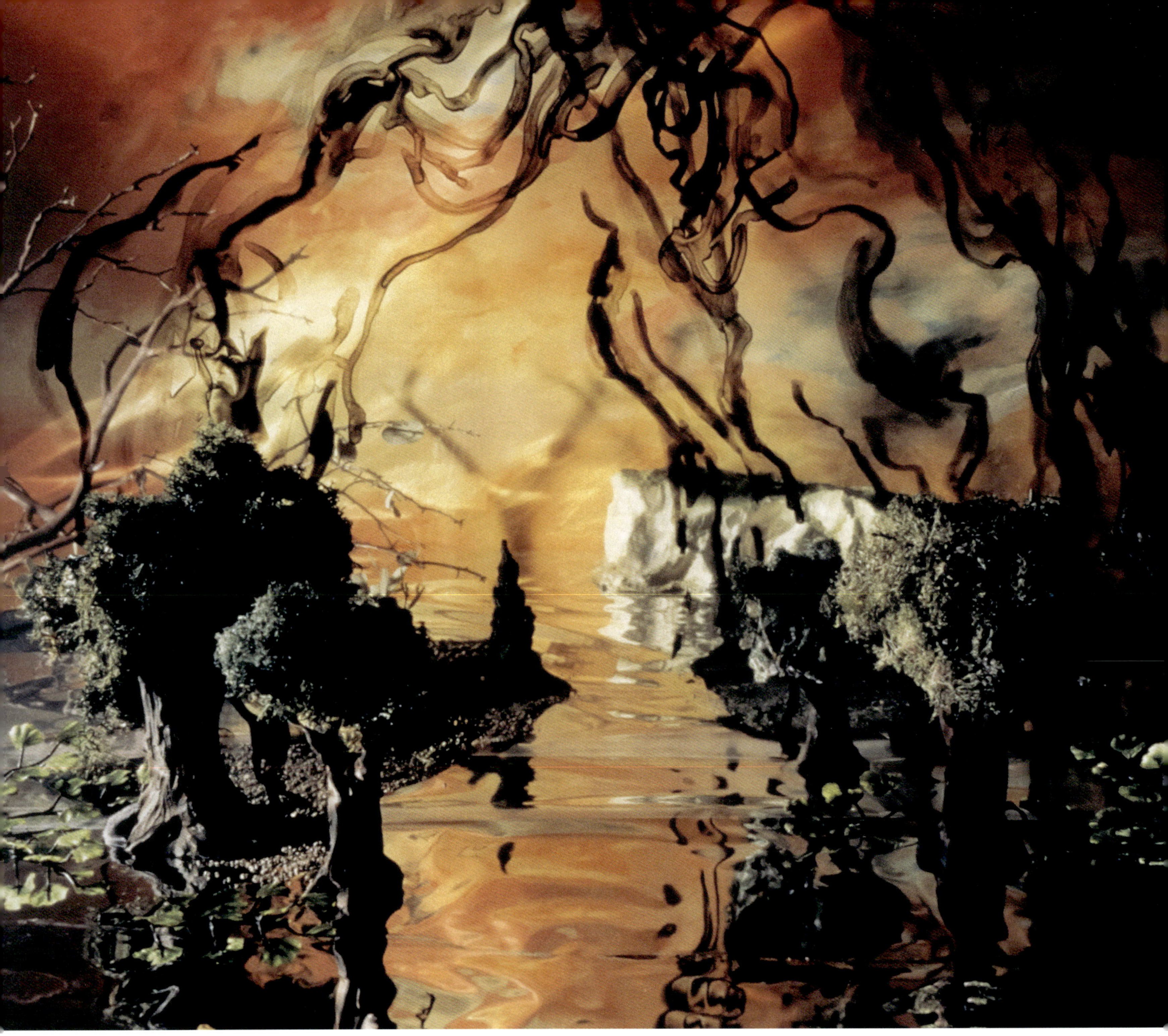

nuancier de textures. Quant à la narration, ce sont toujours les jeux savants de lumière et d'ombre qui la signalent. Ici, le mouvement des eaux, leur trouble presque infini coulent jusqu'à nous, laissant entrevoir sous les apparences bleutées les mystères sous-jacents à notre monde, révélés par des traits semi-abstraits qui miment les dérives des âmes mortes emportées dans une descente vertigineuse vers les abysses, où règne, loin de l'Olympe, le dieu Hadès.

Image : p. 14
Lament, 1999
épreuve à développement chromogène / chromogenic print
153 x 183 cm

En invitant ainsi les dieux dans son atelier, Holly King emprunte métaphoriquement leurs pouvoirs pour insuffler à ses œuvres une puissance fictionnelle qui brouille les frontières entre le réel et l'imaginaire. L'atelier devient un antre de production de paysages qui dorénavant se fixent pour et dans l'image photographique.

IIIe acte : Atelier et construction

En singularisant dans ce corpus de Holly King la série *Realms of Night* (1986-1989), où l'artiste introduit exceptionnellement des composantes architecturales tridimensionnelles à des éléments naturels déposés sur sa table de travail, nous accordons à ces structures le statut d'indices. Tels des présages, les architectures de phare, de pont, de tonnelle qui s'y trouvent signalent la dimension performative de ces « constructions » de paysages, cette dimension constituant l'essence de l'esthétique de l'artiste. Efficaces mises en abyme, ces petites structures révèlent que pour Holly King, l'art est une construction intellectuelle et manuelle. Sans aucun doute, l'artiste se présente comme une *mulier faber* qui invente de sa pensée et de sa main des contes et des outils pour créer et façonner des fictions de paysages. Elle ne cache pas l'illusion. Au contraire, elle rend toujours visibles les traces de fabrication de ses mises en scène. À n'en pas douter, elle est pleinement consciente, et veut que nous le soyons également, que ses gestes se savent apparents : « The "gesture which knows itself to be appearance" is a self-reflexive mirror that reveals the nature of contemporary representation[8]. »

Conséquemment, c'est avec beaucoup de plaisir et de malice qu'elle fait entrer dans son atelier, puis dans ses photographies mises en scène, les ruses du bricolage. Le « bricolage », comme nous l'a rappelé René Payant, rend compte de l'habileté inventive du bricoleur; il appelle les actions de prélèvement, de déplacement, d'intégration, il favorise un dialogue avec un inventaire d'éléments sélectionnés et, comme le mythe, il est une construction qui raconte aussi son auteur[9].

8. Karen Henry, « The Artful Disposition: Theatricality, Cinema, and Social Context in Contemporary Photography », dans *Acting the Part: Photography as Theatre*, op. cit., p. 134-135.
9. Sur ce sujet, nous sommes redevables à René Payant, lui-même inspiré par la lecture de Claude Lévi-Strauss. René Payant, « Bricolage pictural », dans *Vedute, pièces détachées sur l'art 1967-1987*, Laval, Trois, 2003, p. 63.

Image : p. 17
World Beyond the Water, 2009
épreuve à développement chromogène / chromogenic print
122 x 183 cm

Et nous voilà devenus plus attentifs aux innombrables présences de matériaux végétaux, synthétiques ou « patentés » qui posent pour l'objectif, attestant que le travail scénographique s'expose. Brindilles, herbes séchées, fleurs, branches, racines, cailloux sont placés en fonction de leurs formes, de leurs couleurs et de leurs textures. Ils sont ici des natures mortes dont l'artiste va occasionnellement transgresser l'essence en en magnifiant ou amenuisant les dimensions en fonction de l'échelle de ses plateaux de théâtre, crédibles décors miniatures. Ailleurs, la brindille devient frondaison; la racine se fait arche; la mousse, pelouse; l'écorce, tronc; le caillou, rocher. Quand les fruits bruts de ses cueillettes naturalistes ne suffisent pas au réalisme paysager, Holly King convoque à la manière d'une sculpteure le plâtre, l'argile, l'aluminium, le cellophane qu'elle façonne, froisse, découpe, et qui deviennent arbre, forêt, cours d'eau, comme le donnent à voir les séries *Forest of Enchantment* (1997-2000), *Mirages* (2000), *Coming Into View* (2002-2004) ou encore *Twisted Roots* (2005-2007).

Pour donner encore plus de vérité à ses tableaux, elle met en fond de scène des ciels peints aux couleurs spectaculaires – de touchantes références aux grands peintres de paysage anglais et américains.

Mais que seraient toutes ces constructions illusionnistes si l'éclairage n'y installait pas la lumière et les ombres qui complètent, par leurs innombrables et subtiles variations, les moyens de persuasion de la rhétorique plastique ? Car dans une image qui convainc, « le fait peut être faux mais doit être vraisemblable[10]. »

Force est de constater que le nombre volontairement limité de variables matérielles et symboliques, qui constituent le vocabulaire de l'artiste, exigent de celle-ci une parfaite maîtrise de *l'ars combinatoria*. Elle doit constamment recombiner les éléments, en forcer les mutations et créer des représentations renouvelées, comme en témoignent ses grandes photographies.

IVe acte : Paysage et paysages

En 2008-2009, avec la série *Mangroves Floating Between Two Worlds*, Holly King emprunte une nouvelle stratégie. Emportée par les pouvoirs évocateurs de la littérature, elle sort de l'atelier pour aller non pas peindre, mais photographier sur le motif. Les mangroves tropicales lui inspirent alors des paysages horizontaux aux harmonieuses proportions. Cette fois, c'est la nature elle-même qui se dessine, nous tenant à distance de ses calligraphies

10. Ce critère de crédibilité énoncé dans Wikipédia, est fort probablement inspiré du poète Nicolas Boileau à qui nous devons cette formule : « Le vrai peut quelquefois n'être point vraisemblable. »

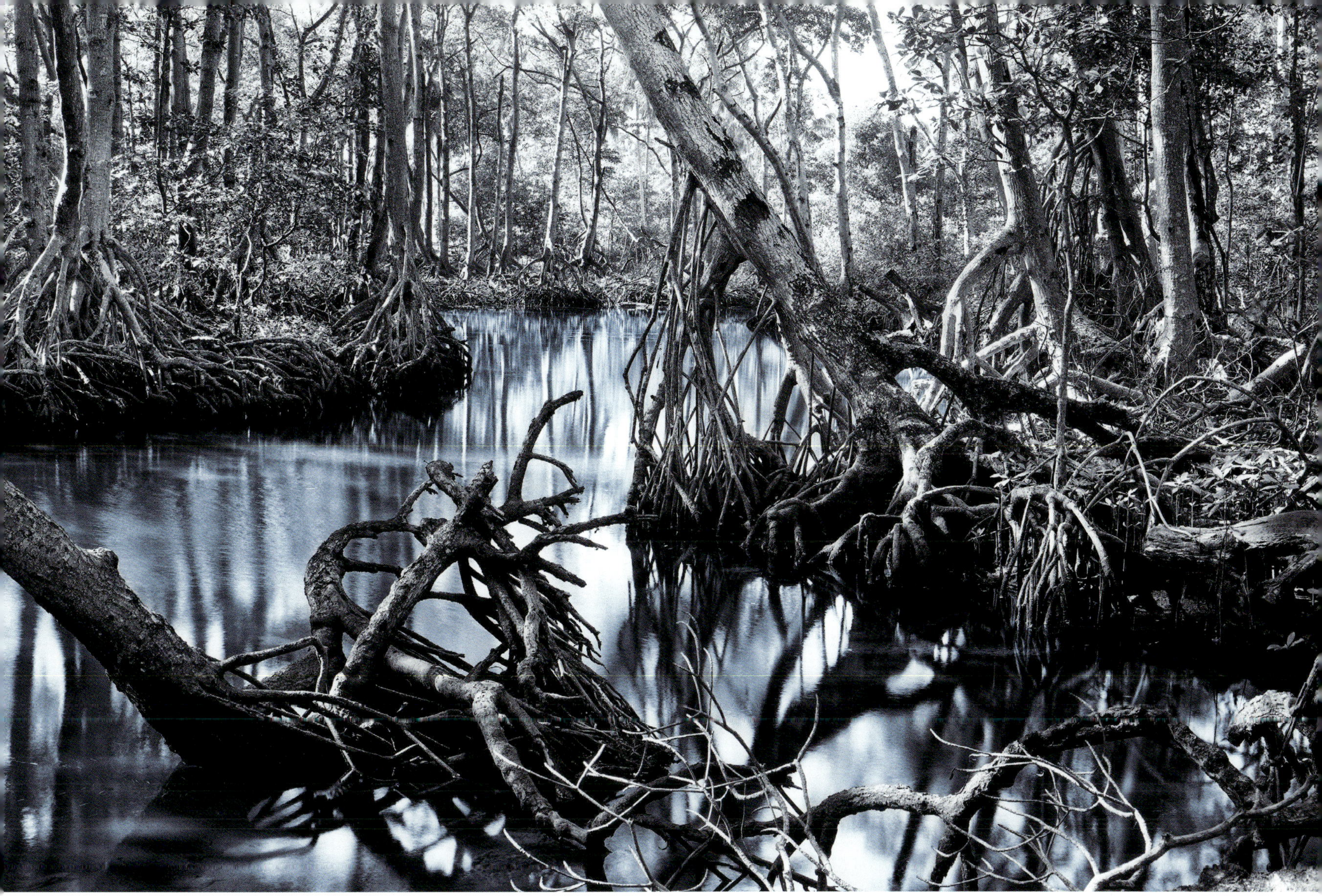

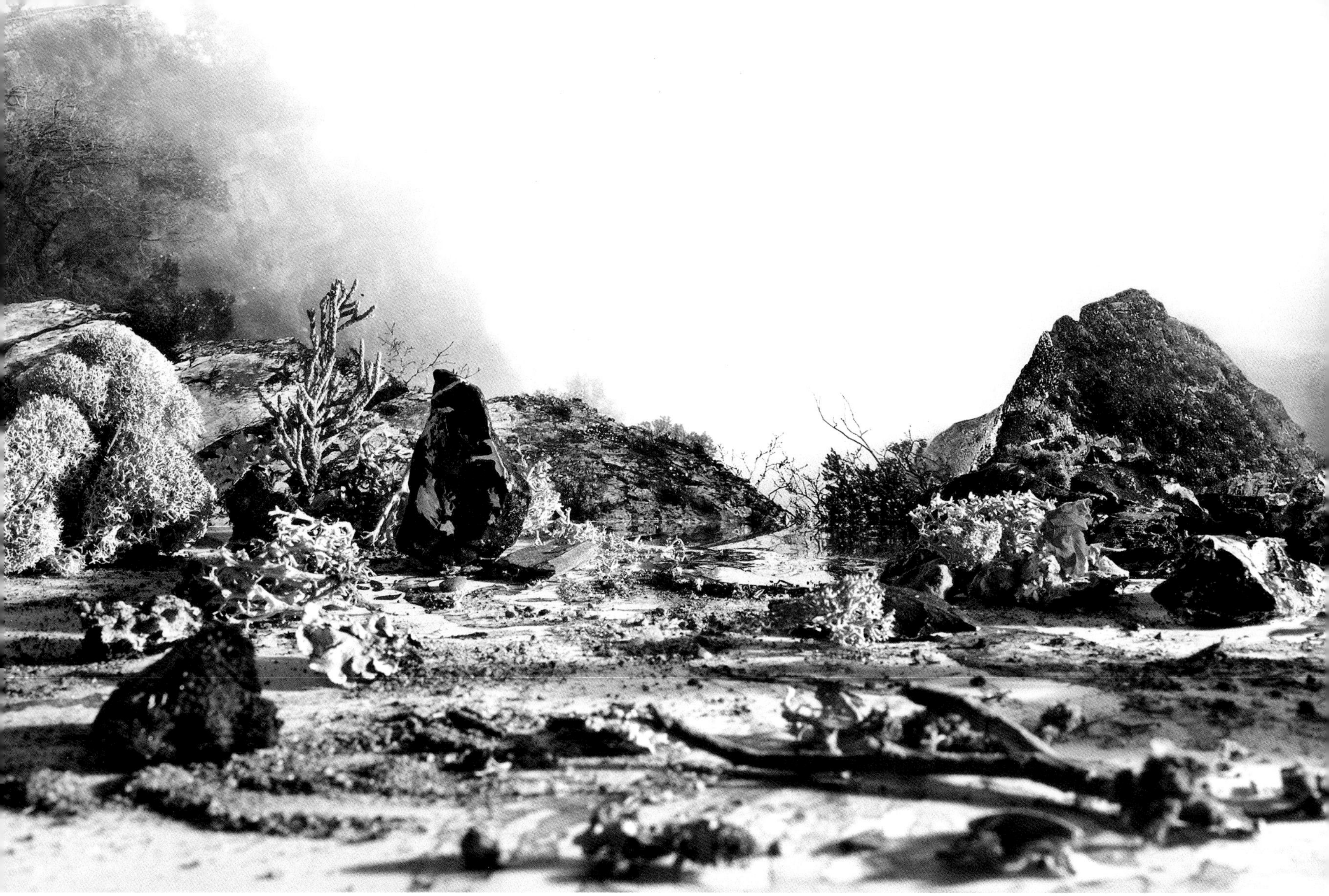

végétales. Difficile pour le spectateur de pénétrer ces paysages touffus de sinuosités, agités et privés d'ouverture perspectiviste, comme si la chaleur torride de l'air limitait l'espace. Même l'eau du premier plan, avec ses jeux de miroir, ne réussit pas à nous offrir les percées visuelles auxquelles Holly King nous a habitués. Par après, à l'issue d'autres missions photographiques, comme celles au Grand Canyon ou sur les côtes anglaises, l'artiste rapporte à l'atelier de grandes diapositives qu'elle installe à l'arrière-scène de la boîte scénique. Cette dernière participe au développement d'une autre avenue conceptuelle, où le miniplateau, toujours ce cube presque magique, devient le contenant d'un nouveau type d'opérations dans lesquelles deux moments, deux paysages se superposent. Un premier, témoin du voyage antérieur et témoin emblématique de la transparence de la photographie, est posé à la verticale. Devant lui, les outils naturels et fabriqués prennent d'autres poses, jouent d'autres rôles dans un second paysage, celui-ci entièrement fictif. Puis, à la tombée du rideau, quand l'artiste démiurge décide du cadrage final, la photographie mise en scène devient troisième paysage, celui qui contient les deux autres – une sorte de paysage gigogne aux pouvoirs évocateurs démultipliés. Voici encore beaucoup de mirages en noir et blanc ou en couleur qui nous appellent, qui ont besoin de nous pour continuer à exister, puisque « nous coopérons, avec l'essentiel de nos pouvoirs de réception et de commémoration, à la régénération et à la perpétuation de l'œuvre de l'artiste, dans la mesure précise où nous faisons, nous aussi, l'expérience de l' "être-là" non maîtrisé d'une instance mystérieuse, d'une création première avec et contre laquelle l'acte d'art s'est produit[11] ».

À terme, se manifeste une incitation aux voyages. Une dramaturgie exacerbée s'ouvre soudainement sur une vastitude, laissant croire que la vérité, la beauté ne sont qu'inventions de mondes où il faut aller. Et ni Holly King ni nous ne savons ce que nous serons au retour.

Image : p. 18
Quiet Monument, 2012
photographie en noir et blanc /
black and white photograph
122 x 183 cm

11. George Steiner, *Réelles présences : les arts du sens*, Paris, Gallimard, 1991, p. 252. (coll. Folio essais, no 255).

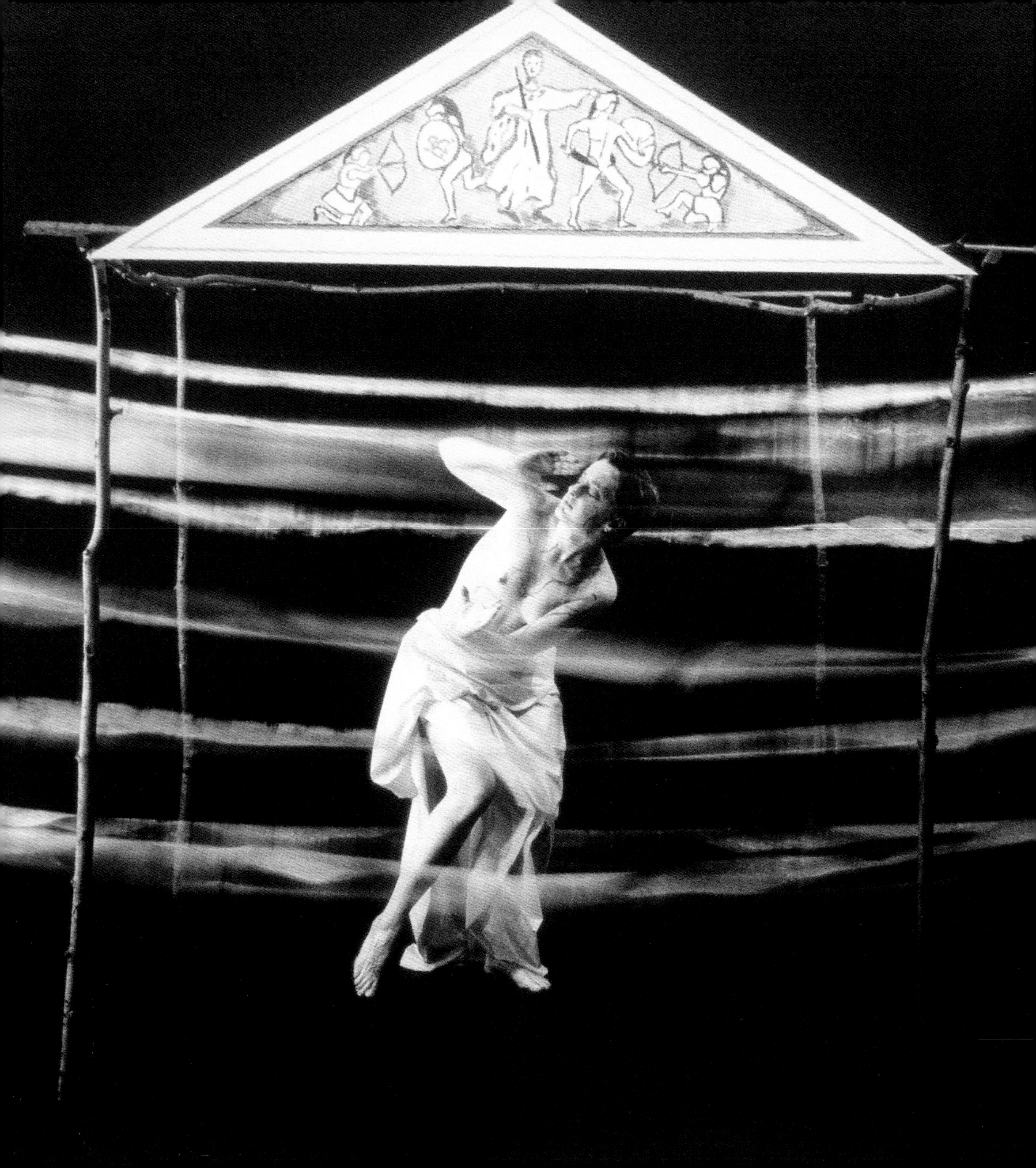

INVENTED LANDSCAPES
THEATRICALITY AND THE STAGED PHOTOGRAPHY OF HOLLY KING

FRANCINE PAUL

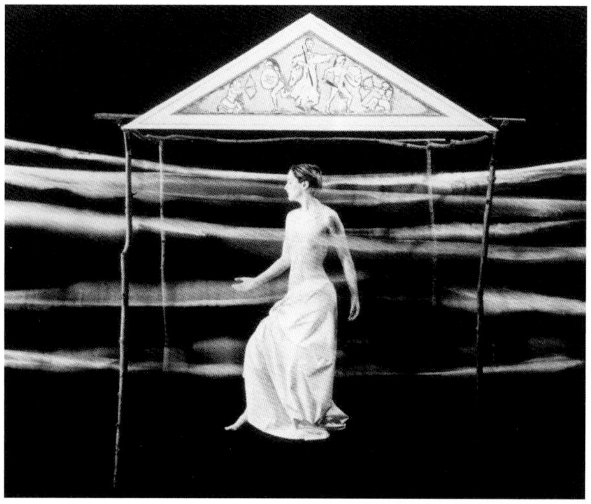 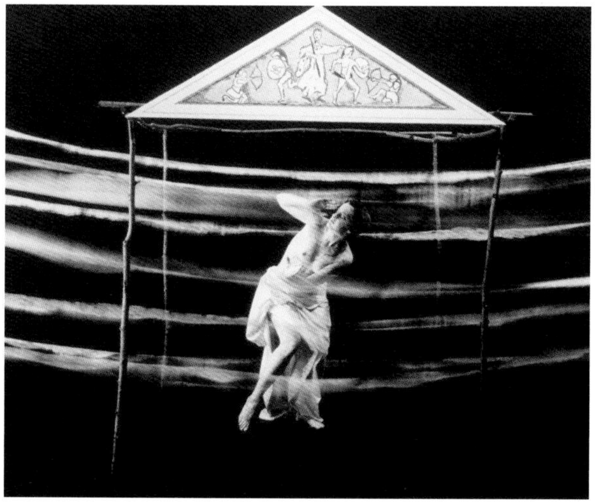

Images : p. 20, 22-23
Hellenic Winds, 1982
épreuves argentiques sur gélatine / silver gelatin prints
102 x 559 cm (ensemble)

Invented Landscapes[1]
Theatricality and the Staged Photography of Holly King

Navigating through an artistic journey as long and sustained[2] as that of Holly King is a tranquil odyssey. The works emerge as a whole due to their powerful interrelation over time, reinforcing the visual unity of the landscape as subject. The use of photographic conventions and scenographic techniques, and the artist's solid foundations in the visual arts, specifically painting and drawing, all confer aesthetic harmony to the large-format works made in series. The titles invite metaphorical wanderings, exposing an inherent theatricality, while giving voice to suggested and imagined meanings.

The quietude of this meandering journey becomes more intense as the works increase in scale and build upon one another, creating fictional worlds. Elements of the natural world appear transformed and reveal arcane characteristics. Are they real or artificial? Are we drawing closer to them or are they receding from view? Like archipelagos, they assume intricate variations, as if the course of life was never-ending, allowing the world to reveal infinite secrets.

From among these works, one always emerges for me, always the same, as enthralling as when I first saw it thirty years ago. *Hellenic Winds* (1982) is one of Holly King's earliest photographic works.

1. Title inspired by this work by Anne Cauquelin: *L'invention des paysages* (Paris: Plon, 1989).
2. Since 1979, Holly King has exhibited over a hundred times, including fifty solo exhibitions. She has also presented seven performances. In parallel with her art, she teaches drawing and painting at Concordia University.

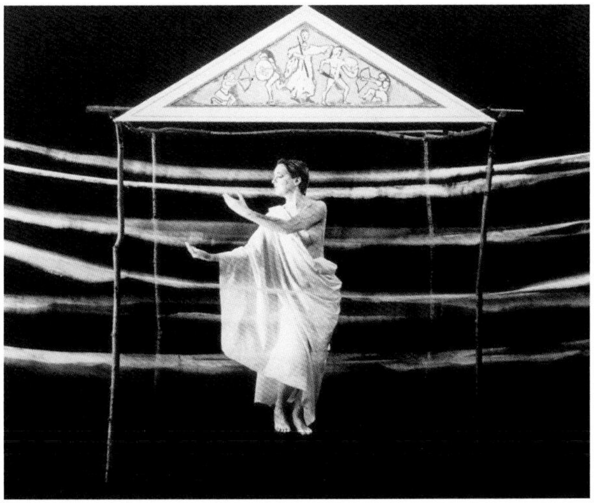

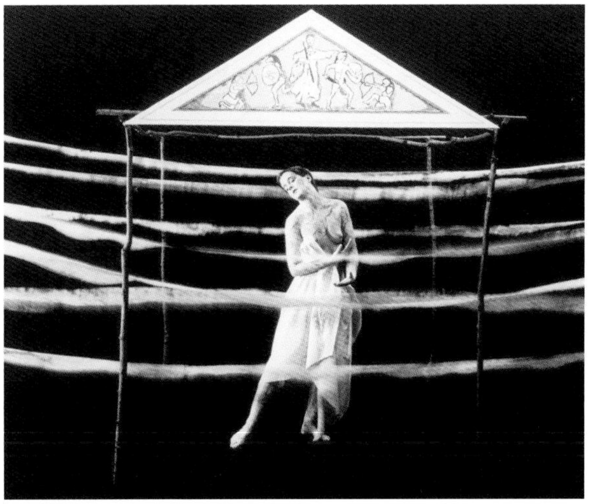

In this series of images, the artist adopts various poses inspired by Greek statuary in simplified architectural iconography reminiscent of ancient Greece. With this choreography, she becomes bard, actress and artist. A drama in four acts, by all appearances we behold tragedy in which the emotional intensity plays off the classicism of the setting, poses and composition. This emblematic piece shows performance as the primary mode of expression, with mythology as inspiration and the studio as the site of all invented spaces. Here, fabulous encounters between painting and photography revel in their theatricality.

Like a demiurge (a half-man god whose immortality is revocable), she reinvents herself and conjures visions.

Act 1: Performance art and theatricality
At the outset of her professional career in the late 1970s, while still a visual arts student at Université Laval, Holly King explored new avenues opening in performance, which defined this art as a process of dematerialization of the object, thereby emphasizing the action by means of which the artist's physical, auditory and gestural presence modulated interaction with the audience.[3] Her earliest performances were staged in 1978, first in tandem with Cyril Reade and then solo before audiences at La Chambre Blanche in Québec City, followed by the Musée d'art contemporain in Montréal and the Grange Arts and Performance Toronto in 1981.

3. I borrow these elements of the definition from Guy Sioui Durand, "Notes critiques sur l'ambiguïté des performances au Québec," Inter, art actuel 58 (fall 1993): 5.

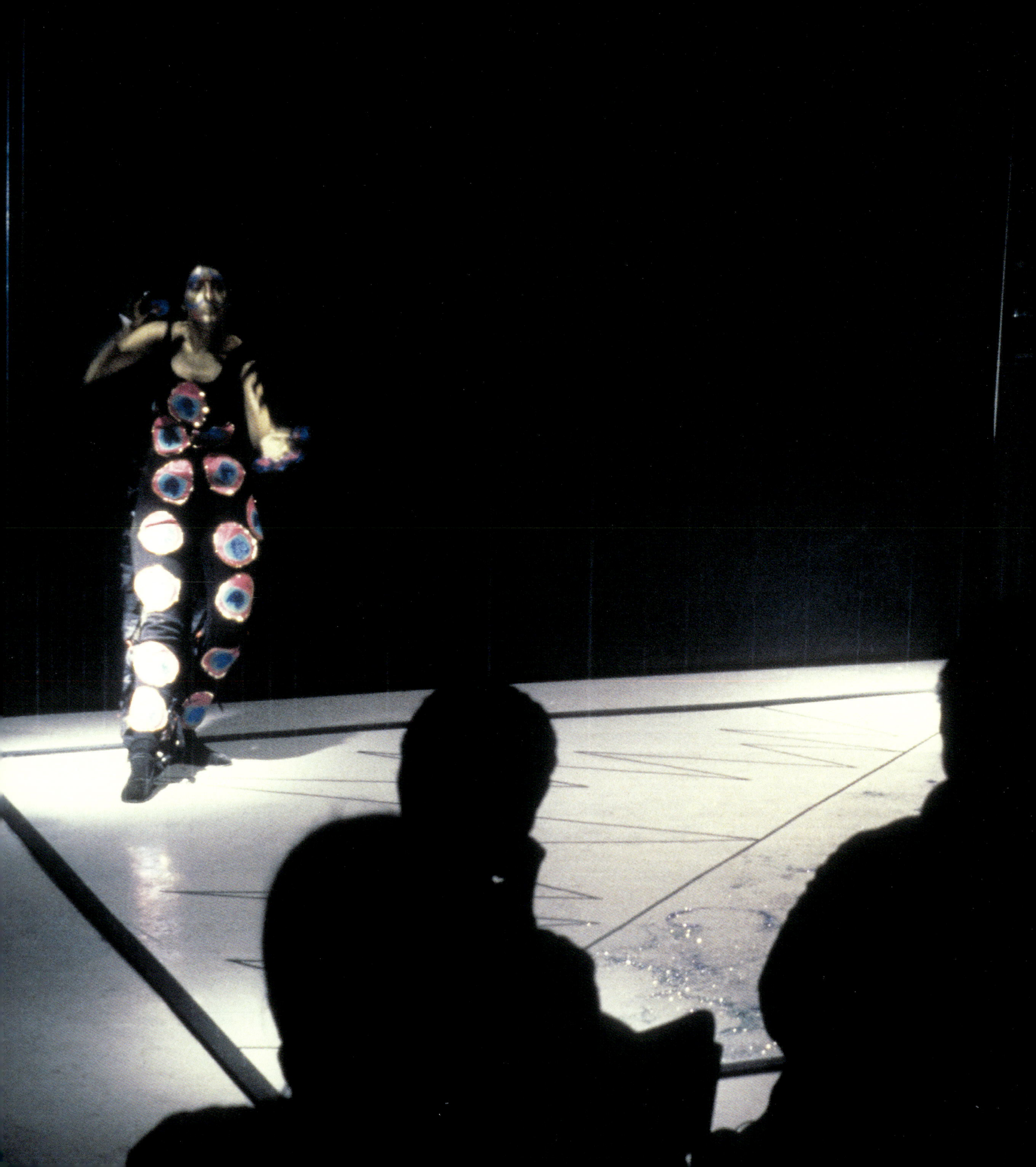

In her solo performances, she drew inspiration from the works of Freud and Jung on psychology and symbols to script the action and develop the content of her pieces. She would casually define the space using simple props, creating the costumes and gestural idioms. She would also vary the length, sound effects, lighting, slideshow and score of action to adapt to spatial limitations and lighting. These are all the strategies of a body in action in space, which constitutes the foundation for her approach, as evidenced in *Two Characters* (1980).

Image : p. 24
Two Characters, 1980
performance
The GAP, Toronto, ON

In fact, by the time she takes to the stage in her studio in 1982 for *Hellenic Winds*, Holly King is familiar with the audience vantage and knows how to integrate it for a frontal perspective. As well, she has discovered the most effective and expressive poses and how to render emotion in her gestural idioms and facial expressions. Moreover, she is familiar with how to create the illusion of movement, plan a sequence and determine the correct proportions for an architectural composition. Therefore, when she sets her camera on a tripod in her studio, which she does as actress, artist and raconteur of a theatrical performance played out in front of the camera lens, thanks to her performance background she has already understood and assimilated all the components of staged photography.

Staged photography, as explained by the publication edited by Lori Pauli, *Acting the Part: Photography as Theatre*,[4] can rely heavily on the use of actors and models, narration, or even theatricality, as was formerly the case with painting and sculpture.[5] This type of photography, akin to a film still, has undergone a resurgence since the 1960s, among other reasons since contemporary photographers delight in offering the viewer the possibility of completing the narrative for these dramatic moments frozen in time.[6] As for theatricality's contribution to contemporary photography, independent curator Karen Henry explains the conceptual complexity as follows:

> Theatricality in early twenty-first-century photography makes no effort to deny the audience or its own constructed fictions. Rather, it invites viewers to participate in an imaginative engagement with representation itself and with the state of affairs in society in general…They reveal the techniques of illusion while reaffirming the possibility of meaningful representation. Like classic tableaux, they imply the continuing project of imminent transformation.[7]

4. Lori Pauli, ed., *Acting the Part: Photography as Theatre* (London: National Gallery of Canada, Merrell Publishers, 2006).
5. Lori Pauli, "Setting the Scene," in *Acting the Part: Photography as Theatre*, 13.
6. *Ibid.*., 18: "[T]he way that staged photography, like painting—or probably more accurately, like the film still—leaves the completion of the narrative up to the viewer. The staged photograph has become once again a dramatic moment frozen in time."
7. Karen Henry, "The Artful Disposition: Theatricality, Cinema, and Social Context in Contemporary Photography," in *Acting the Part: Photography as Theatre*, 154.

Image : p. 27
River on Fire, 1986

As we will see, from the 1980s Holly King has made an original and sustained contribution to staged photography, not through the directing of actors or models, but by the construction of dramatic scenes in which landscape plays the lead role and viewers are invited to imagine the drama about to unfold.

Act 2: Landscape and mythology
Starting in 1985–86, Holly King's studio became the setting for her pictorial and photographic pursuits, her artwork having concentrated until then on drawing and painting on paper.
The artist invited the epic tales of Greek mythology to inhabit her studio, accompanied by their pantheon of gods and goddesses making and unmaking the world along with the heroes that inhabit it. At times fierce, often excessive, they steal into the works and a few of their fantastic stories infuse the narrative. The driving forces of human tragedy—fears, compulsions, dreams and aspirations—intimated their way into the landscapes, finding them fertile ground to explore the inextricable paradoxes between action and inaction.

This inquiry led Holly King to gravitate to expressionism, finding this great landscape tradition most suited to her dramatic material. Thus, disjointed gestural strokes in bright and often contrasting colours sketch summary approximations of natural object forms, attesting to the artist's apparent subjectivity rather than complying with the objective imperatives of diligent mimesis. Free from the tacit obligation to describe, these lyrical flights of fancy unlock expressivity in terms of colour, form, movement and light, thereby releasing a vast range of emotion and inner conflict.

Quite frequently in the artist's paintings, particularly in *River on Fire* (1986), from the series *Rivers of Hades*, the landscape is clearly defined, with diagonals that compel our gaze to peer into the depths of the scene or seek out the horizon. The high-angle perspective favoured for the foregrounds bids us to enter the landscape whose successive planes delineate a delusion of depth. Delightful elements of the natural world abound, highlighted by a superb play of textures. As for the narrative, skillful juxtapositions of light and shadow direct our gaze. Here in particular, the rising and almost infinite watery depths flow to the edge of consciousness. But beneath the bluish tinges are hints of the mysteries underpinning our world, suggested by semi-abstract evocations of dead souls cascading into the underworld abyss ruled by Hades.

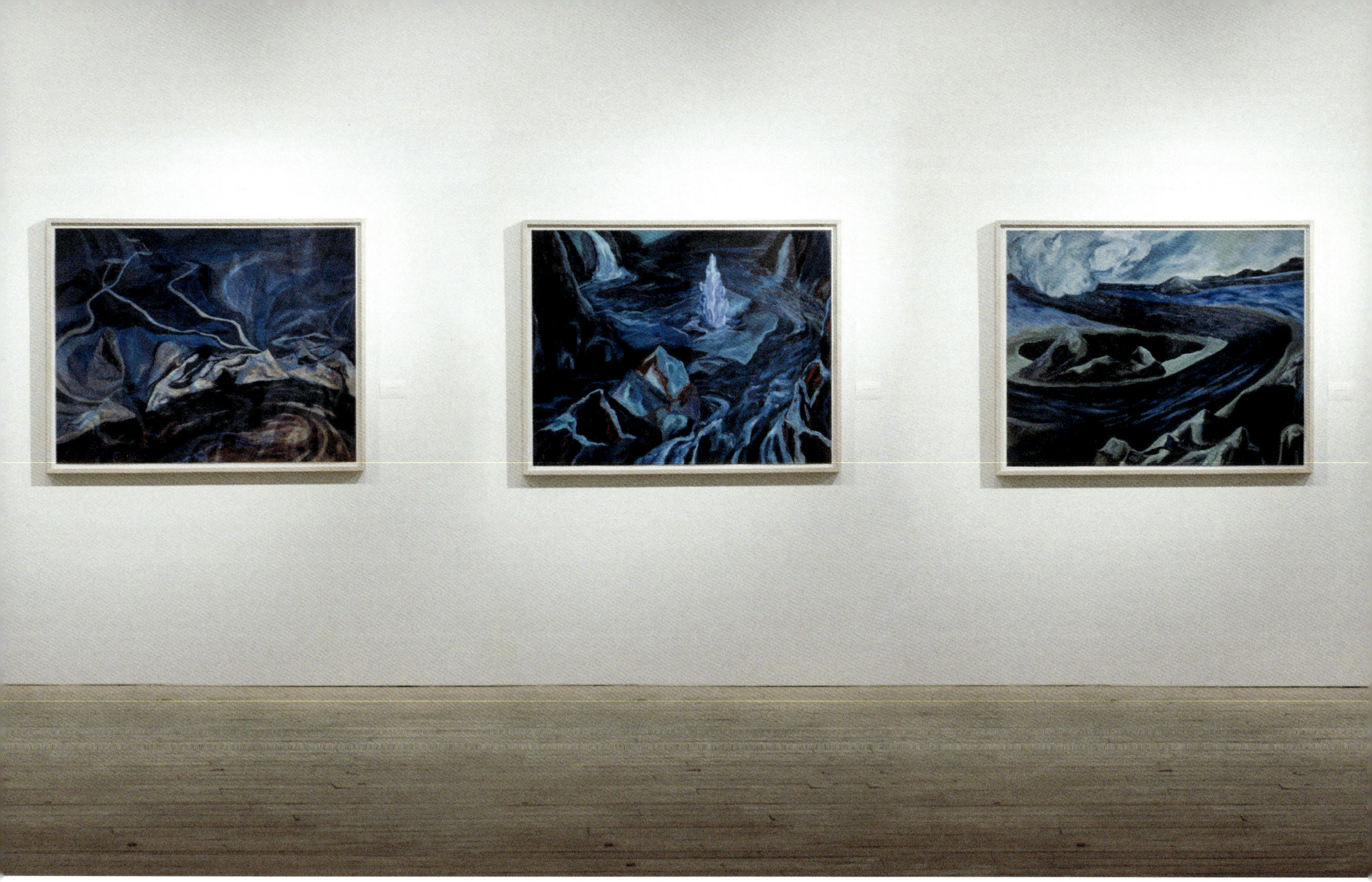

By inviting the gods into her studio, Holly King has metaphorically borrowed their powers to infuse her works with a fictional force that obscures the margin between the real and imaginary. In these terms, the studio becomes a cave dedicated to the production of landscapes that will henceforth be created for and immortalized by photographic imagery.

Act 3: The studio and construction
Closer examination of the series *Realms of Night* (1986–89), in which the artist exceptionally introduced three-dimensional architectural components to the natural elements arranged on her work table, leads us to grant these structures the status of

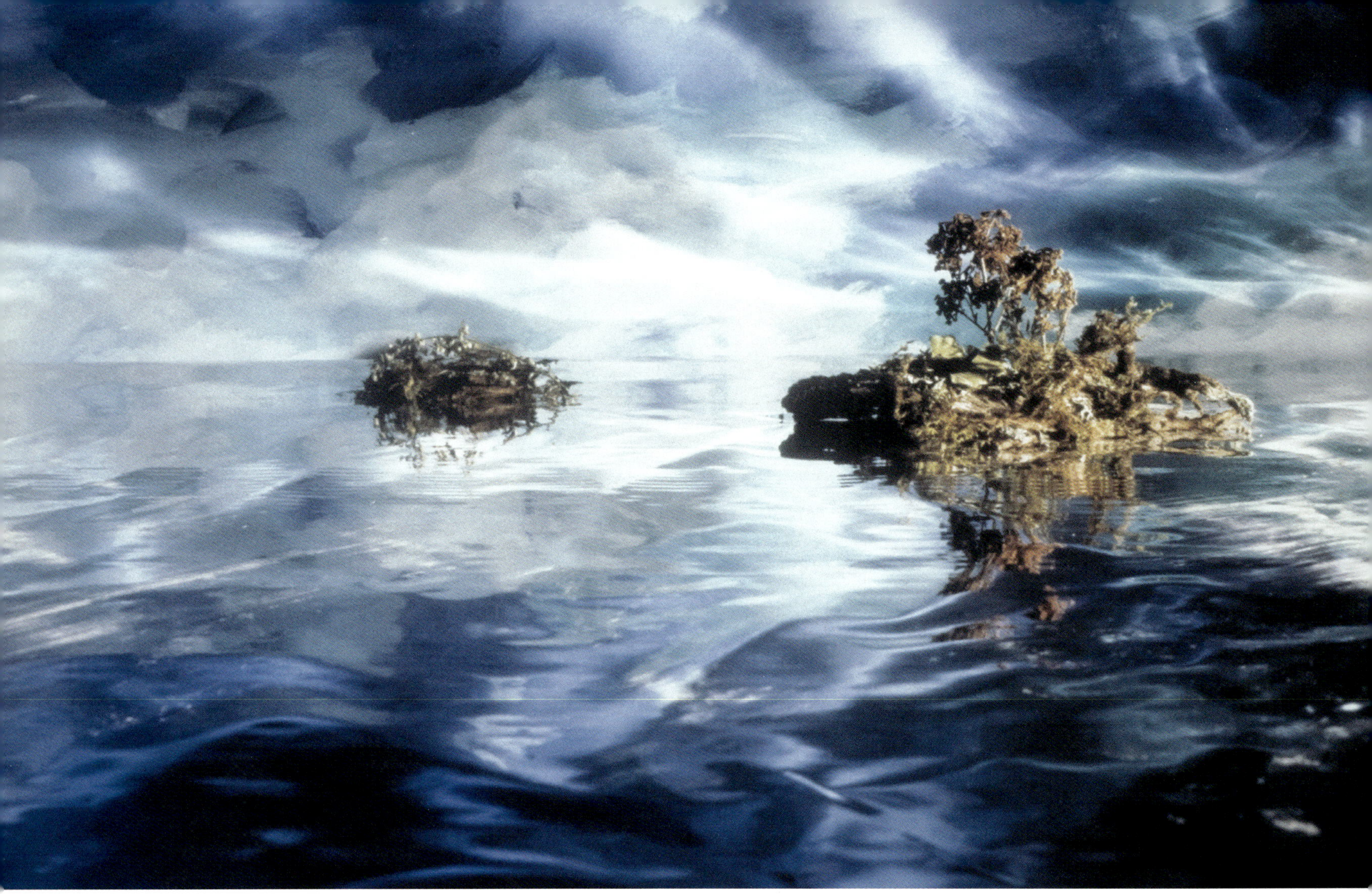

clues. Like precursors, the structures of the lighthouse, bridge and arbour point to the performance dimension of these landscape "constructions," evoking the artist's aesthetic nucleus. Serving as effective self-referential deconstructions, these small tabletop sets reveal that for Holly King, art is an intellectual and manual construction. There is no doubt that the artist presents herself as a mulier faber, the architect of her own fortune who concocts ideas and fashions tools for her imaginary tales, with mind and hand allied to devise and mould landscape fictions. She does not hide the illusion. On the contrary, she consistently makes her theatricality apparent. There is little doubt she is fully aware and wants us to know that she is cognizant of her gestures: "The 'gesture which knows itself to be appearance' is a self-reflexive mirror that reveals the nature of contemporary representation."[8]

8. Karen Henry, "The Artful Disposition: Theatricality, Cinema, and Social Context in Contemporary Photography," in *Acting the Part: Photography as Theatre*, 134–35.

Consequently, she derives great pleasure from the mischief of introducing fabricated props into her studio and then ultimately into her staged photographs. Artistic constructions, as René Payant reminds us, depend on the inventive skill of the craftsperson/artist, relying on their talent for collecting, integrating and staging. This process engages in a dialogue with an inventory of found objects and, like myth, is a construction that also reveals the storyteller.[9]

Continuing on our journey, we suddenly find ourselves more attentive to the countless presences of natural materials that pose for the camera, exposing the scenographer's craft. Twigs, dried grasses, flowers, branches, roots and pebbles are positioned depending on their shapes, colours and textures, composing miniature still lifes whose essence the artist occasionally transgresses by magnifying or shrinking dimensions to suit the scale of her theatrical productions, creating believable landscape vistas. Elsewhere the twig becomes foliage, the root an arch, the bark a tree trunk, or the pebble a boulder. These natural findings heighten the desired landscape realism, complementing the scenes which Holly King has previously conceived in a sculpture genre using plaster, clay, aluminum, or cellophane that she shapes, wrinkles and patterns into trees, forests and streams, as seen in the series *Forest of Enchantment* (1997–2000), *Mirages* (2000), *Coming Into View* (2002–04), or even *Twisted Roots* (2005–07).

Further, to give even more verisimilitude to her collage constructions, she paints strikingly colourful skies in the background, a tender homage to the great English and American landscape painters.

But what would become of these illusionist creations if the lighting did not add its play of light and shadow to complete the tableaux with countless subtle variations, using the rhetoric of visual seduction? While "at times truth may not seem probable,"[10] for an image to be effective, though, the effect must not appear so.

Clearly, we must conclude that the voluntarily limited number of physical and symbolic variables allowed to enter into the artist's vocabulary requires a constant mastery of *ars combinatoria*. Skilled in this hybrid form, she must constantly recombine components, force mutations and renew representational forms, as explored in her large-format photographs.

Image : p. 28
Solitude, 2000
épreuve à développement chromogène / chromogenic print
99 x 168 cm

9. On this topic, we are indebted to René Payant, who was in turn inspired by his reading of Claude Lévi-Strauss. René Payant, "Bricolage pictural," in *Vedute, pièces détachées sur l'art 1967–1987* (Laval: Trois, 2003), 63.
10. This criterion for credibility listed on Wikipedia is likely paraphrased from the poet Nicolas Boileau, to whom we are indebted for this classical episteme: "Le vrai peut quelquefois n'être point vraisemblable."

Image : p. 31
Ascent to the Edge, 2011
photographie en noir et blanc / black and white photograph
163 x 91 cm

Act 4: Landscape and landscapes

In 2008–09, with the series *Mangroves: Floating Between Two Worlds*, Holly King embarked on a new strategy. Enthused by the evocative powers of literature, she left the studio not to paint, but to photograph actual landscapes. She found that tropical mangroves inspired horizontal compositions with harmonious proportions. This time, it is nature that draws itself, keeping us at bay before its vegetal calligraphy. The viewer is not accorded an aperture to penetrate these dense, sinuous landscapes, tortured and unyielding, without the benevolence of welcoming perspective, as if the torrid heat swallowed all space. Even the reflective play on the water in the foreground offers none of the visual openings to which Holly King has accustomed us.

Subsequently, following other photographic expeditions, such as to the Grand Canyon or the English seacoast, the artist reintroduced large-format slides to the studio, installing them as the backgrounds in constructed sets. This practice gave rise to another conceptual step where the viewing boxes became the arena for a new format, where two moments, two landscapes are superimposed. The first, witness to the previous journey and symbolic witness to photography's transparency, is positioned at the back of the set. Before this scene, natural and fabricated elements play other roles in a second, entirely fictitious landscape. With the fall of the curtain, when the artist demiurge decides on the final framing, this results in the staged photograph becoming a third landscape, one combining and encompassing the two others, a sort of Russian doll of landscapes layered with multiple evocative powers. Here again, we discover myriad mirages in black and white, which summon us, needing us to continue to exist, since "we collaborate, to the best of our receptive and commemorative means, in the regeneration and perpetuation of the artist's work, precisely to the extent that we too experience the unmastered 'thereness' of a secret sharer, of a prior creation with and against which the art-act has been effected."[11]

Finally, we are invited on a fictitious journey. With heightened dramatic artistry, the curtain abruptly unveils a distant horizon, compelling us to seek truth and beauty in the imaginary world to which we must travel. And neither Holly King nor we know who we will be upon our return.

11. George Steiner, *Real Presences: Is There Anything in What We Say?* (Boston and London: Faber & Faber, 1989), 212.

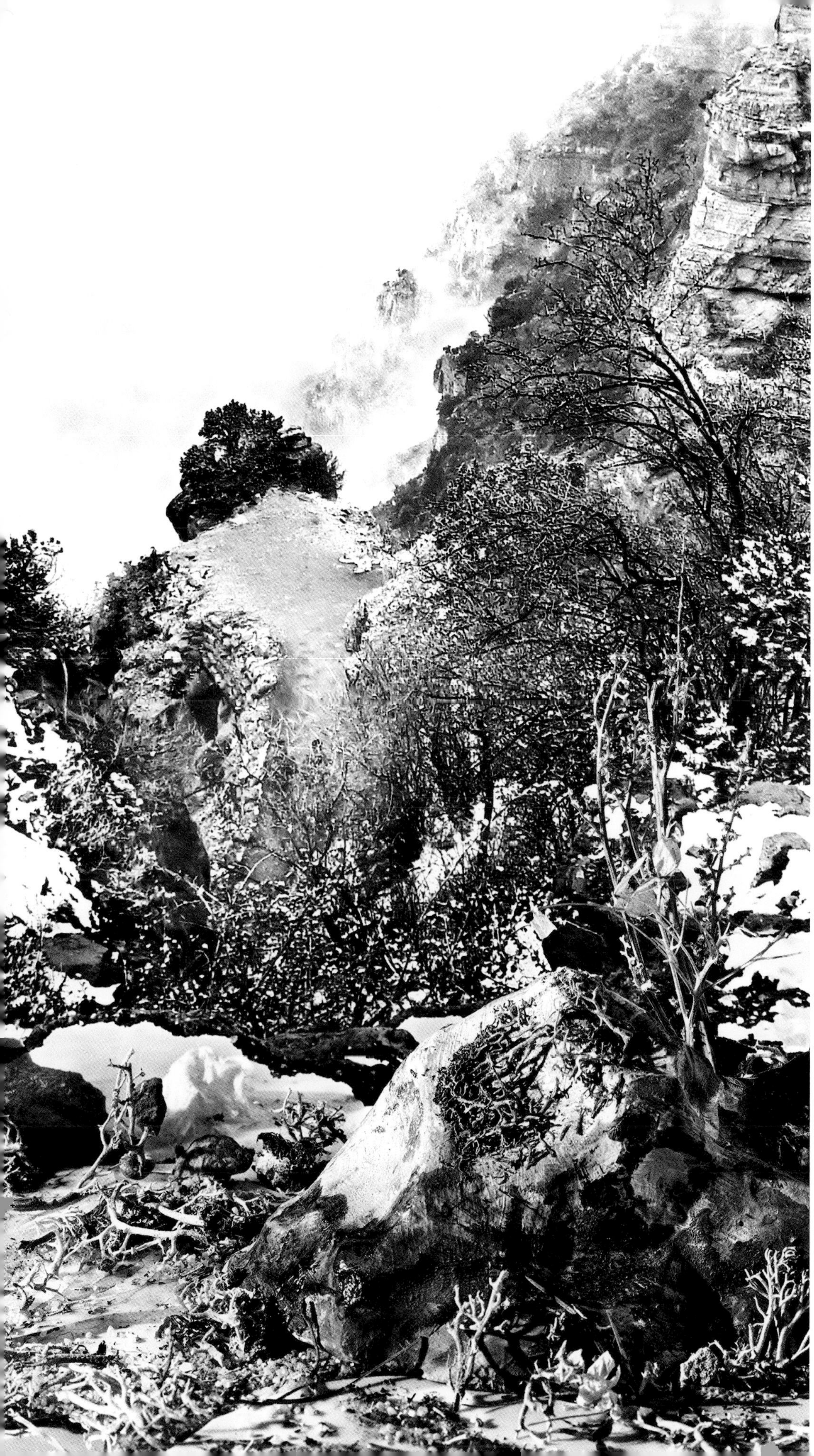

PORTFOLIO I

THE REALMS OF NIGHT

THE GARDENS

MINING PROJECT

THE VIEWLESS WINDS

FOREST OF ENCHANTMENT

MIRAGES

COMING INTO VIEW

THE TRANSCENDENT SUBLIME

THE REALMS OF NIGHT

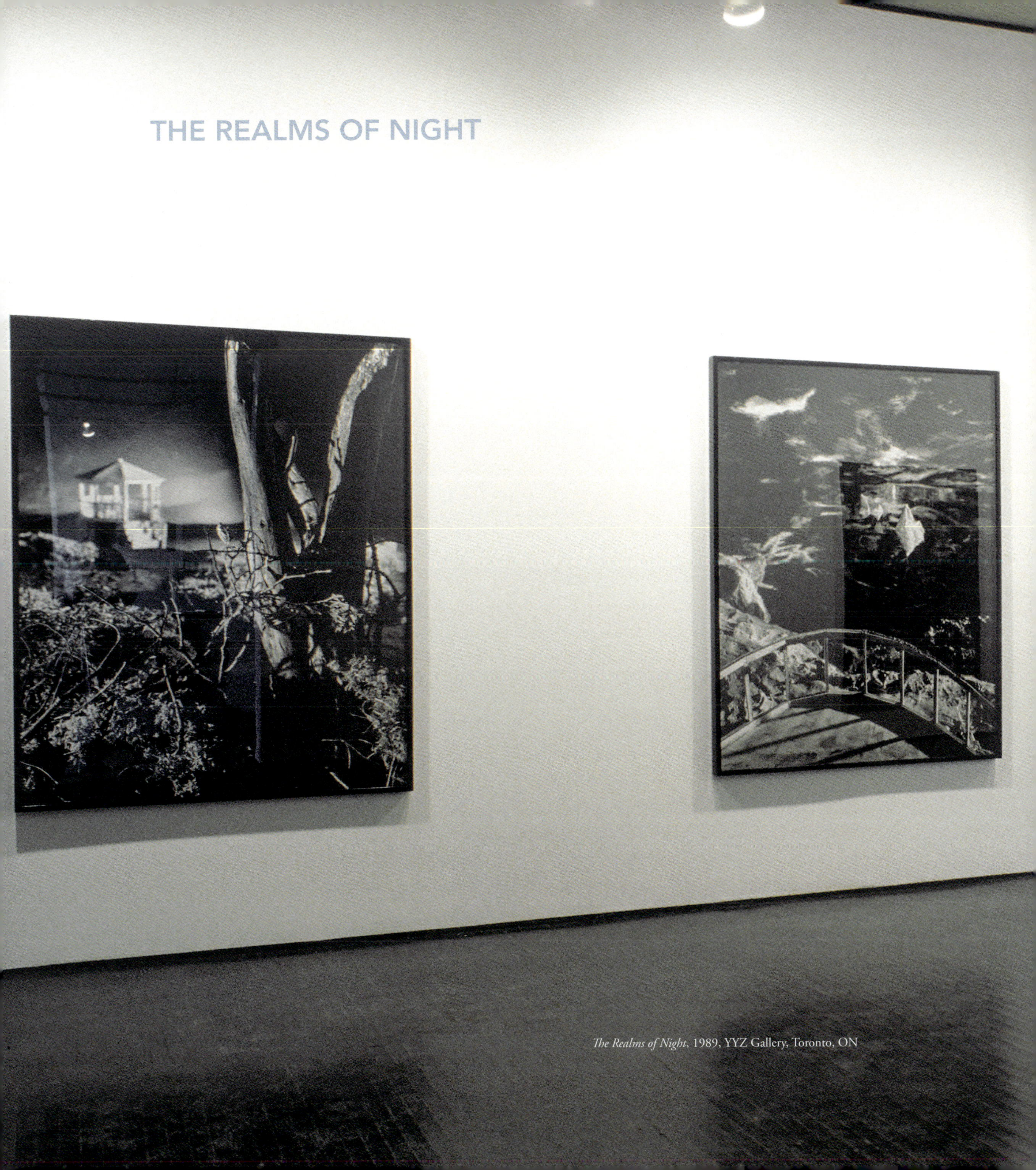

The Realms of Night, 1989, YYZ Gallery, Toronto, ON

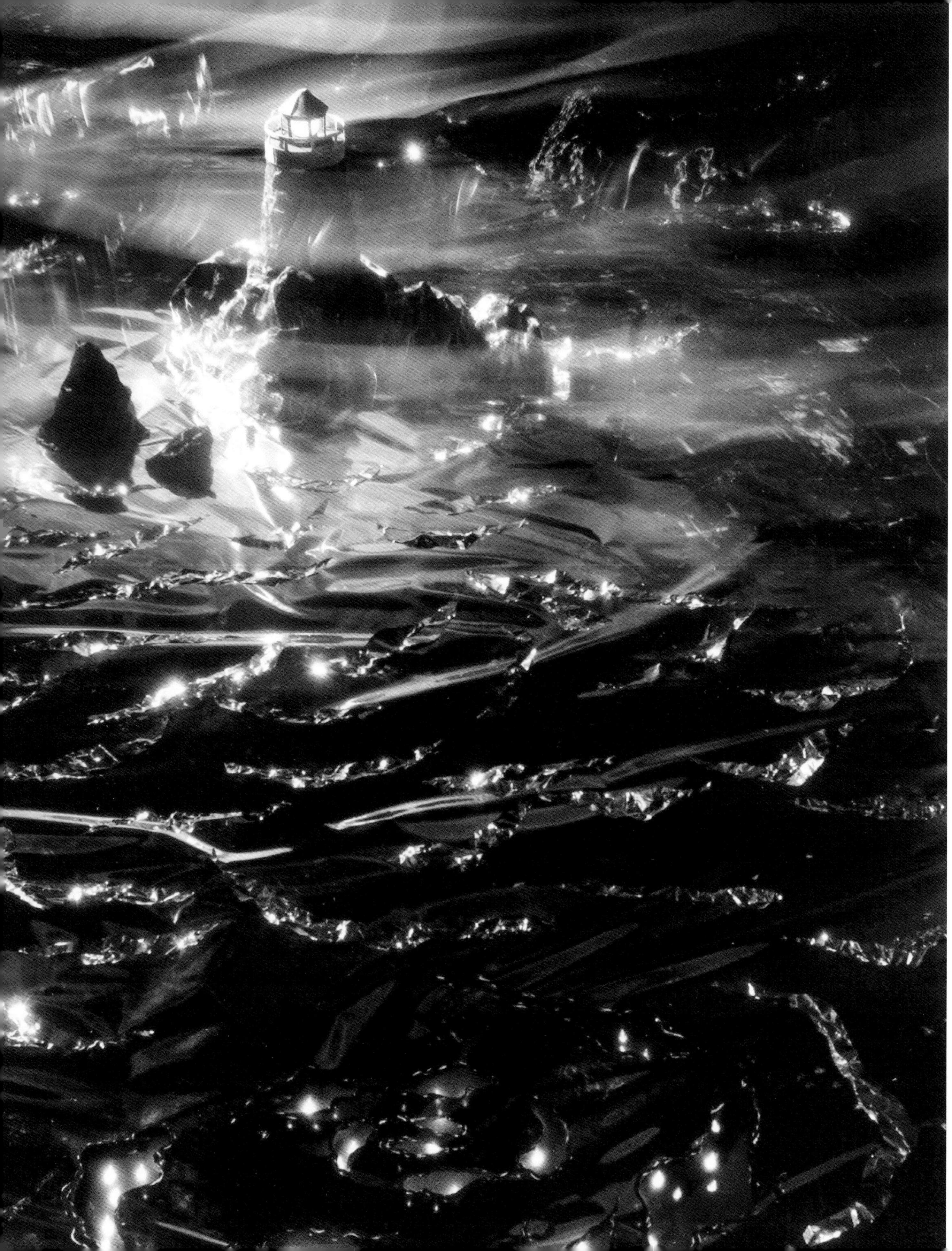

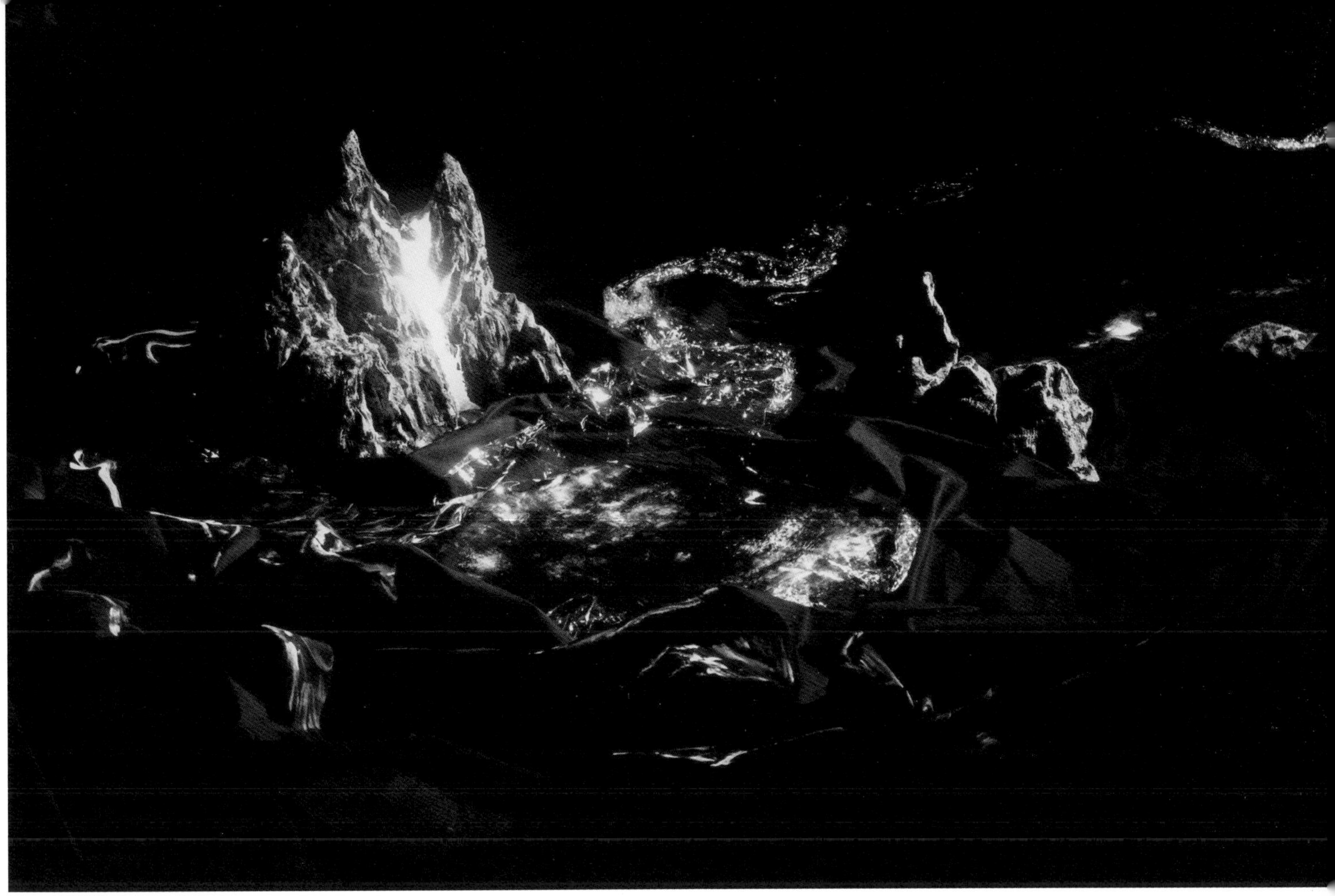

Image : p. 34
Lighthouse Furies, 1986
épreuve argentiques sur gélatine /
silver gelatin print
159 x 122 cm

Image : p. 35
Schism, 1986
épreuve argentiques sur gélatine /
silver gelatin print
122 x 184 cm

THE GARDENS

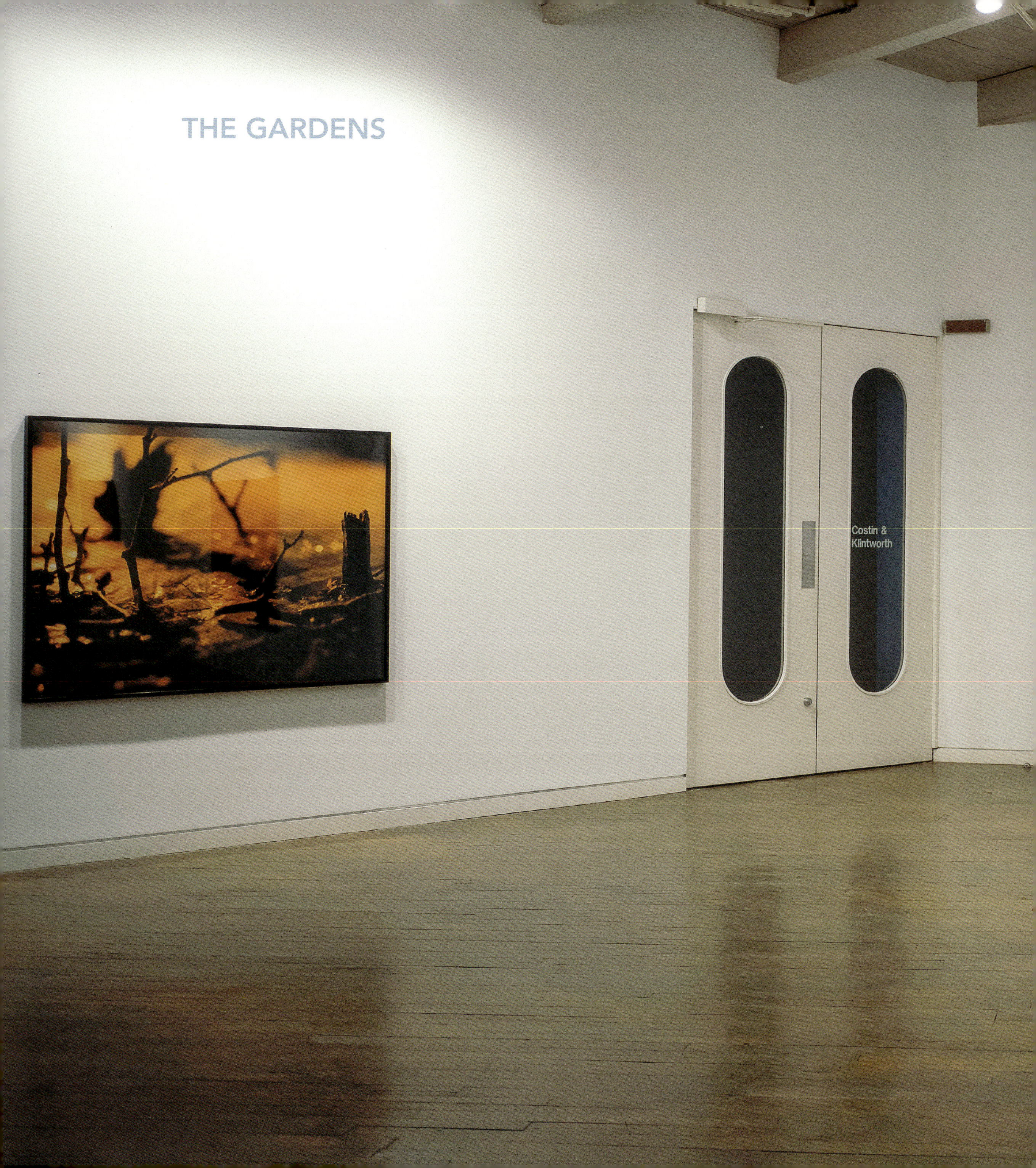

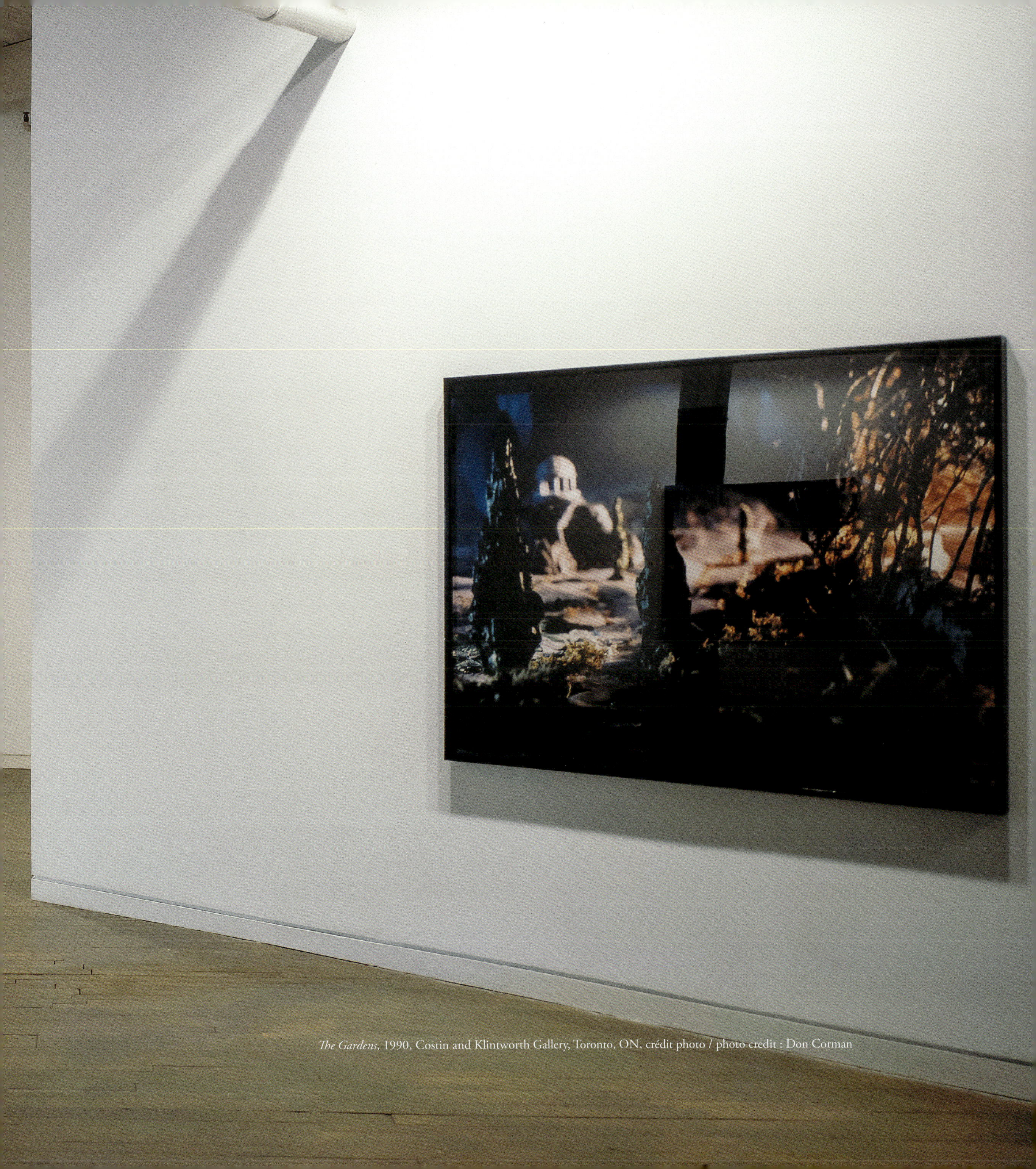

The Gardens, 1990, Costin and Klintworth Gallery, Toronto, ON, crédit photo / photo credit : Don Corman

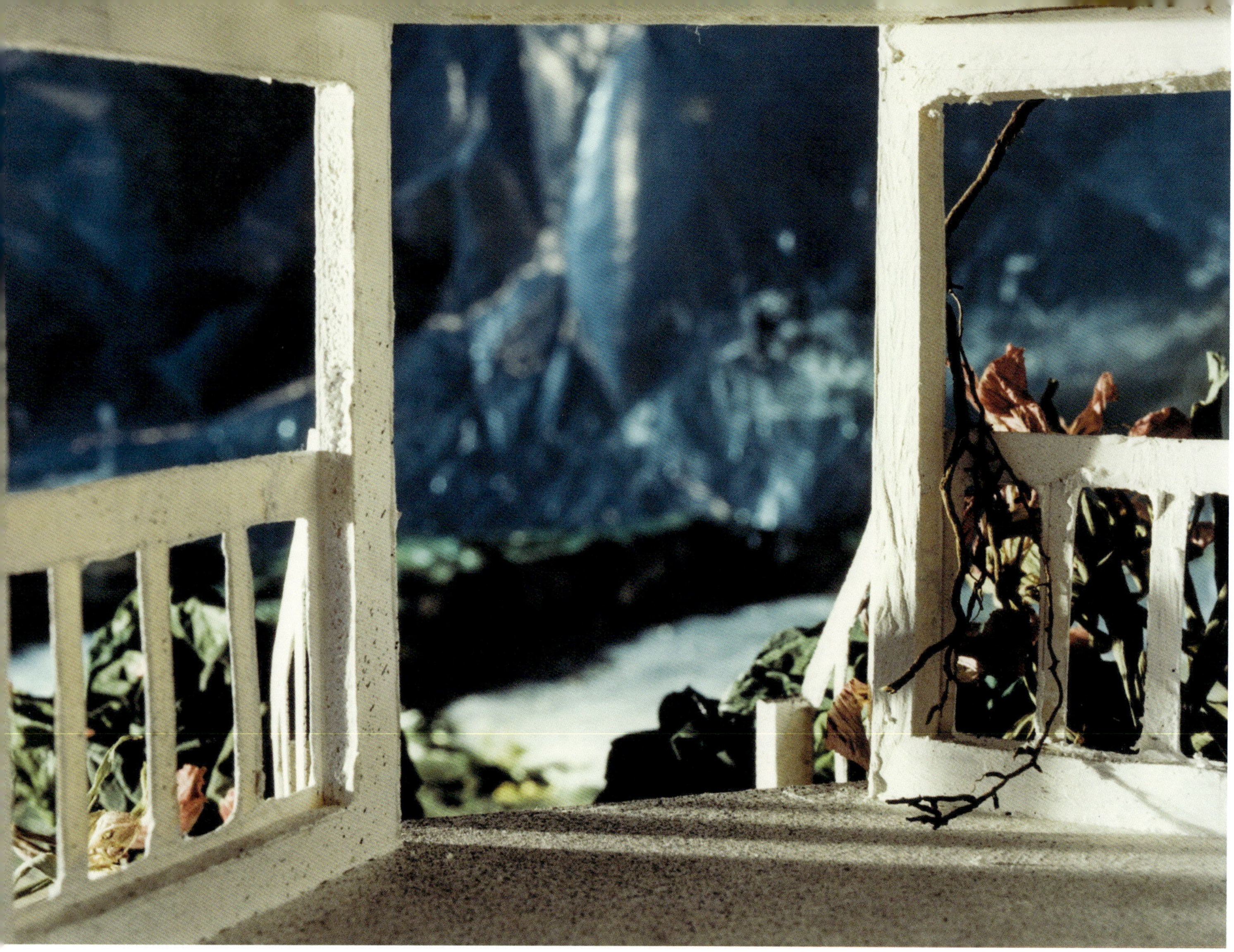

Encroaching Panorama, 1990
épreuve à développement chromogène /
chromogenic print
122 x 158 cm

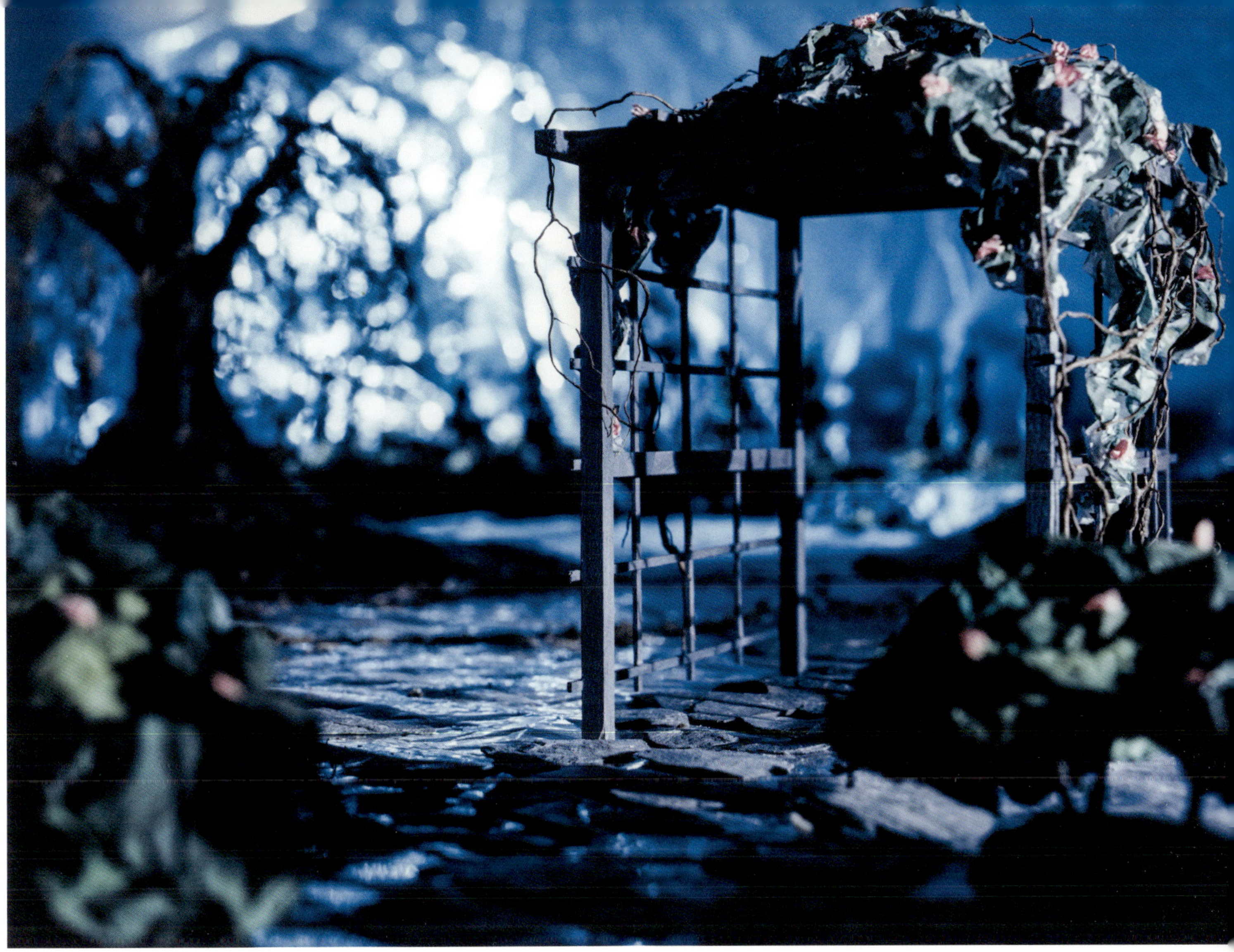

Moonlit Pergola, 1990
épreuve à développement chromogène /
chromogenic print
122 x 158 cm

THE MINING PROJECT

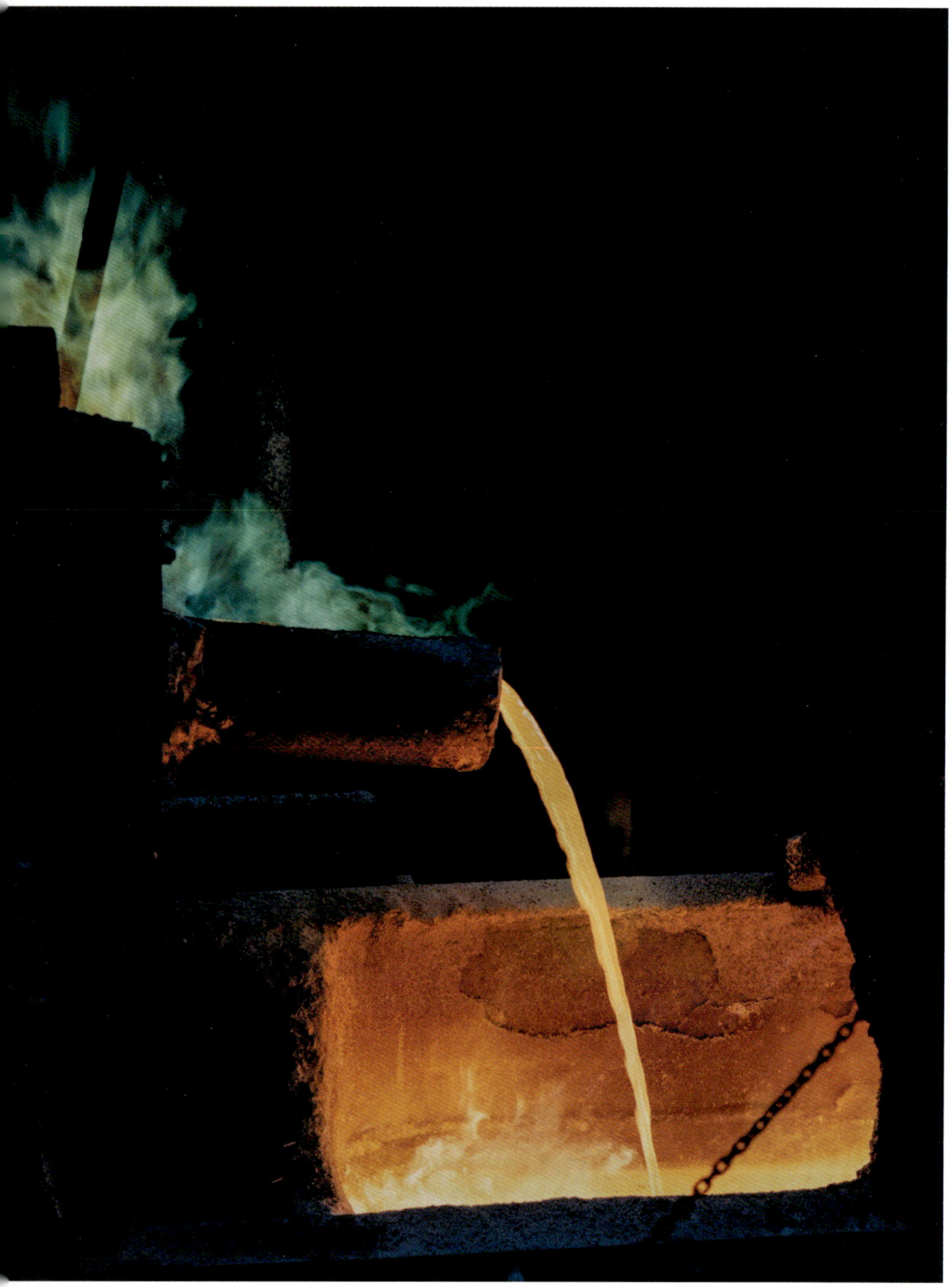

Image : p. 40
Metallurgical Pour, 1993
épreuve à développement chromogène /
chromogenic print
122 x 158 cm

Image : p. 41
Chamber of Passage (série Mining), 1993
épreuve à développement chromogène /
chromogenic print
158 x 122 cm

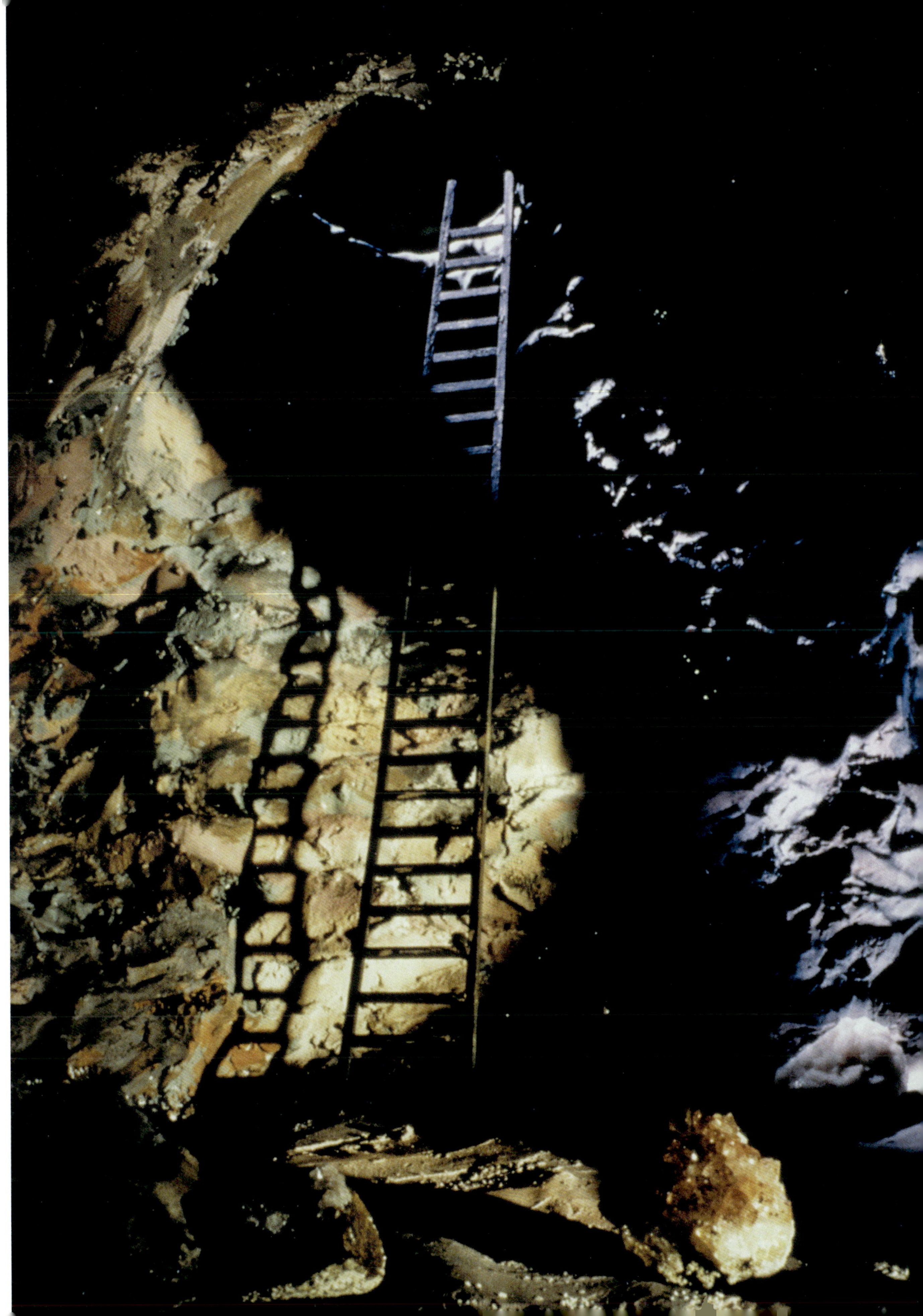

THE VIEWLESS WINDS

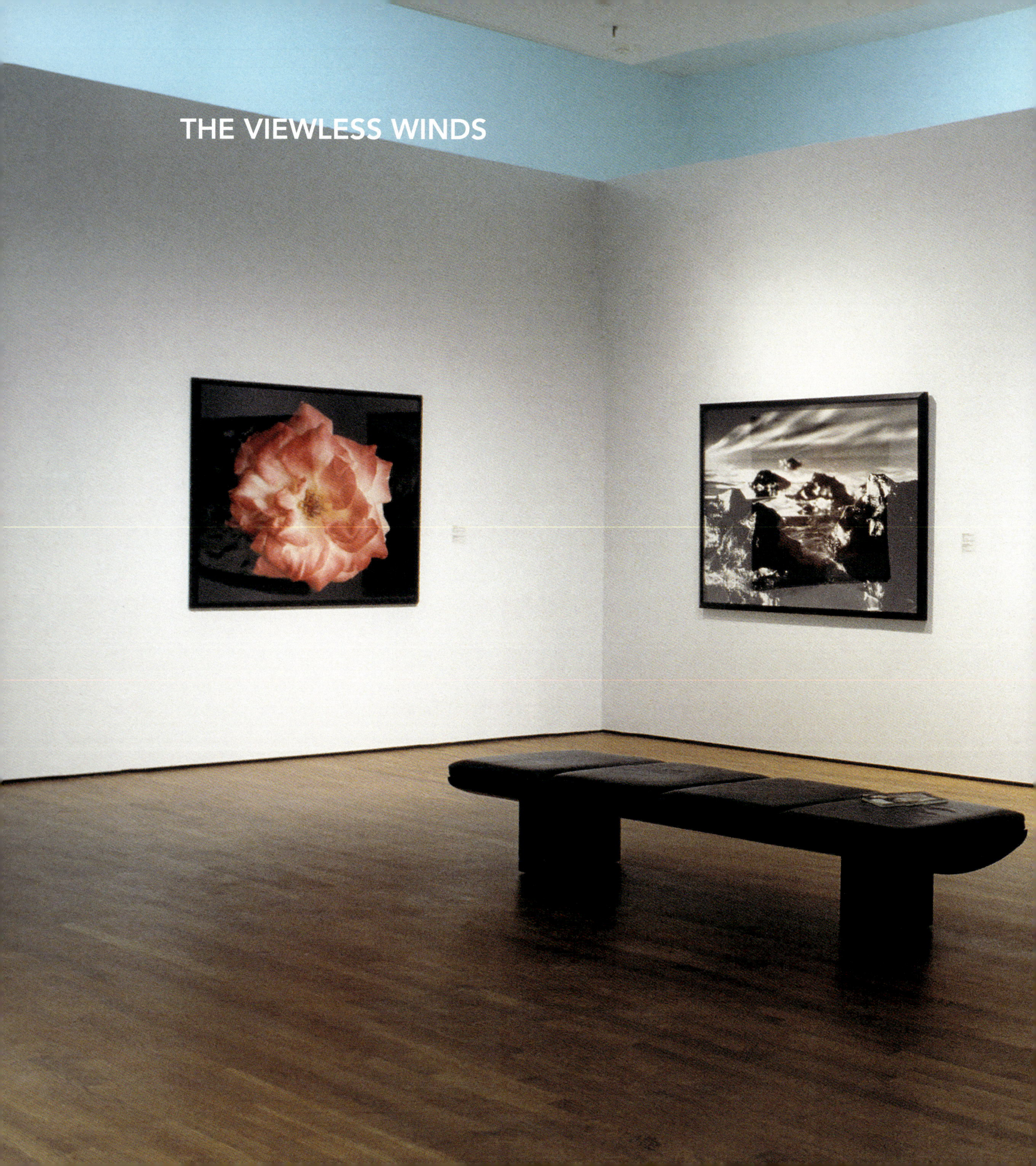

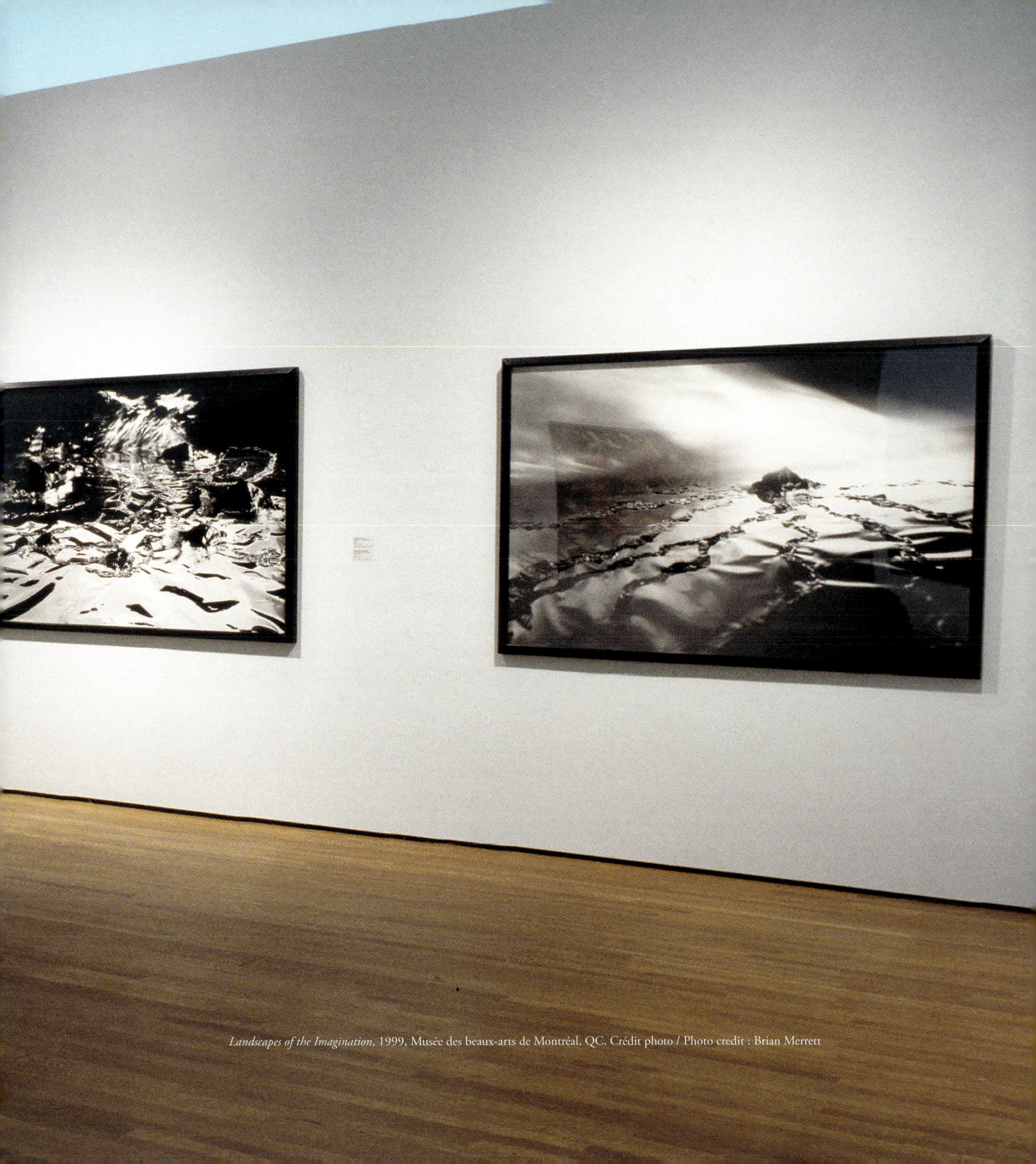

Landscapes of the Imagination, 1999, Musée des beaux-arts de Montréal, QC. Crédit photo / Photo credit : Brian Merrett

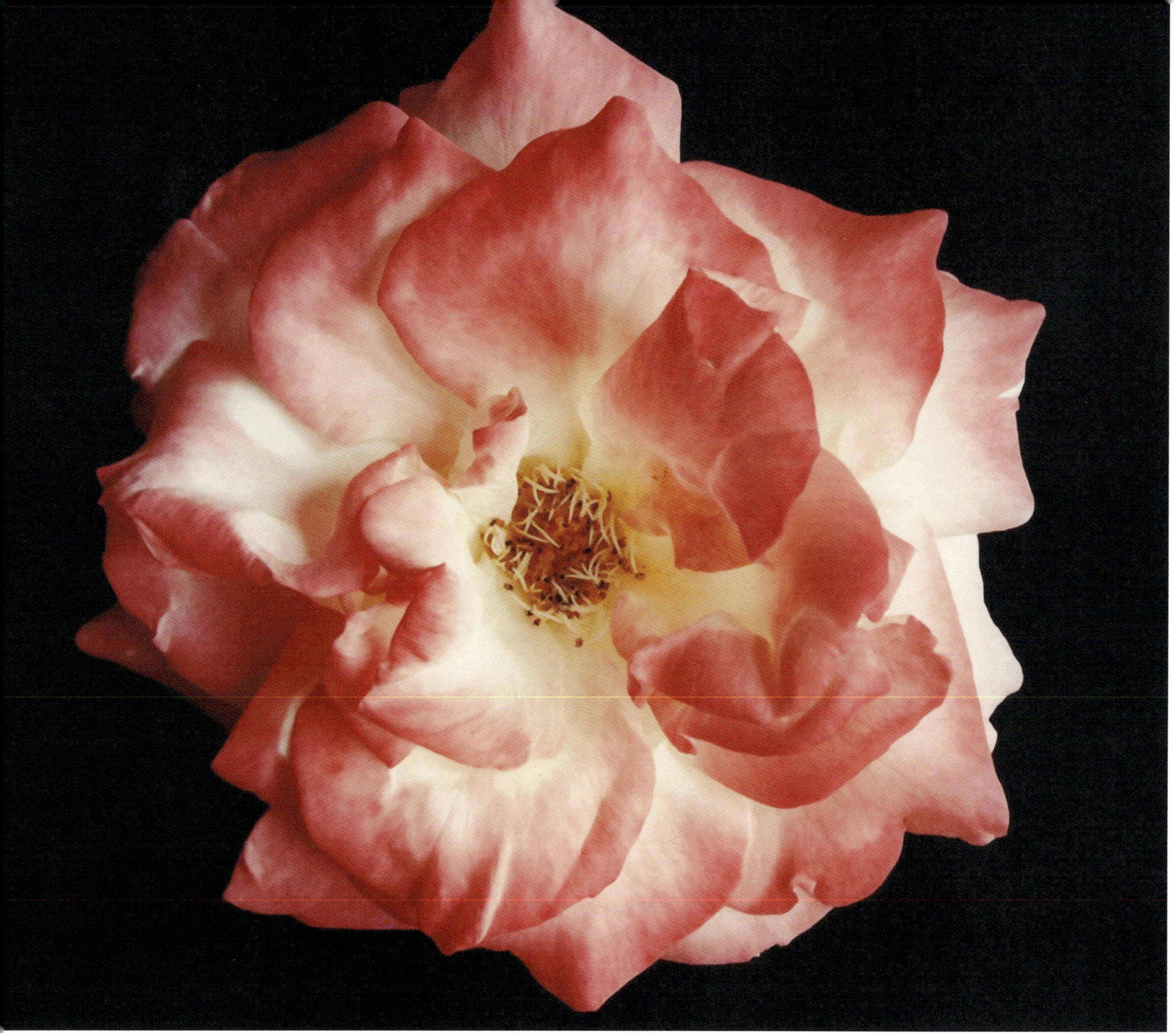

Rose Bloomed, 1995
épreuve à développement chromogène /
chromogenic print
122 x 150 cm

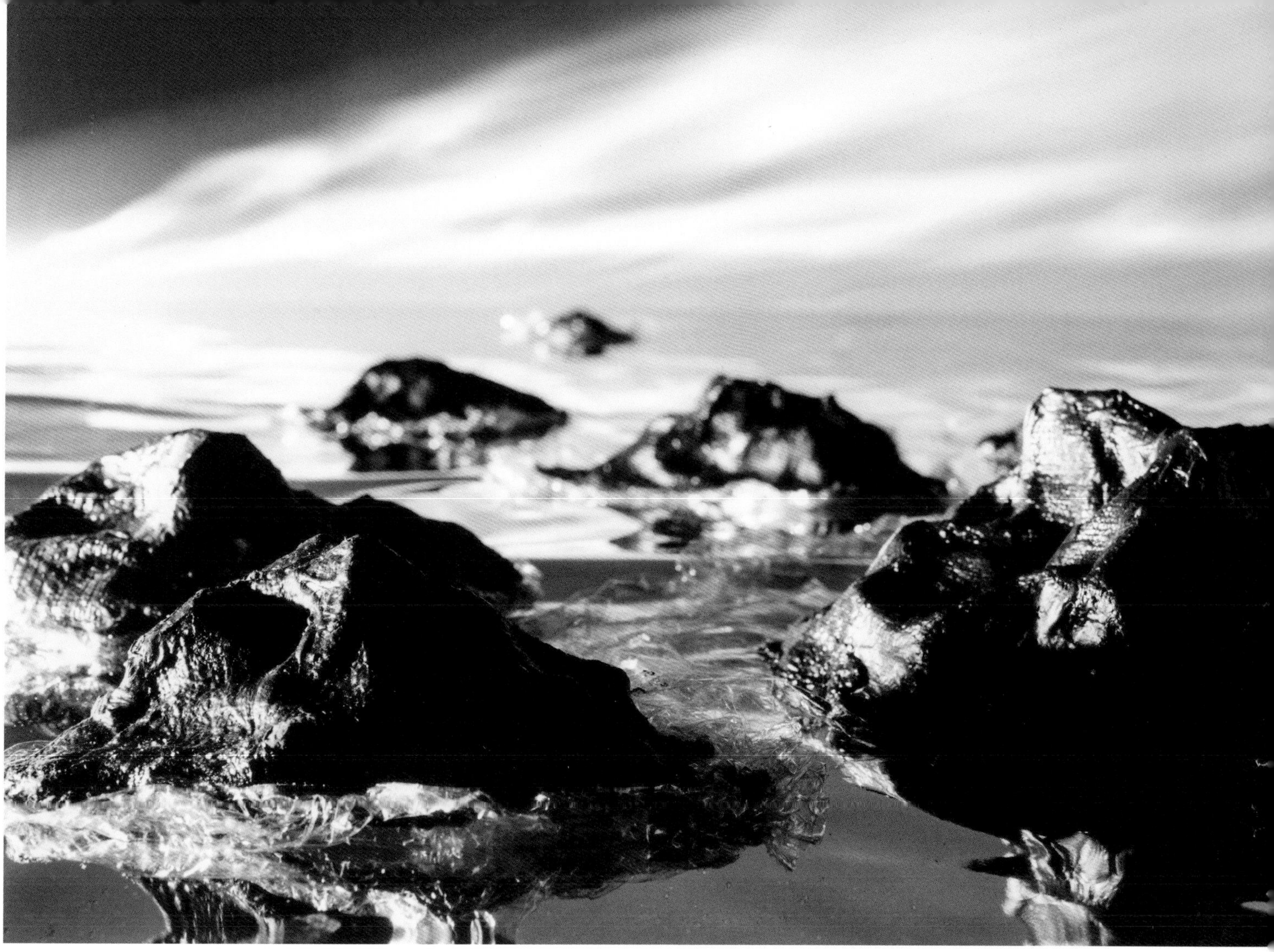

The Viewless Winds, 1995
photographie en noir et blanc /
black and white photograph
122 x 183 cm

THE FOREST OF ENCHANTMENT

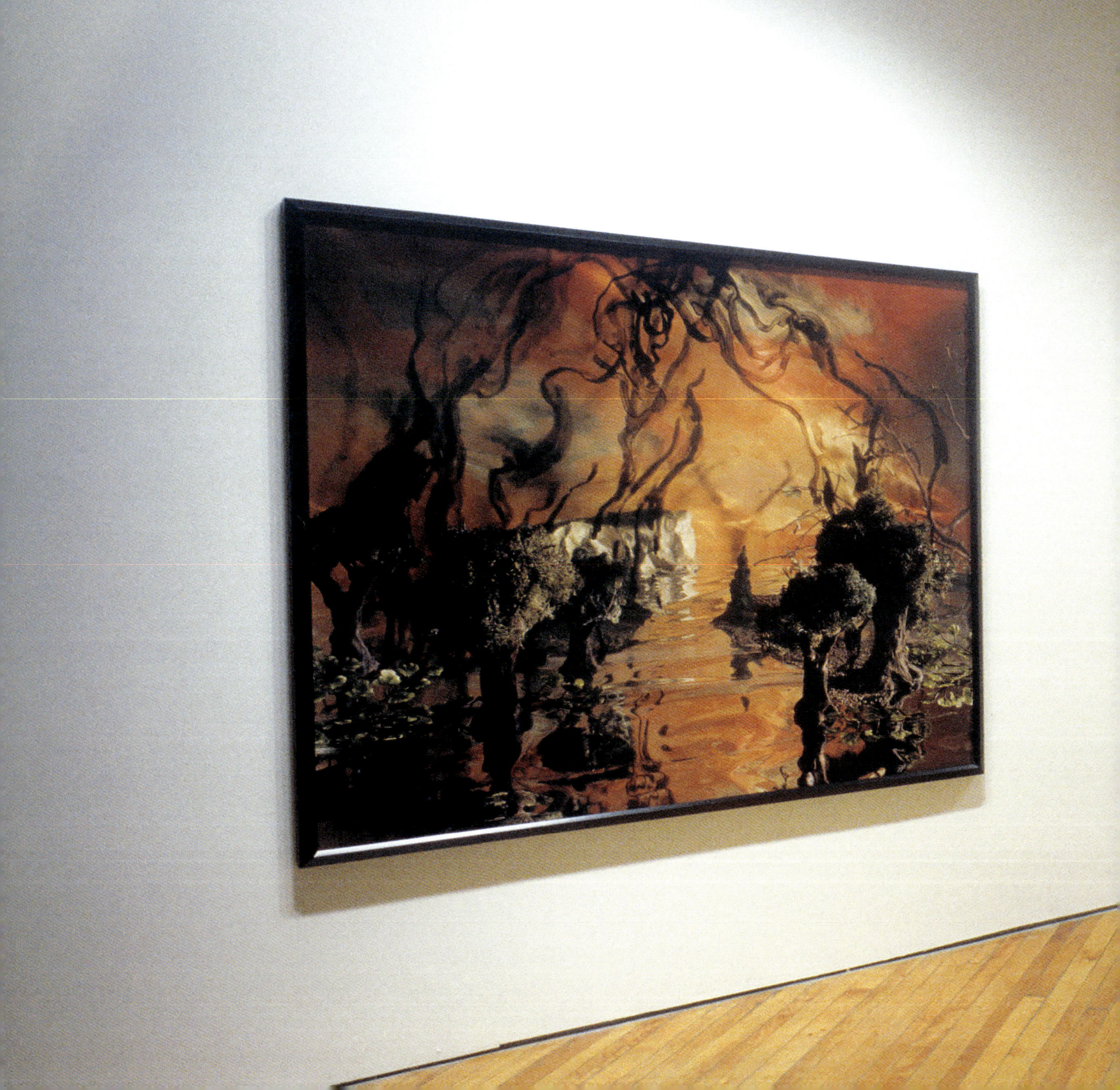

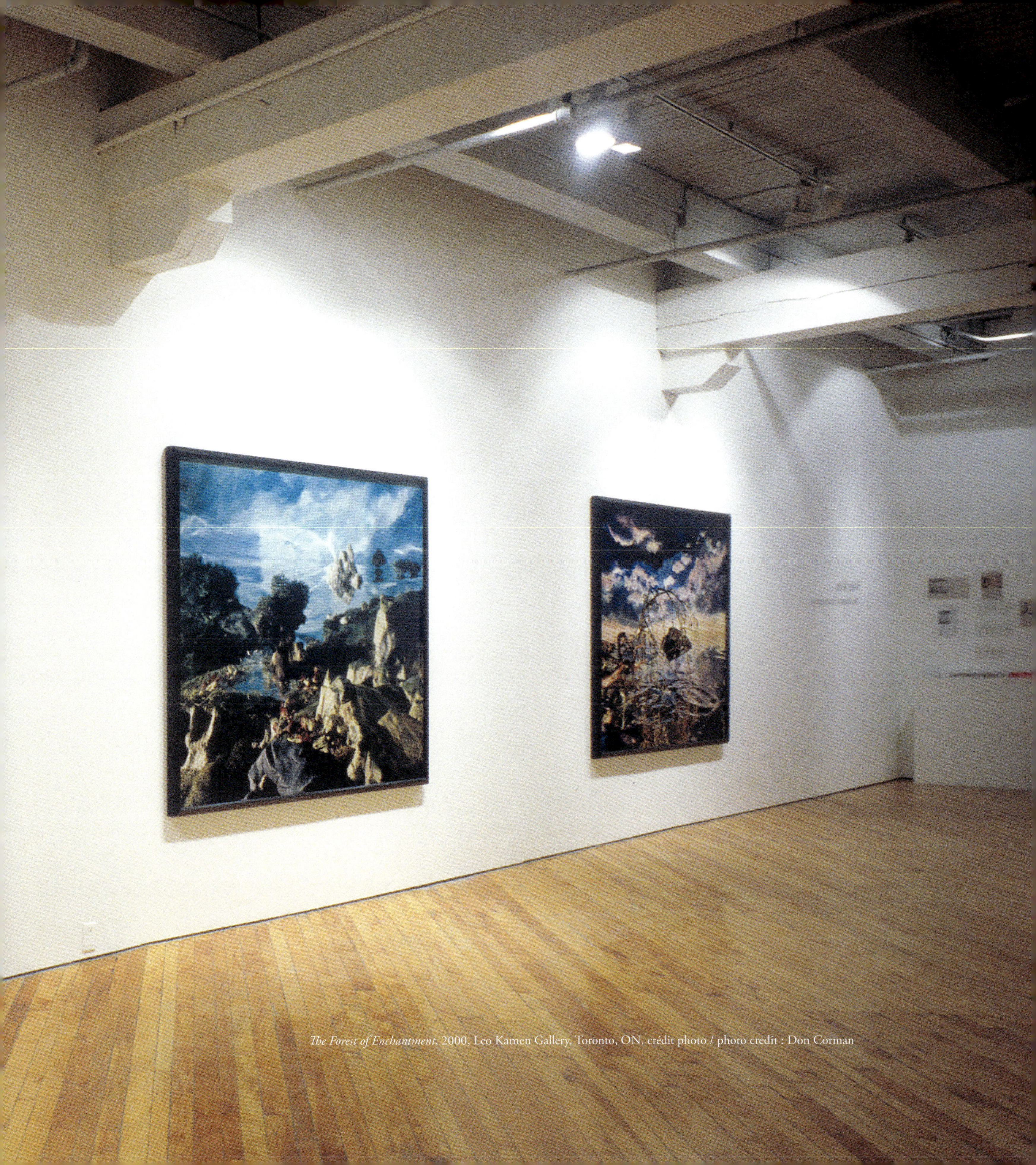

The Forest of Enchantment, 2000, Leo Kamen Gallery, Toronto, ON, crédit photo / photo credit : Don Corman

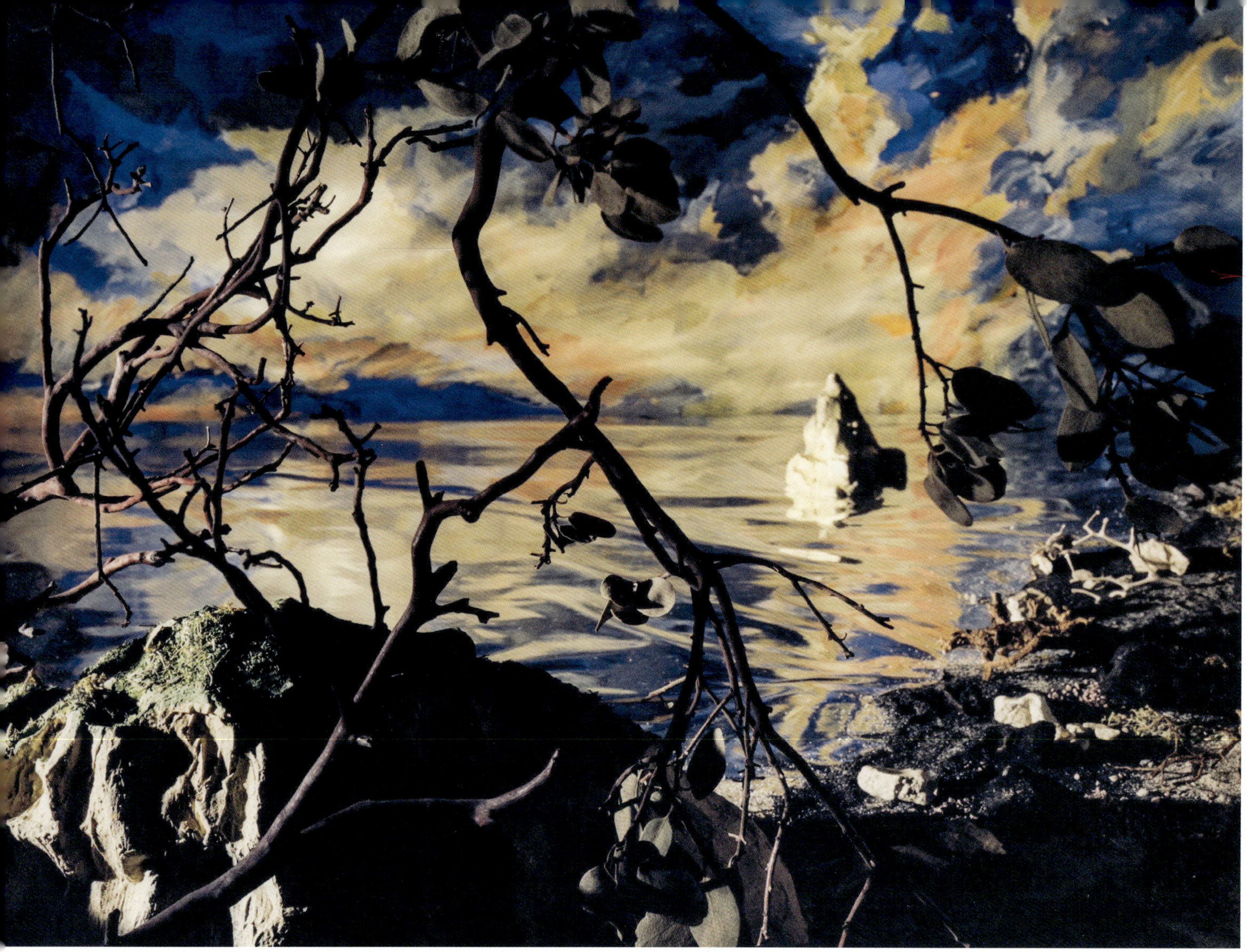

Lament, 1999
épreuve à développement chromogène /
chromogenic print
153 x 183 cm

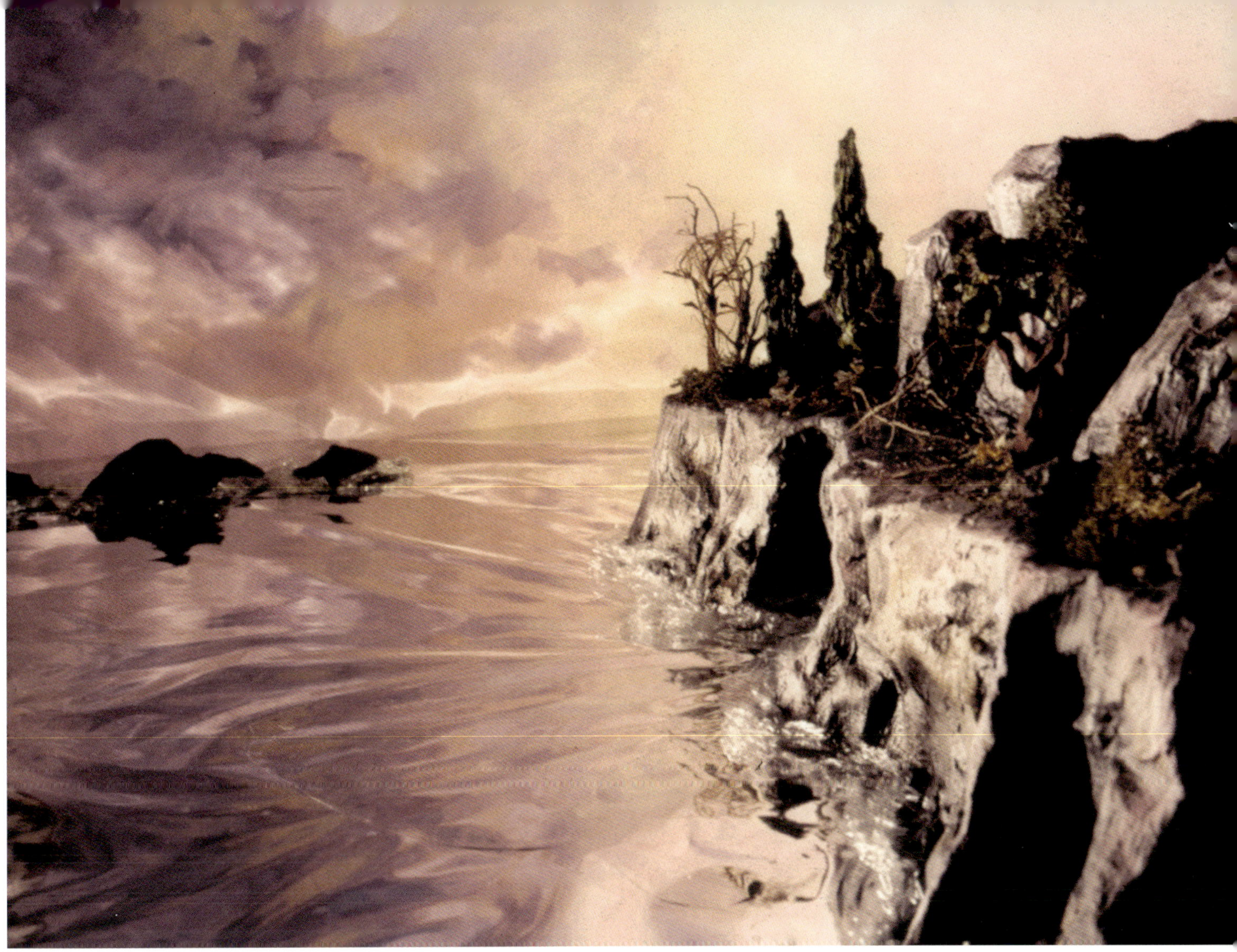

Roseate, 1999
épreuve à développement chromogène /
chromogenic print
153 x 183 cm

MIRAGES

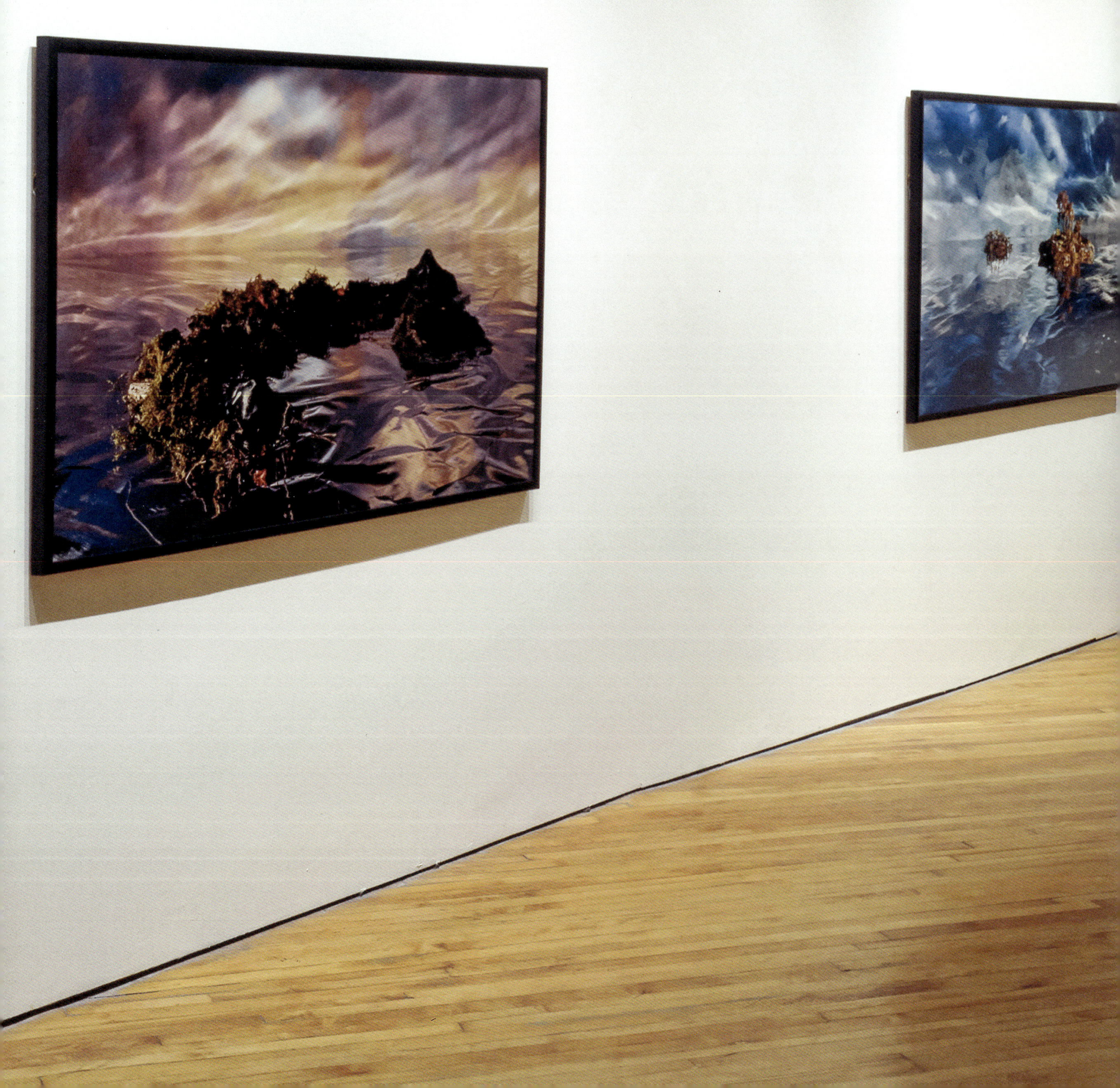

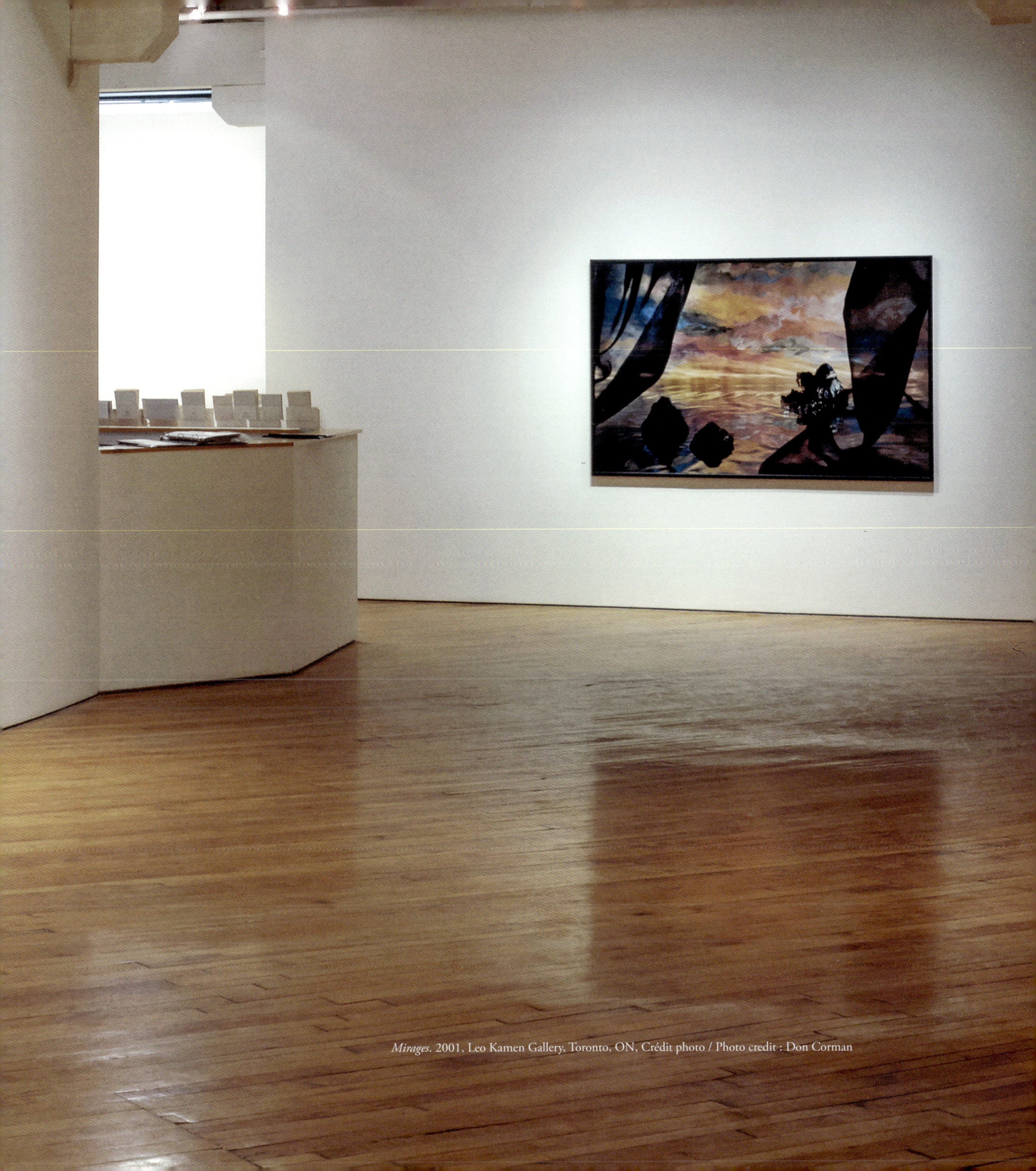

Mirages. 2001, Leo Kamen Gallery, Toronto, ON, Crédit photo / Photo credit : Don Corman

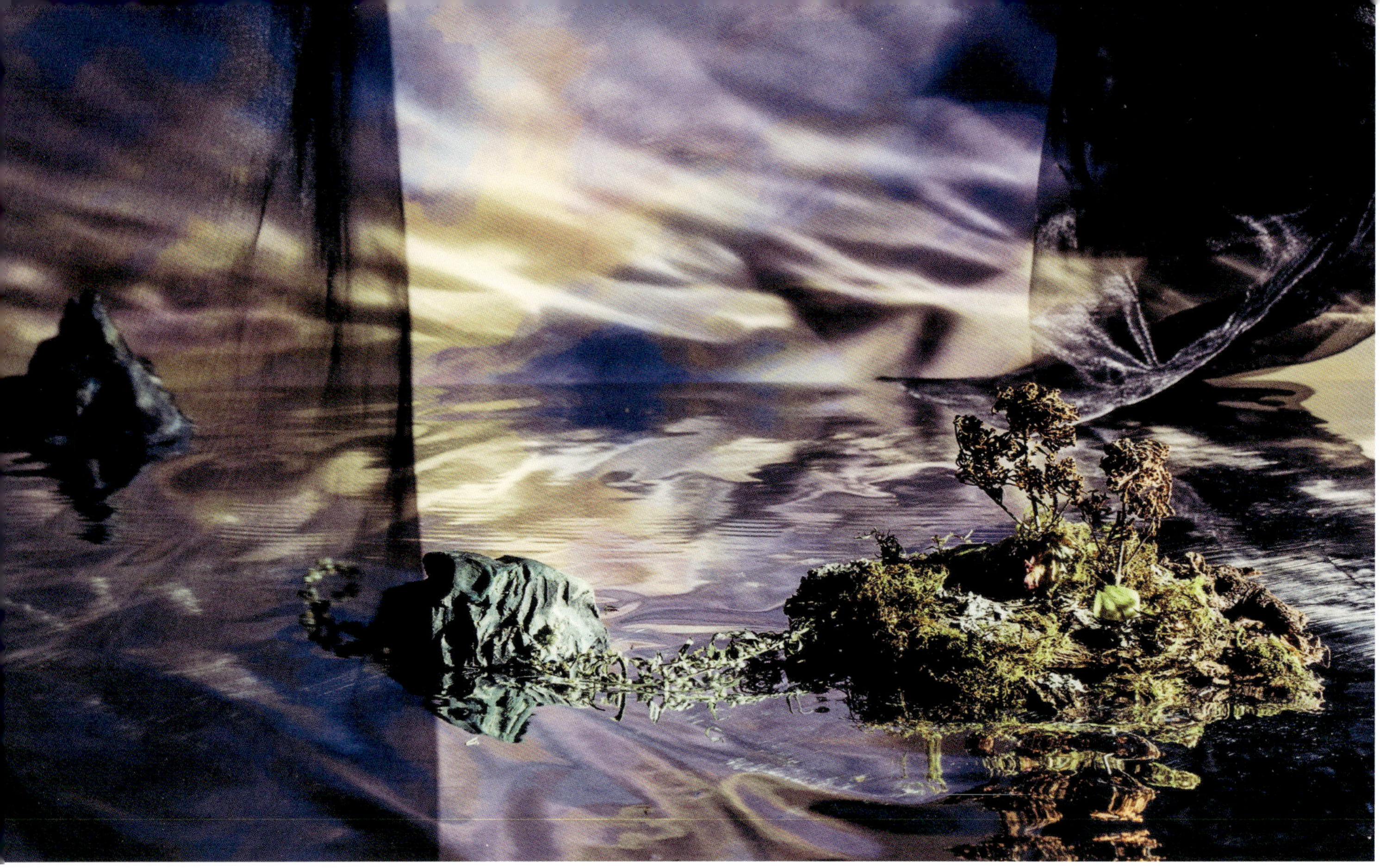

Vision, 2000
épreuve à développement chromogène /
chromogenic print
123 x 183 cm

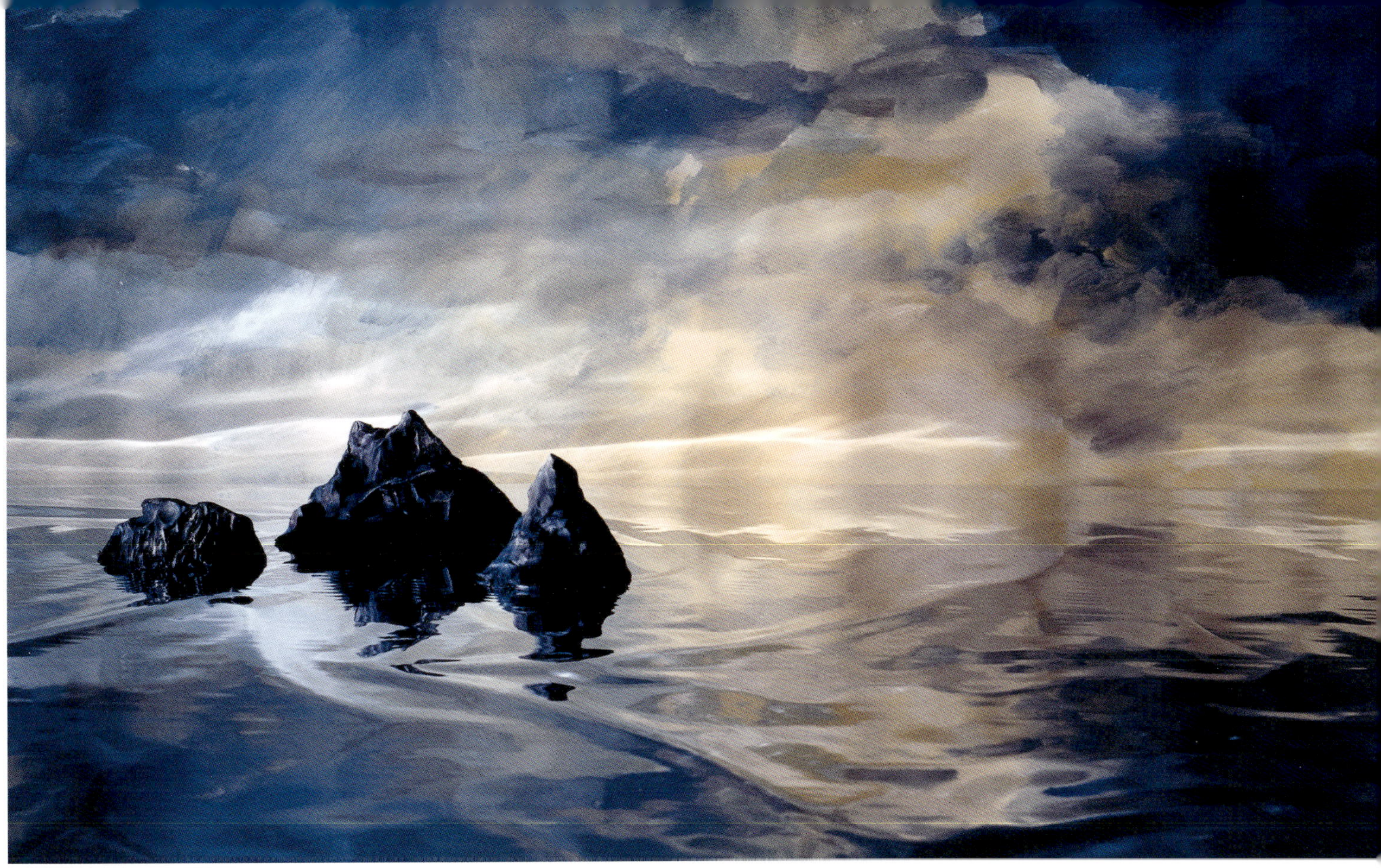

Behold (série *Mirages*), 2001
épreuve à développement chromogène /
chromogenic print
122 x 163 cm

COMING INTO VIEW

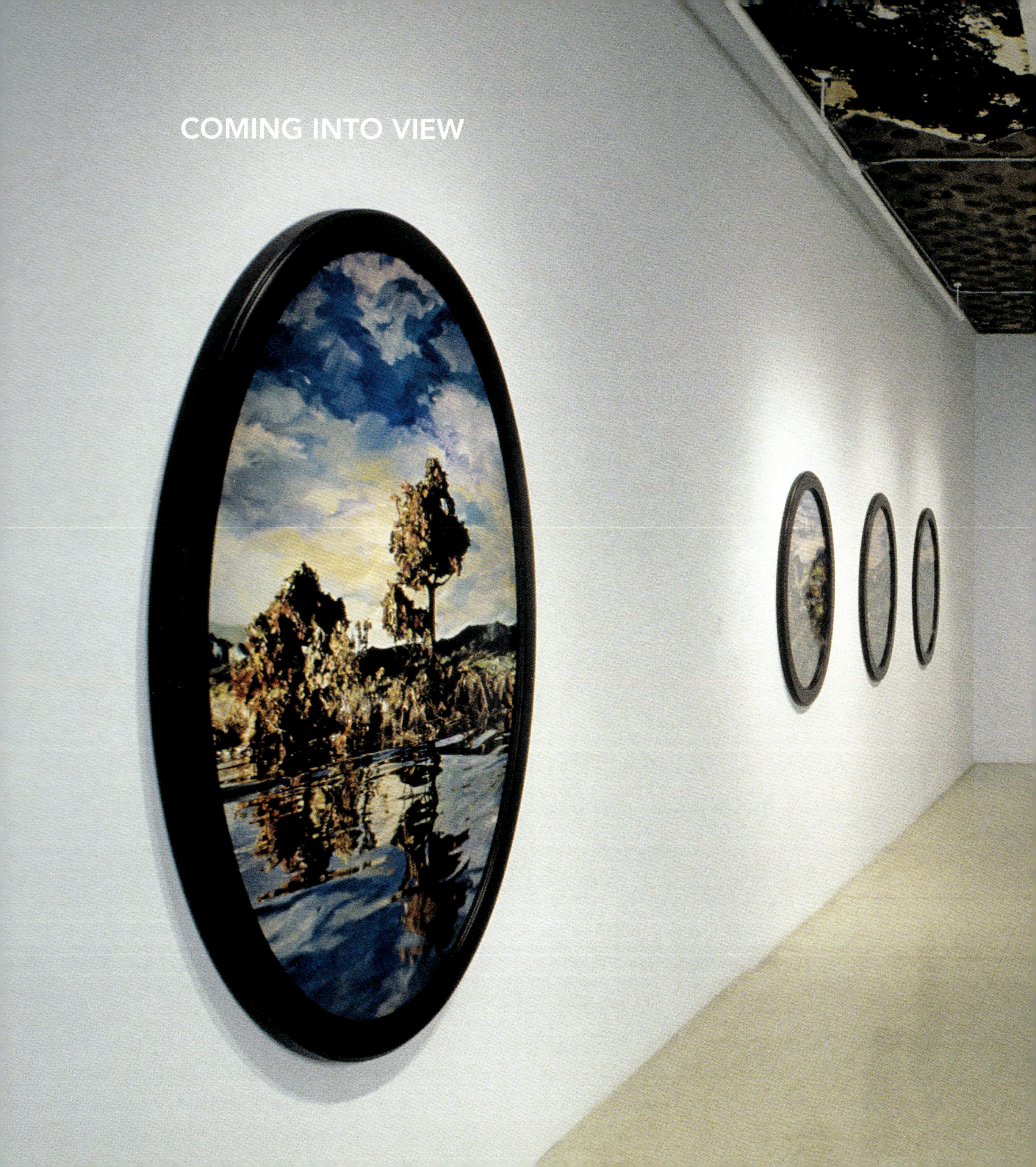

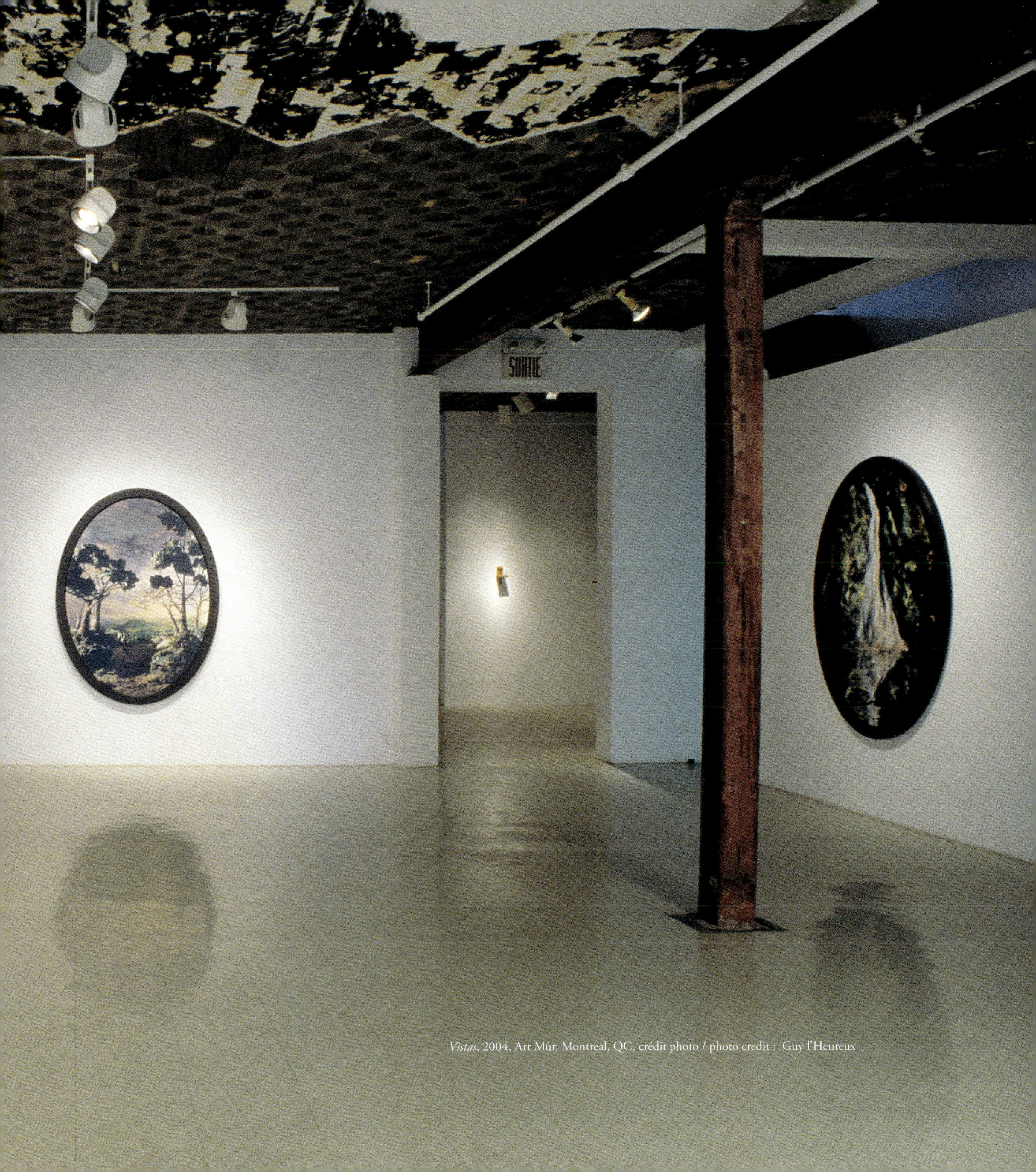

Vistas, 2004, Art Mûr, Montreal, QC, crédit photo / photo credit : Guy l'Heureux

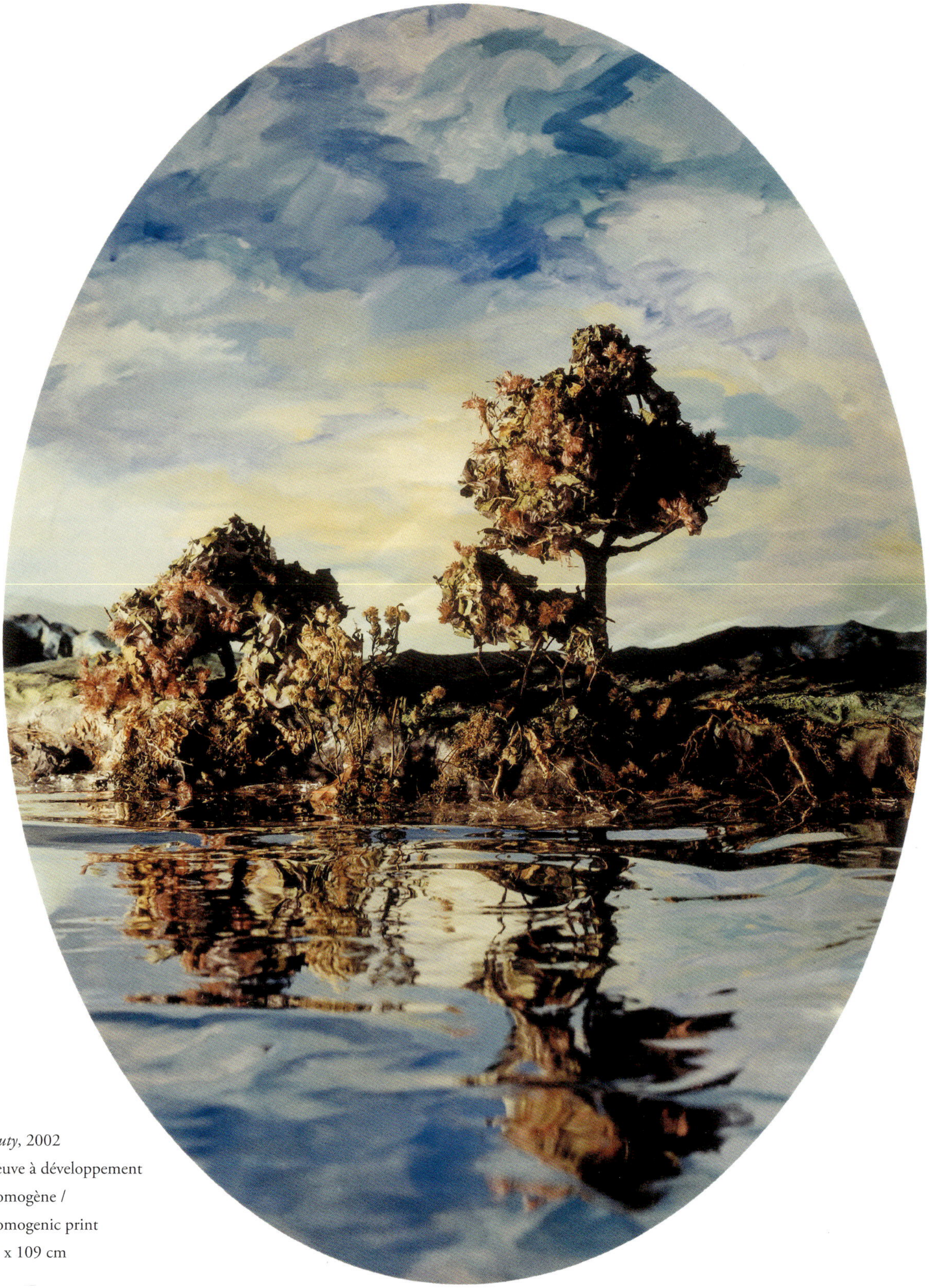

Beauty, 2002
épreuve à développement chromogène / chromogenic print
152 x 109 cm

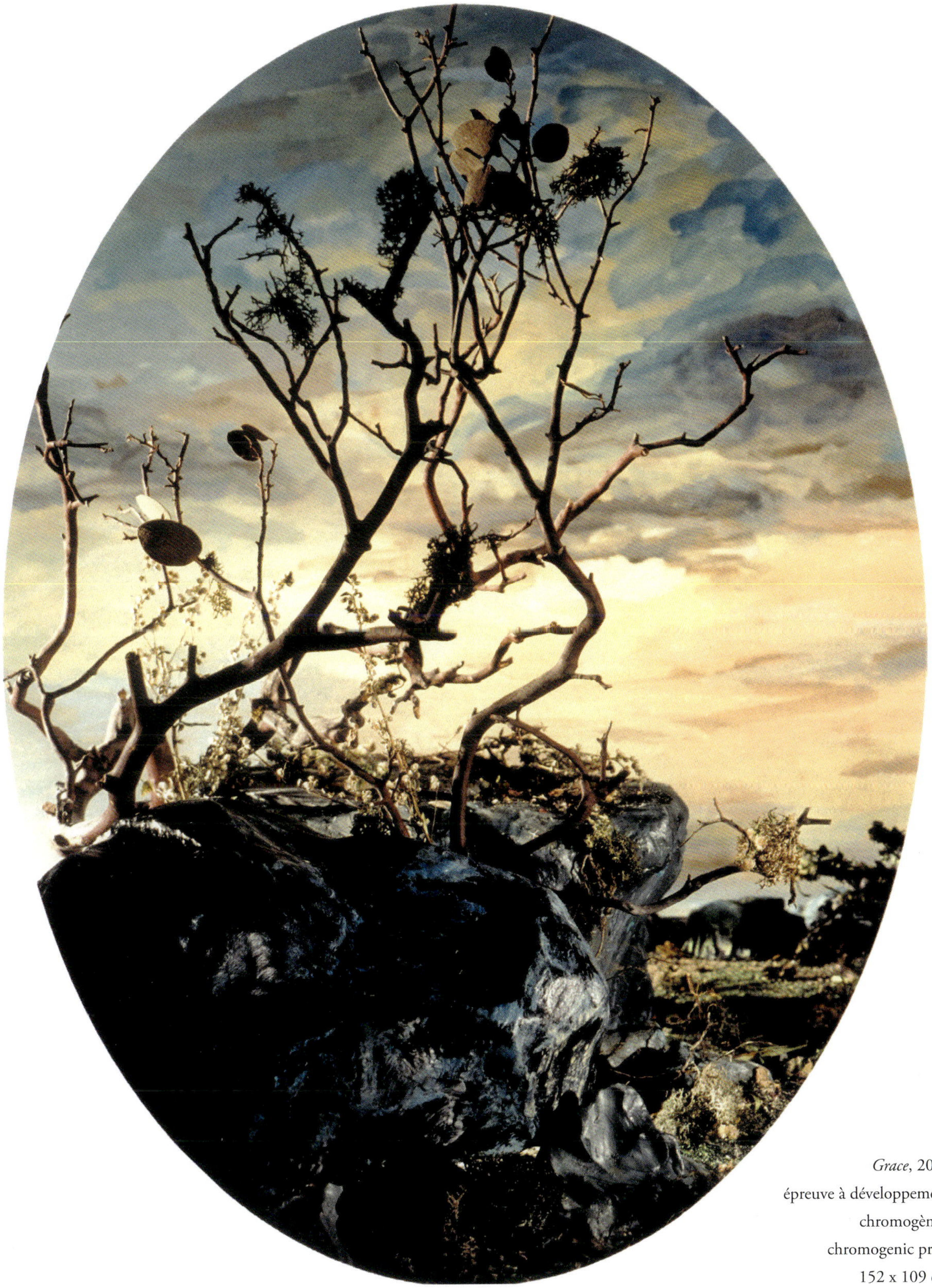

Grace, 2002
épreuve à développement
chromogène /
chromogenic print
152 x 109 cm

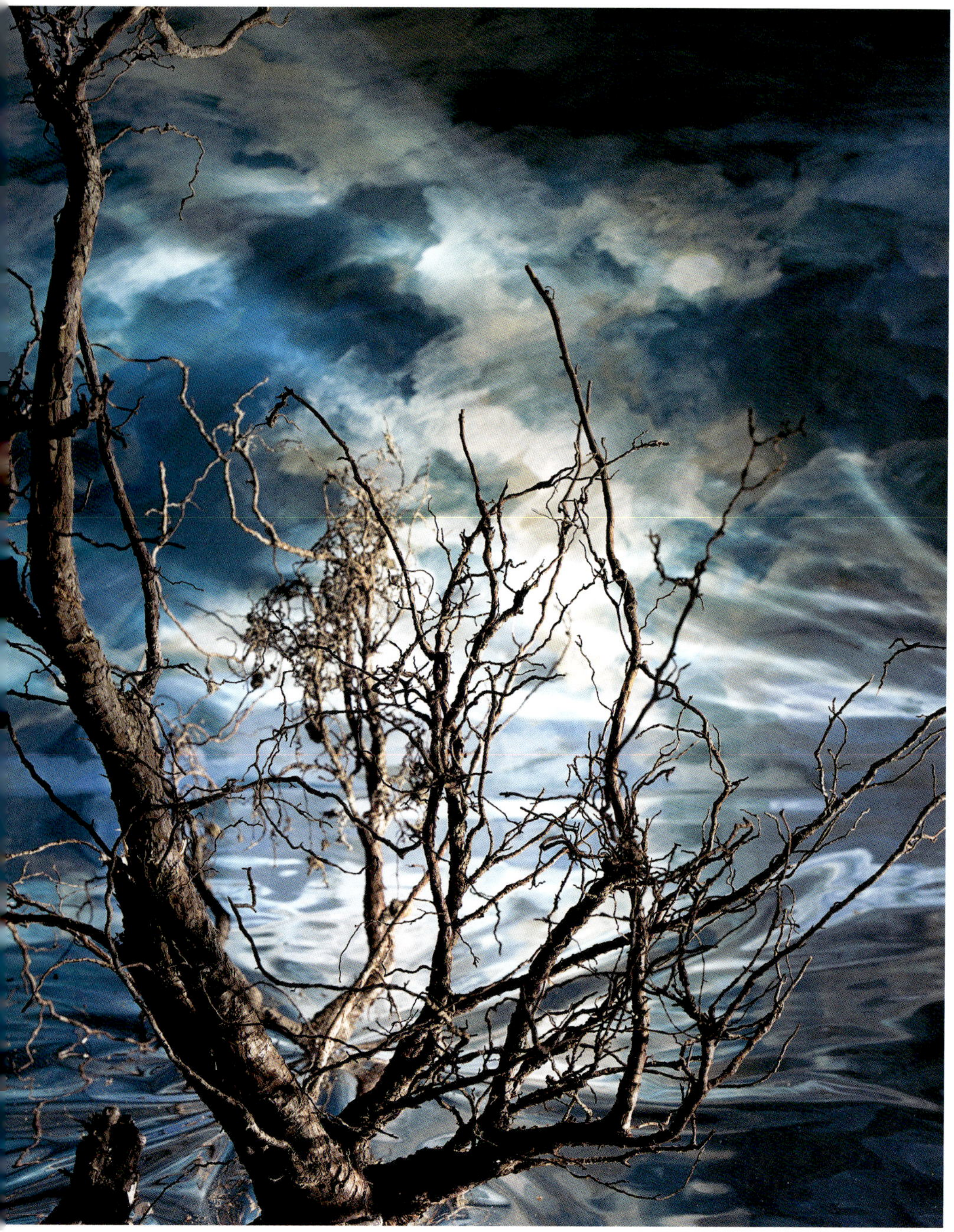

Verdigris Suspended, 2005
impression giclée sur papier aquarelle /
giclée print on watercolour paper
109 x 80 cm

Image : p. 81
Azure, 2005
impression giclée sur papier aquarelle /
giclée print on watercolour paper
109 x 80 cm

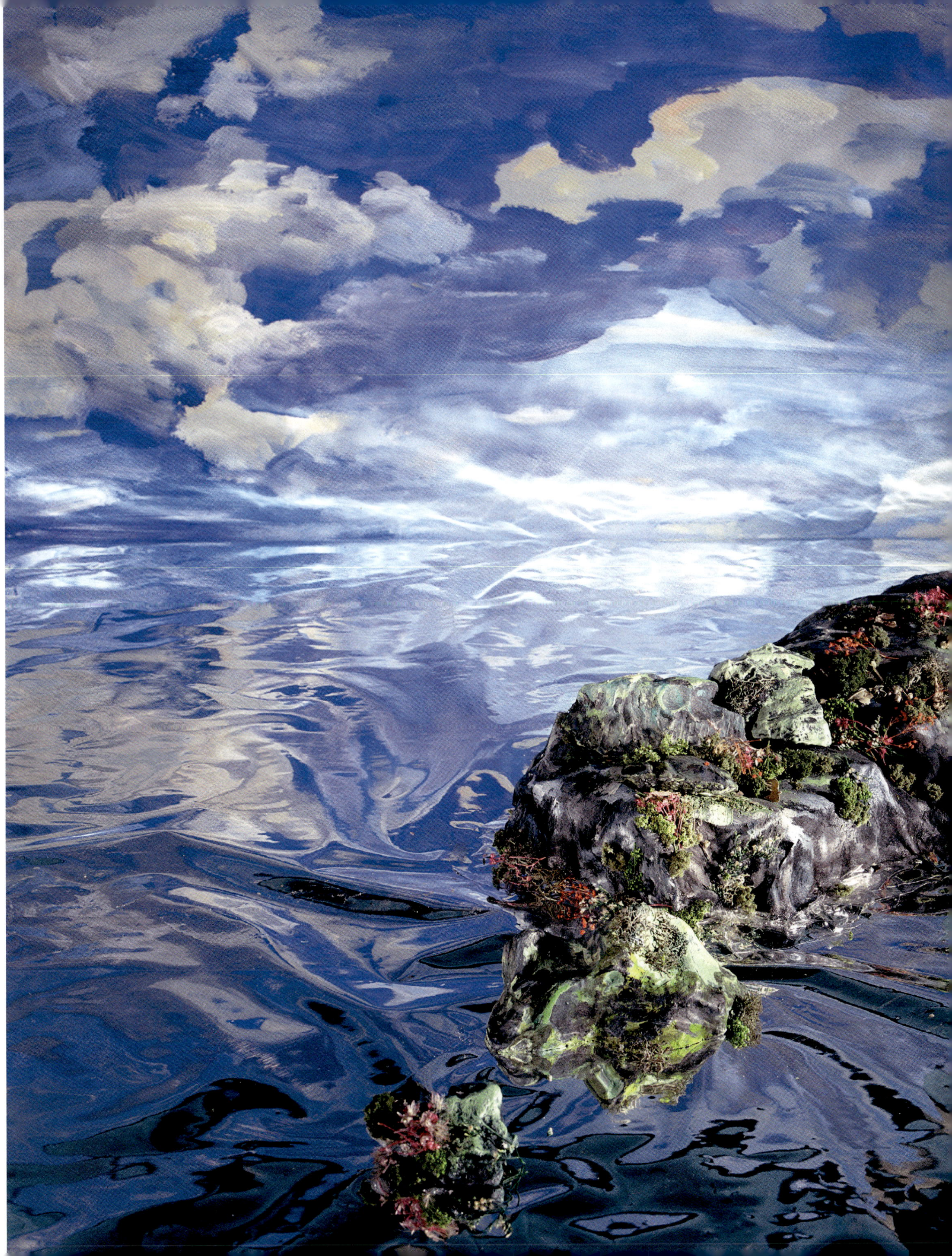

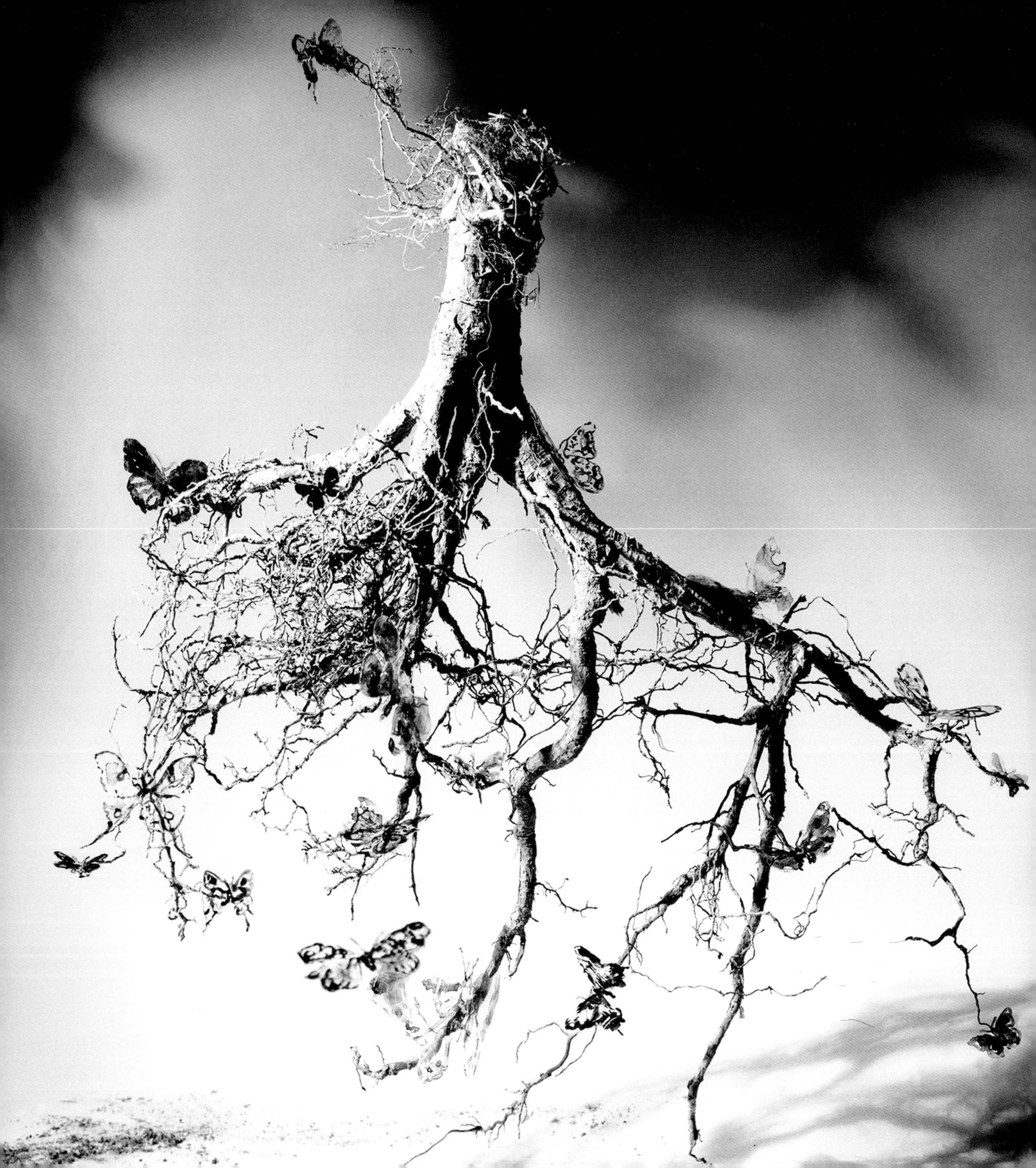

THE SUBLIME AND BEAUTIFUL IN THE WORK OF HOLLY KING

LINDA JANSMA

Image : p. 60
Impossible Sanctuary, 2006
épreuve à jet d'encre sur papier Hahnemuhle / ink jet print on Hahnemuhle paper
132 x 99 cm

Image : p. 63
Tender Cradle, 2007
épreuve à jet d'encre sur papier Hahnemuhle / ink jet print on Hahnemuhle paper
99 x 168 cm

The Sublime and Beautiful in the Work of Holly King

The concept of the sublime was first written about by Pseudo-Longinus, a first-century Greek teacher of literature. While his manuscript focuses on literary criticism, it has widely been used to address the sublime in various art forms:

> Sublime does not persuade the audiences but rather transports them out of themselves. Invariably what inspires wonder casts a spell upon us and is always superior to what is merely convincing and pleasing.[1]

Beautiful, sublime and picturesque landscapes are most often associated with British painting of the eighteenth century, culminating in the work of J. M. W. Turner, and later mid-nineteenth century American landscape painters including Albert Bierstadt, Thomas Cole and Frederic Edwin Church. At that time, the term "sublime" dealt with the differences between it and beauty, the latter making reference to feeling and formlessness, the former to form and taste. Eighteenth century philosopher Immanuel Kant stated that since a painting was a representation of nature, it could not be, itself, sublime. It could present sublime aspects of nature, but could only be beautiful. Abstract Expressionist painter Barnett Newman (significant, in particular, to The Robert McLaughlin Gallery's mid-twentieth century Modernist mandate) felt that the American painter should distance him/herself from a European model that sought to combine beauty and the sublime by freeing the work from the burden of beauty. Rather than include a small human to denote the sublime in nature, as had been the model, Newman expanded the scale of the painting itself and requested that the viewer look at it up close—enveloping herself in the experience—thus creating sublimity "out of our own feelings."[2]

Montreal-based artist Holly King is not alone in celebrating the sublime within the context of contemporary art. The sublime is often referenced in the work of artists Anselm Kiefer, Denyse Thomasos, Anish Kapoor, Edward Burtynsky and Andreas Gursky. Critic Julian Bell writes about the beauty/sublime dilemma in contemporary art:

> Can the sublime in art, I might ask, also at once be the beautiful? … [H]ow can they not? How can any sublime that is presented through art not get bound up in the take-it-or-leave-it luxury of spectatorhood, how can it not be complicit in sheer showmanship?[3]

1. As cited in ed. Umberto Eco, *History of Beauty* (New York: Rizzoli International Publications, 2004), 278.
2. Barnett Newman, "The Sublime in Now," *Tiger's Eye* (December, 1948) as cited in *Barnett Newman: Selected Writings and Interviews*, ed. John P. O'Neill, (New York: Alfred A. Knopf, 1990), 173.
3. Julian Bell, 'Contemporary Art and the Sublime,' in eds. Nigel Llewellyn and Christine Riding, *The Art of the Sublime*, Tate Research Publication, January 2013, https://www.tate.org.uk/art/research-publications/the-sublime/julian-bell-contemporary-art-and-the-sublime-r1108499, (accessed August 10, 2015.)

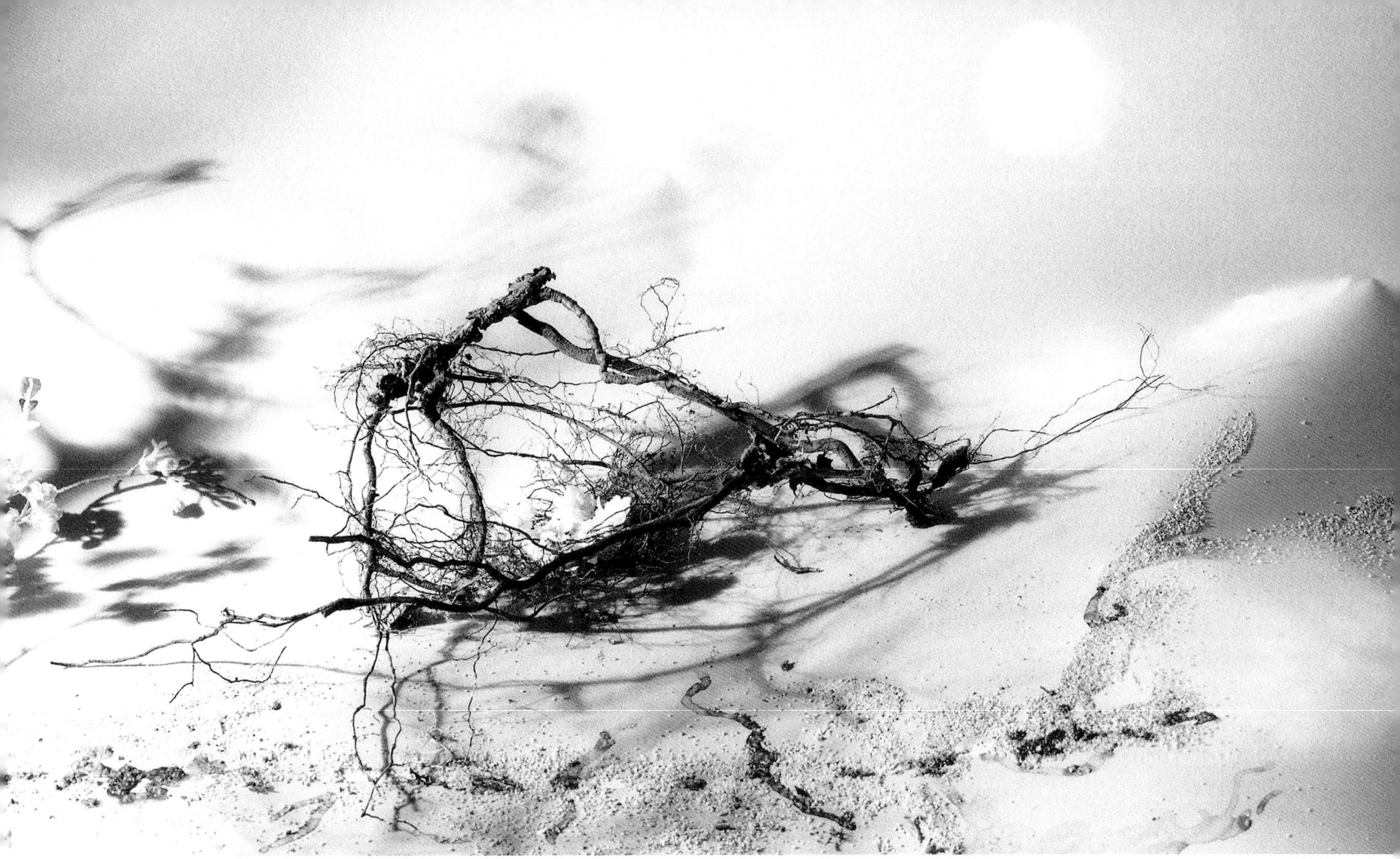

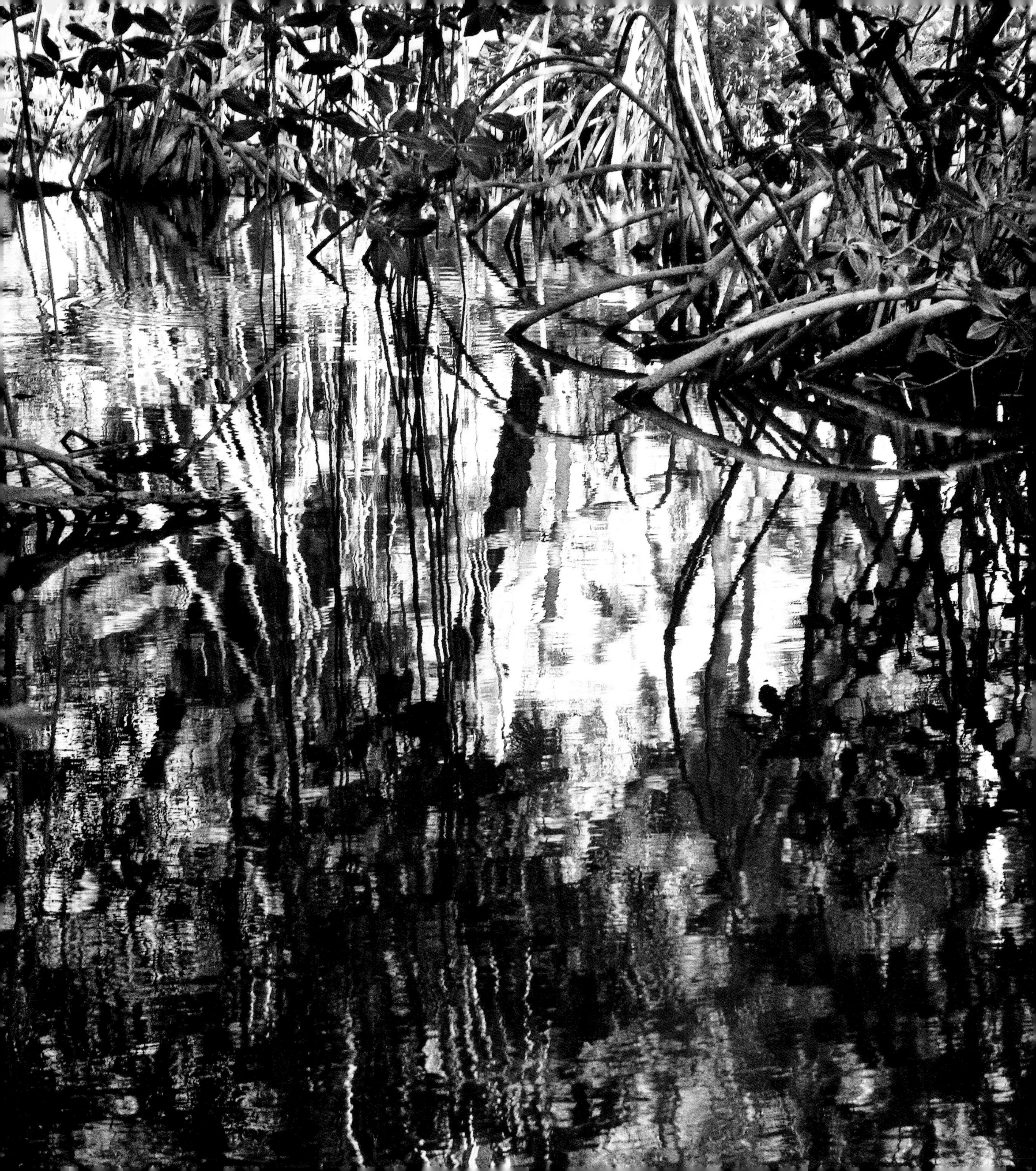

When discussing the sublime within the context of contemporary photography, as compared to painting or other studio-based practices, Bell writes: "Photography outside the studio, being tethered to external, real-world processes, has a weighting unlike other art forms: it can persuade us that it is those processes which beautify, rather than individual human volition."[4] The work in this exhibition is a continuation of King's constructed /manufactured landscapes, yet veers, for the first time, "outside the studio"; in a theatrical sense, she has broken the fourth wall.

This ten-year, mid-career retrospective of the photographs of Holly King is comprised of four of her most recent series: *Twisted Roots*, *Mangroves: Floating Between Two Worlds*, *Grand Canyon: Unseen* and the recently completed *English Cliff* series. Two of the series more clearly represent her constructed works, while the other two are based more obviously in reality. King states that her photographs are a "celebration of sublime beauty in nature," aware that it is not a particularly popular direction to take within the context of contemporary art.[5] Yet, despite Kant and Newman, beauty has its place, and Jonah Lehrer, when speaking of beauty, speaks also to the sublime as an emotional reaction: "I see beauty as a form of curiosity that exists in response to sensation, and not just information. It's what happens when we see something and, even though we can't explain why, want to see more."[6]

> "There is never the intent to create a complete illusion."
> —Holly King

Holly King manufactures both the beautiful and sublime, and is interested in "the tension between artifice and illusion generated."[7] *The Twisted Root* series harkens most closely to her earlier work and acts as an appropriate segue to the newer series. In these black and white photographs, King builds sets from the roots of apple trees, combining them with frosted Mylar and moths that she made and painted. Some, like *Impossible Sanctuary* and *Tender Cradle*, are constructed with a shallow depth of field; all are lit in a particularly theatrical way. The fine roots are reminiscent of drawing, and, in a sense, these photographs are more about drawing than landscape. The thin lines of the roots cast a shadow, those lines now blurred and softened against the backdrop. The work reminds us that King is not, in a real sense, just a photographer, as she has studied the more hands-on processes of painting, drawing, performance and dance. As much as the camera is her tool, so are tweezers and

Image : p. 64
Jacquard, 2009
épreuve à développement chromogène / chromogenic print
66 x 76 cm

4. Julian Bell, 'Contemporary Art and the Sublime,' in eds. Nigel Llewellyn and Christine Riding, *The Art of the Sublime*, Tate Research Publication, January 2013, https://www.tate.org.uk/art/research-publications/the-sublime/julian-bell-contemporary-art-and-the-sublime-r1108499, (accessed August 10, 2015).
5. Holly King, interview by author, Montreal, April 22, 2015.
6. Jonah Lehrer, "Why Does Beauty Exist," *Wired*, http://www.wired.com/2011/07/why-does-beauty-exist/ (accessed July 22, 2015).
7. Holly King, Artist Statement, http://www.hollykingart.com/new-page/ (accessed August 12, 2015).

Image : p. 67
Reflections Tantalize, 2011
photographie en noir et blanc / black and white photograph
183 x 122 cm

magnifying glass. These images give little to the viewer as a frame of reference, and are clearly sets from the imagination, denying the viewer a conventional landscape and requesting that we see beauty in the impossible.

The 2009 series *Mangroves: Floating Between Two Worlds* was conceived while King was reading Amitav Ghosh's novel *The Hungry Tide*. The story is set within a maze of small islands in the Bay of Bengal, and the author goes into great detail to describe the swamps and swiftly growing mangrove trees.

> Staring at it [the mangrove forest] now, she was struck by the way the greenery worked to confound the eye. It was not just that it was a barrier, like a screen or a wall: it seemed to trick the human gaze in the manner of a cleverly drawn optical illusion. There was such a profusion of shapes, forms, hues and textures that even things that were in plain view seemed to disappear, vanishing into the tangle of lines....[8]

King researched and chose to photograph mangroves in the Dominican Republic and the resulting large-scale prints were the first that did not include her signature constructed landscapes. Yet there remains an artificiality about these images; the work resembles a theatre or movie set with the action just waiting to start (*Heavenly Invitation* actually contains a proscenium arch stretched across the top of the composition). Although photographed with film—King feels that film gives a depth to shadow and light that is lost in digital production—she went back into the works and added colour, digitally. The resulting monochromatic image—greens, blues—are hauntingly eerie and their set-like quality lends itself to narrative. Stylistically, they follow the *Twisted Roots* series through their linearity: the image comprised of patterns of twisted and intertwining lines of roots reminiscent of drawing. King notes that trees seem to grow "both up and down at the same time,"[9] and it is this, combined with the strangeness of the colour and entanglement of roots, that creates moody, disquieting, yet hauntingly beautiful photographs.

The scale of King's photographs is an important aspect of her practice. While her set pieces, used to create works like the *Twisted Root* series, are quite small, the resulting photographs are printed large-scale. The viewer, as with Barnett Newman's abstractions, is lost in size of the work, the monumentality of the imagery. As King says: "the large size of the photographs

8. Amitav Ghosh, *The Hungry Tide* (New York: Houghton Mifflin, 2005), 125.
9. Gary Michael Dault, "Eerie photographs play like drawings," *The The Globe and Mail*, February 27, 2010, R15.

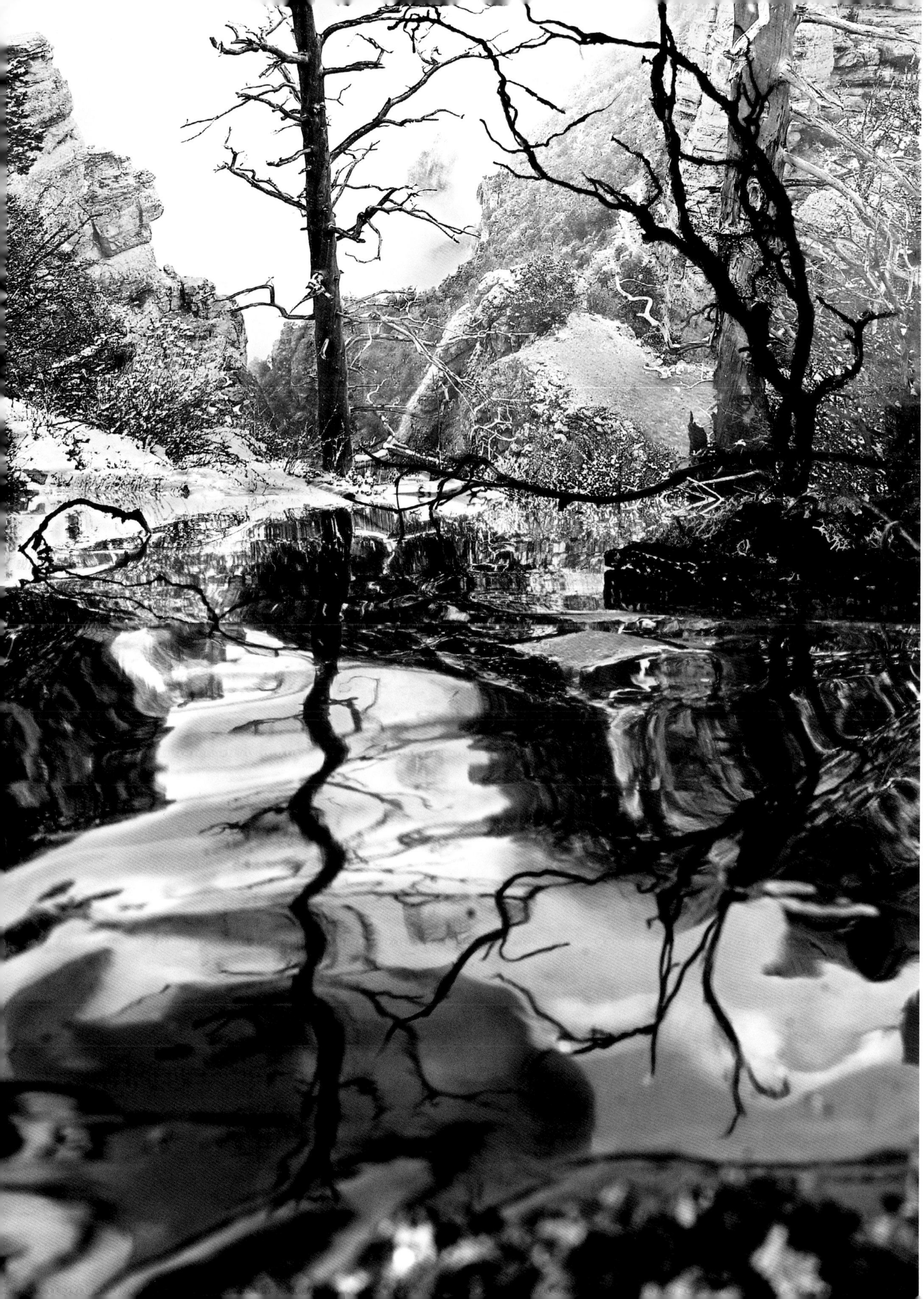

Image : p. 69
Chalk Shoreline, 2013
épreuve à développement chromogène / chromogenic print
122 x 152 cm

allows the viewer to imagine projecting themselves into these imaginary places."[10] That transformation of scale is partly what the work is about: the contradiction between the miniature and the monumental.

The *Grand Canyon: Unseen* series was intended to follow the example of the *Mangrove* series—shot on location and modeling the great American Hudson River School of painters in the creation of the sublime in the presence of the grandeur of nature. The series was sparked by American filmmaker Ken Burns's documentary *The National Parks: America's Best Ideas*, wherein the director speaks about the importance of the national park system and how the landscapes are an "incredibly powerful force."[11] The ironic thing was that the edge of the canyon, the place where that sublime landscape would be revealed, was inaccessible when King visited due to an unexpected, unseasonal snowstorm. The storm created a black and white world that King thought interesting—the *Grand Canyon* series would be a return to black and white images. Of missing that look over the canyon's edge, King writes: "the viewer must imagine the rugged landscape that is barely visible beyond the edge of the abyss."[12] This series represents the first time that King combined the use of actual photographs with foreground details that she fabricated in her studio. By placing a 30 x 40 centimetre slide behind her "set" of handmade rocks, tiny branches that represent trees, as well as Mylar bodies of water on which she has drawn with ink, she has created a tension between readings of reality and artifice. She challenges the viewer's understanding of the photograph—the fog-enshrouded background versus the crisp outlines of hand-drawn reflections and pebbles that resemble massive slabs of rock. *Pathway to an Illusion* and *Reflections Tantalize* are examples from the series that show this dichotomy of readings: the unworldly studio lighting, the dizzying perspective that has the landscape fall into the foreground, and then the beautiful, misty background image, which shrouds the entire photograph in mystery. There is no thought of deception; indeed, the final photographs are reminiscent of early science fiction movie and television sets—simultaneously off-kilter and mood-enhancing—giving us enough for our imaginations to hold on to.

King's most recent photographs make up the *English Cliff* series. In it, she returns to colour and continues to combine photographs taken in the landscape with constructed imagery. The great height of cliff edges that she photographed in Cornwall and Essex, England (she wanted to shoot particular

10. Artist Statement, May, 2015.
11. http://www.pbs.org/kenburns/films/the-national-parks, (accessed August 14, 2015).
12. Artist Statement, May, 2015.

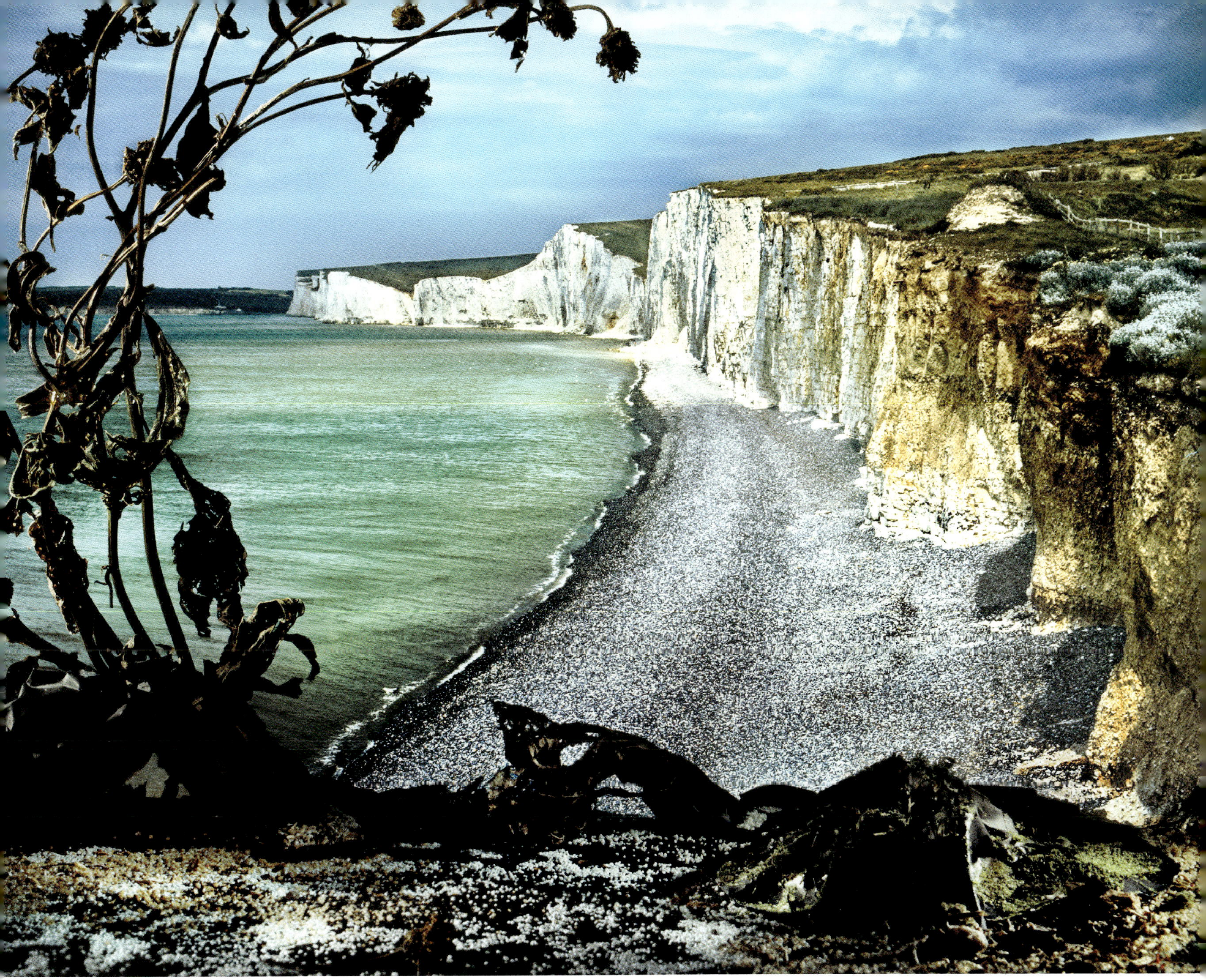

Image : p. 71
Viewing Box, 2015
bois, métal, paysage miniature, DEL / wood, metal and miniature 3d landscape, LED lights
46 x 32 x 92 cm

cliffs—granite, basalt, chalk and slate), reminded her of her own studio practice in that the land formations below the cliffs were miniaturized, not unlike her small studio sets. By standing on the cliff's edge, King felt that "you're in the landscape, but you can't really claim it. I was aware … that I was both experiencing and separating myself from it, an important distinction."[13] King fabricates the foliage around the front of the image, framing it in an Art Nouveau patterning of branches and foliage. Despite the reality of the background photograph, when she looks at the resulting images, they always feel like a constructed set. And they do. *Chalk Shoreline*'s colour is deeply saturated: turquoise water, grey beach and multi-hued cliffs seem constructed below the blue of the sky. The foreground is scattered with tiny pebbles that mimic the beach below, yet are simply grains of salt. The sheer vastness of the landscape, the endless curve of both cliffs and water, are impossibly beautiful—a set for an elusively grand narrative. *Basalt Cliff* and *Crowned Seascape* take the viewer to the verge of the cliff, dangerously close to the edge, with a sense of how simultaneously terrible and spectacular the scenes are. King's added fragments of landscape seem surreal in the context of the majesty of the original photographs—peculiar branches, trees and bushes are developed from her imagination. She takes a few steps back in *Tree and Field*, a traditionally composed landscape of fore-, middle- and background, with the cliffs in the far distance. The foreground elements, fabricated by King, are cast in shadow, emphasizing the saturation of the colour in the original photograph. The photographs in this series feel like a digitally re-mastered film: colour added decades later to entice the viewer into a second look. In the end, it is not only the foreground elements that seem manufactured but the entire scene. Perhaps such a sublime view is simply too grand to be true.

While King is not out to deceive the viewer with her constructed landscapes, her sets have, until now, remained in the studio. With this exhibition, she has included two viewing boxes: elegantly designed cabinets into which one peers and sees a landscape built using forced perspective. Her meticulously rendered "rocks and trees" are visible to all, outside the context of her enlarged photographs. The box becomes a personal space for the viewer, a point of contemplation. King notes that with this structure she hopes to "construct a partially believable poetic place."[14]

Holly King has said that her work is a "search for a deep silence."[15] We return to Pseudo-Longinus's assertion that the

13. Artist Statement, May, 2015.
14. *Ibid.*.
15. Holly King, interview by author, Montreal, April 22, 2015.

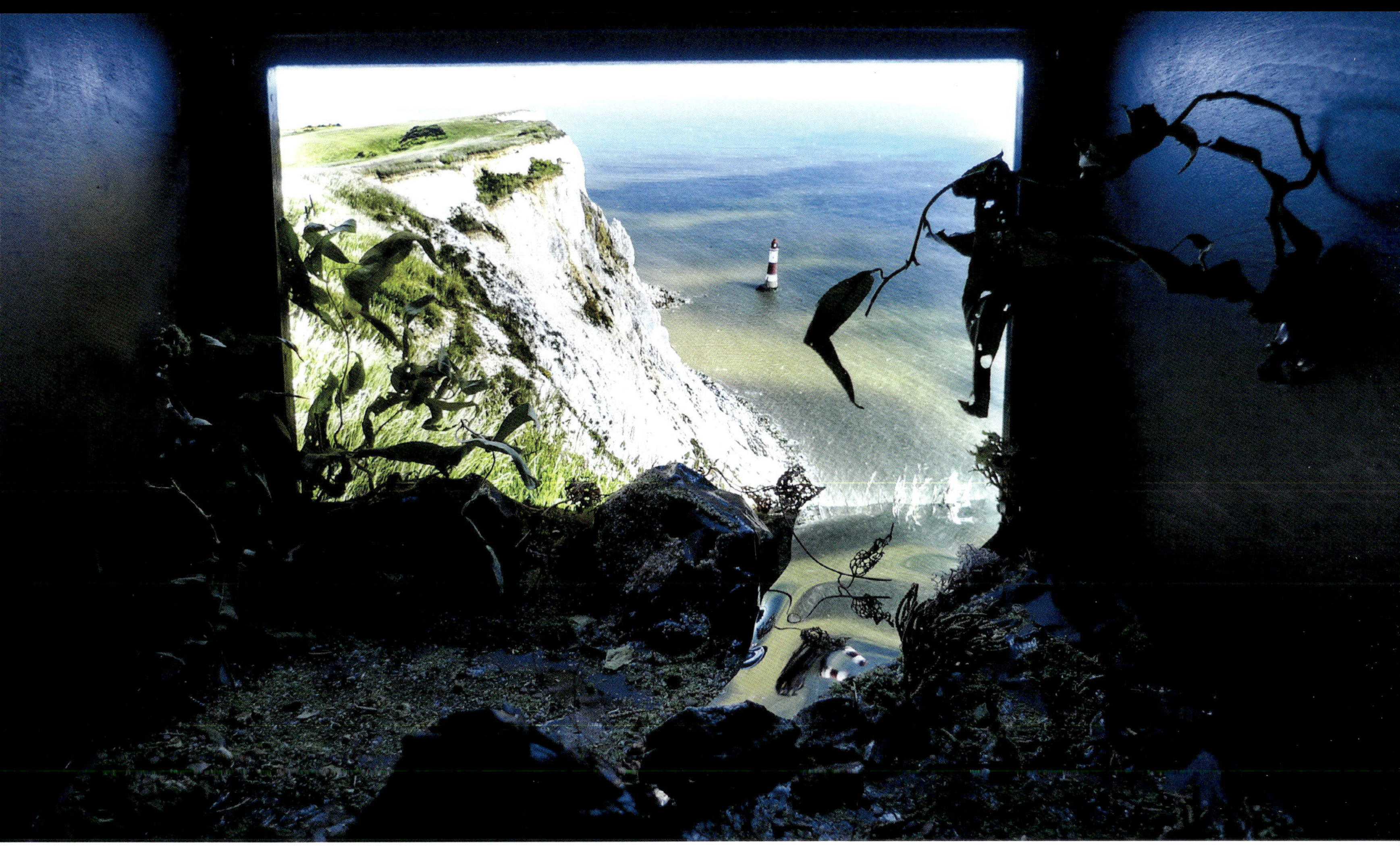

“Sublime does not persuade the audiences but rather transports them out of themselves.” King’s photographs, both constructed and real, serve, through a vastness of scale, a depth of colour or the richness of the blacks in her monochromatic work, to allow the viewer to delight in the beautiful, and to savour the silence in the face of the sublime.

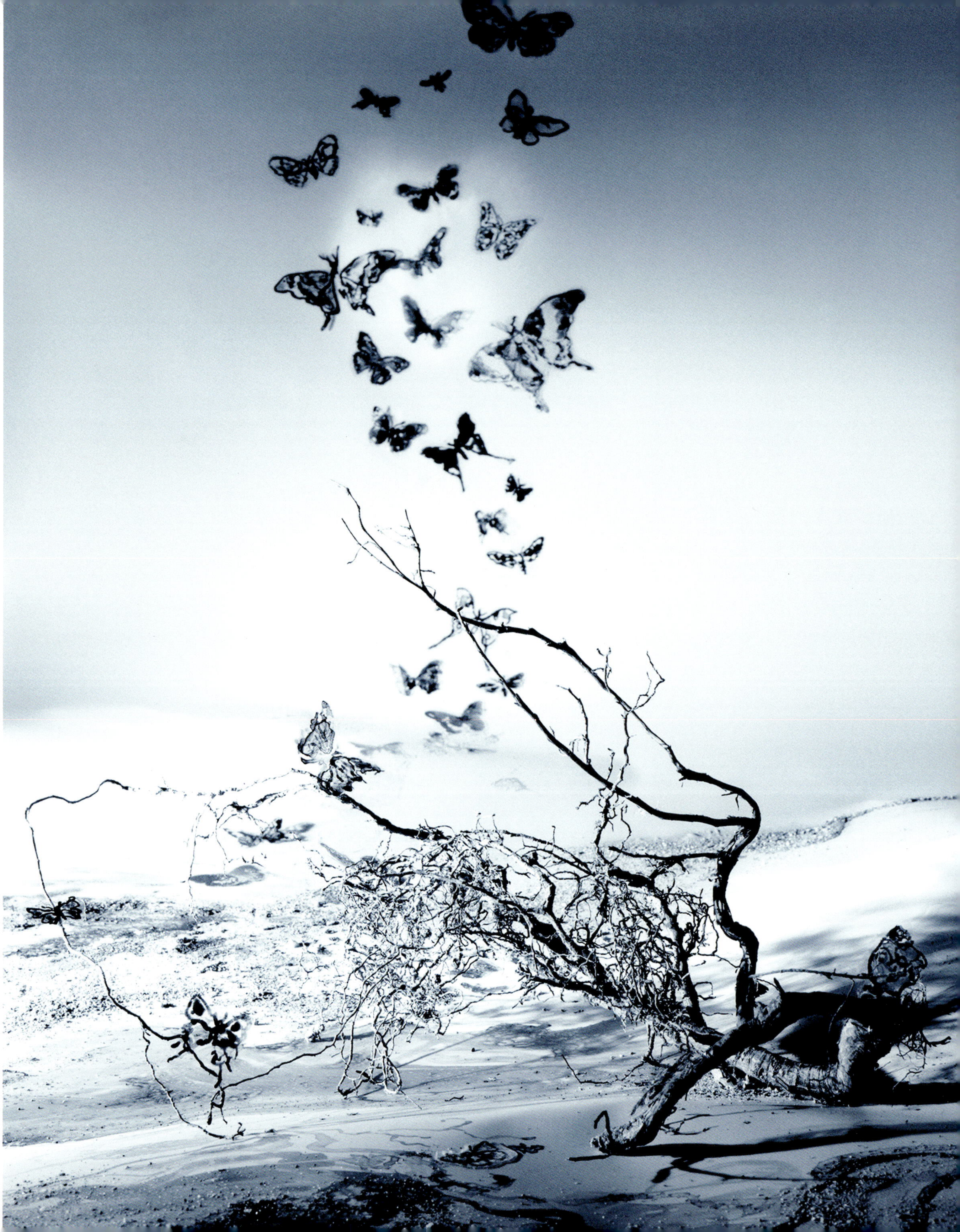

LE SUBLIME ET LE BEAU DANS L'ŒUVRE DE HOLLY KING

LINDA JANSMA

Image : p. 72
Heightened Release, 2006
épreuve à jet d'encre sur papier Hahnemuhle / ink jet print on Hahnemuhle paper
132 x 99 cm

Image : p. 75
Sans titre (série *Loosened Roots*), 2006
techniques mixtes, encre et papier photographique / Mixed media, ink, photographic paper

Le sublime et le beau dans l'œuvre de Holly King

C'est Pseudo-Longin, auteur du Ier siècle, qui a été le premier à écrire sur le sublime. Même si son traité porte sur la critique littéraire, il a beaucoup servi à aborder le sublime dans différentes disciplines artistiques :

> *[Le sublime] ne persuade pas proprement, mais il ravit, il transporte, et produit en nous une certaine admiration mêlée d'étonnement et de surprise, qui est toute autre chose que de plaire seulement, ou de persuader*[1].

Les paysages beaux, sublimes et pittoresques sont la plupart du temps associés à la peinture anglaise du XVIIIe siècle, dont l'œuvre de J.M.W. Turner constitue l'apogée, et aux peintres de paysage américains du XIXe siècle, comme Albert Bierstadt, Thomas Cole et Frederic Edwin Church. À cette époque, on évoquait avec le terme sublime ses différences avec la beauté, celle-ci renvoyant au sentiment et à l'informe, et lui, au goût et à la forme. Immanuel Kant, philosophe du XVIIIe siècle, a affirmé que, la peinture étant une représentation de la nature, elle ne pouvait pas elle-même être sublime. Elle pouvait présenter des aspects sublimes de la nature, mais ne pouvait être que belle. Le peintre expressionniste abstrait Barnett Newman (figure importante dans le cadre du mandat moderniste du XXe siècle de la Robert McLaughlin Gallery) estimait que tout peintre américain devait se distancier d'un modèle européen qui cherchait à combiner la beauté avec le sublime, et ce, en libérant l'œuvre du fardeau de la beauté. Plutôt que d'inclure un être humain en miniature pour dénoter le sublime dans la nature, comme le dictait le modèle, Newman a élargi l'échelle de la peinture en soi et a demandé du spectateur et de la spectatrice qu'ils regardent de plus près, qu'ils s'imprègnent de l'expérience, pour créer ainsi du sublime « à partir de [leurs] propres sentiments[2] ».

Holly King, artiste établie à Montréal, n'est pas seule à célébrer le sublime dans le contexte de l'art contemporain. En effet, l'on rencontre souvent le sublime dans les travaux d'Anselm Kiefer, de Denyse Thomasos, d'Anish Kapoor, d'Edward Burtynsky et d'Andreas Gursky. Le critique Julian Bell écrit ce qui suit sur le dilemme beau/sublime en art contemporain :

> *Le sublime en art, pourrais-je demander, peut-il également être beau ? [...] Comment le contraire est-il possible ? Comment le sublime présenté en art ne peut-il pas se faire happer par le luxe du « tout ou rien » du spectacle,*

1. Cité dans Umberto Eco (dir.), *Histoire de la beauté*, Paris, Éditions Flammarion, 2010 (2004), p. 278.
2. Barnett Newman, « The Sublime in Now », *Tiger's Eye* (décembre 1948), cité dans John P. O'Neill (dir.), *Barnett Newman: Selected Writings and Interviews*, New York, Alfred A. Knopf, 1990, p. 173. [Notre traduction.]
3. Julian Bell, « Contemporary Art and the Sublime », dans Nigel Llewellyn et Christine Riding (dir.), *The Art of the Sublime*, Tate Research Publication, janvier 2013, https://www.tate.org.uk/art/research-publications/the-sublime/julian-bell-contemporary-art-and-the-sublime-r1108499, consulté 10 août 2015.

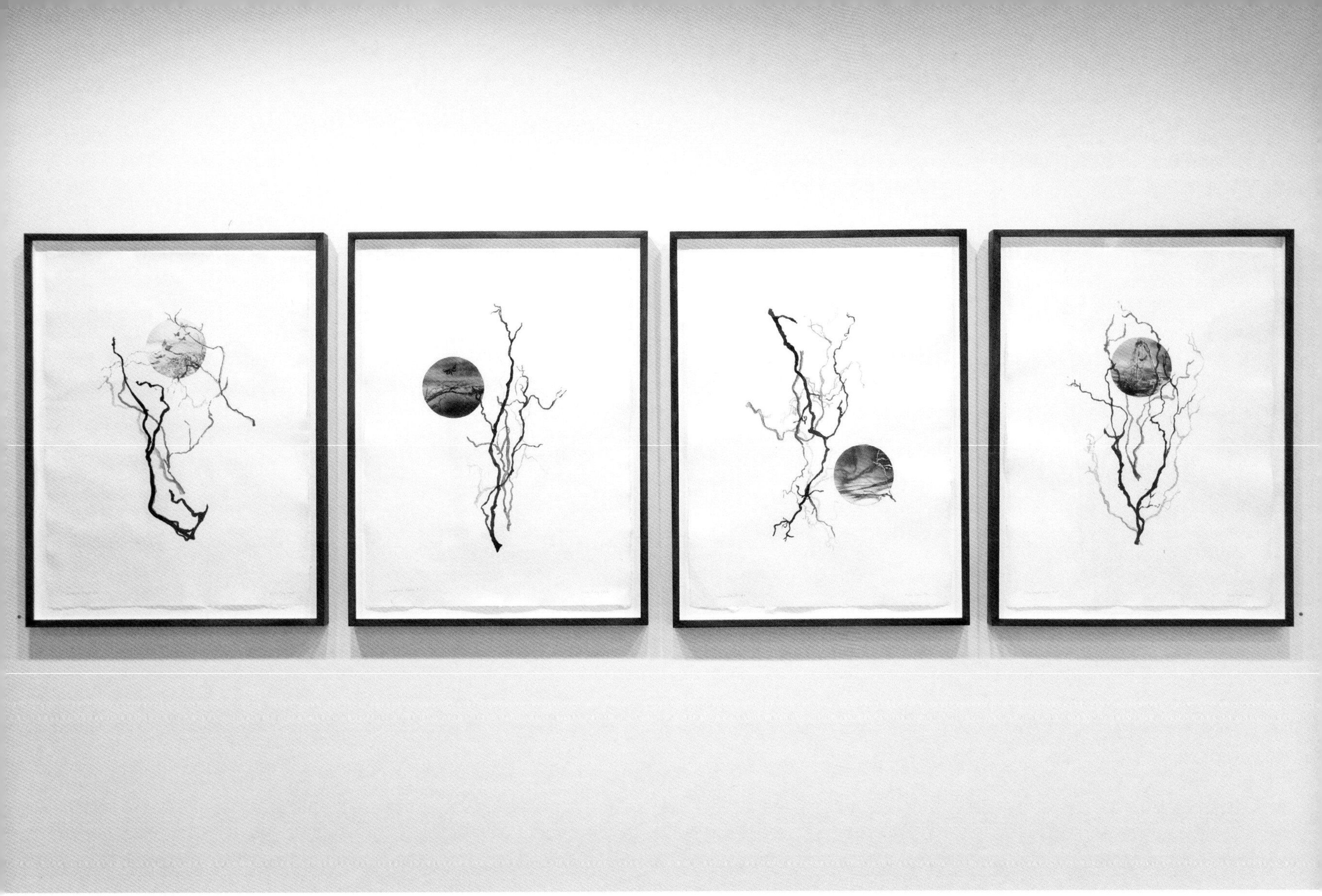

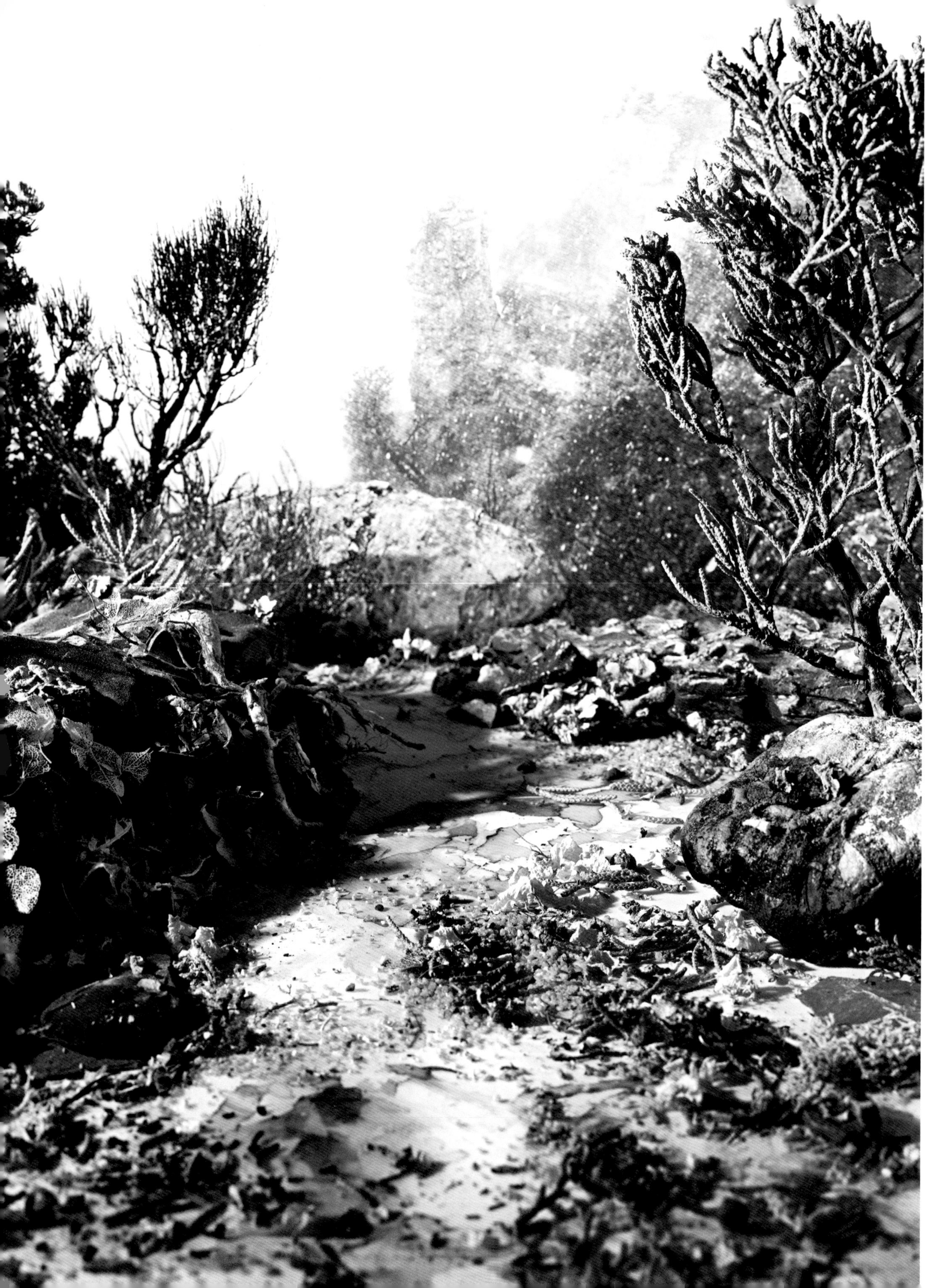

comment ne peut-il pas être complice de l'art même de la mise en scène[3] *?*

Au sujet d'une discussion sur le sublime dans le contexte de la photographie contemporaine plutôt que dans celui de la peinture et d'autres pratiques d'atelier, Bell écrit : « La photographie hors de l'atelier, en étant rattachée aux processus externes du monde réel, a un poids différent des autres formes artistiques : elle peut nous persuader que la beauté découle de ces processus plutôt que de la volonté humaine individuelle[4]. » Les œuvres dans la présente exposition sont en continuité avec les paysages construits et fabriqués de King, mais elles « sortent », pour la première fois, de l'atelier; on dirait, en termes théâtraux, que King a fait tomber le quatrième mur.

Cette rétrospective de dix ans de photographie de Holly King, artiste à mi-carrière, comprend quatre de ses plus récentes séries : *Twisted Roots*, *Mangroves : Floating Between Two Worlds*, *Grand Canyon : Unseen* et la série récemment achevée *English Cliffs*. Deux des séries font clairement partie de ses séries construites, alors que les deux autres s'appuient plus nettement sur la réalité. King dit de ses photographies qu'elles sont « une célébration de la beauté sublime dans la nature », tout en étant consciente que ce n'est pas une direction particulièrement populaire dans le monde de l'art contemporain[5]. Pourtant, n'en déplaise à Kant et à Newman, la beauté a sa place et Jonah Lehrer, parlant de beauté, parle également du sublime en tant que réaction émotionnelle : « Je vois la beauté comme une forme de curiosité qui existe en réaction à une sensation, et non comme un simple renseignement. C'est ce qui se produit quand on voit une chose et que, sans pouvoir se l'expliquer, on veut en voir davantage[6]. »

L'intention n'est jamais de créer une illusion totale.
— Holly King

Holly King fabrique à la fois du beau et du sublime, et elle s'intéresse à « la tension créée entre artifice et illusion[7] ». C'est la série des *Twisted Roots* qui se rapproche le plus de ses œuvres antérieures et qui sert de trait d'union approprié aux nouvelles séries. Dans ces photographies en noir et blanc, King construit des décors à partir de racines de pommiers qu'elle combine à du mylar givré et à des papillons de nuit qu'elle a fabriqués et peints. Quelques-unes d'entre elles, par exemple *Impossible Sanctuary* et *Tender Cradle*, ont très peu de profondeur de champ; toutes sont éclairées de façon particulièrement théâtrale. Les fines racines rappellent le dessin et, d'une certaine manière, ces photographies

Image : p. 76
Pathway to an Illusion, 2011
photographie en noir et blanc / black and white photograph
183 x 122 cm

4. Julian Bell, « Contemporary Art and the Sublime », dans Nigel Llewellyn et Christine Riding (dir.), *The Art of the Sublime*, Tate Research Publication, janvier 2013, https://www.tate.org.uk/art/research-publications/the-sublime/julian-bell-contemporary-art-and-the-sublime-r1108499, consulté 10 août 2015.
5. Conversation entre l'artiste et l'auteure, 22 avril 2015, Montréal.
6. Jonah Lehrer, « Why Does Beauty Exist », Wired, http://www.wired.com/2011/07/why-does-beauty-exist/, consulté 22 juillet 2015. [Notre traduction.]
7. Holly King, texte de démarche de l'artiste, http://www.hollykingart.com/new-page/, consulté 12 août 2015. [Notre traduction.]

Image : p. 79
Arch and Sea, 2015
épreuve à développement chromogène / chromogenic print
122 x 152 cm

ont plus à voir avec le dessin qu'avec le paysage. Les lignes minces des racines projettent une ombre, s'estompent et s'adoucissent contre la toile de fond. Ces œuvres nous rappellent que King n'est pas, à proprement parler, seulement une photographe, puisqu'elle a étudié dans les disciplines plus tactiles de la peinture, du dessin, de la performance et de la danse. Autant l'appareil photo est son outil, autant le sont les pinces fines et la loupe. Ces images nous donnent peu en termes de référents et il s'agit nettement de décors issus de l'imagination, qui nous refusent un paysage conventionnel et nous demandent de voir la beauté dans l'impossible.

La série *Mangroves: Floating Between Two Worlds*, de 2009, a été conçue par King pendant qu'elle lisait le roman d'Amitav Ghosh intitulé *The Hungry Tide* [Le pays des marées]. L'histoire se déroule dans un labyrinthe de petites îles dans la baie du Bengale et l'auteur y va de nombreux détails pour décrire les marécages et les palétuviers qui poussent très vite.

> *Elle était frappée maintenant par la manière dont la végétation travaillait à tromper l'œil : non seulement bannière, écran ou mur, elle semblait aussi tromper le regard humain à la façon d'une illusion d'optique intelligemment conçue. Elle offrait une telle profusion de formes, de couleurs, de textures que même les choses pleinement visibles semblaient disparaître, s'évanouir dans le fouillis des lignes [...]*[8].

Après avoir fait des recherches, King décide de photographier des palétuviers en République dominicaine; les grandes épreuves qui en ont résulté sont les premières à ne pas inclure les paysages construits qu'on lui connaît. Elles conservent toutefois une certaine artificialité; les images ressemblent à un décor de théâtre ou de film où l'on attend le début de l'action (*Heavenly Invitation* contient en fait un cadre de scène qui s'étend dans la partie supérieure de la composition). Bien que les images aient été captées sur pellicule – King estime que la pellicule donne une profondeur à l'ombre et à la lumière qui se perd dans la production numérique –, l'artiste y est intervenue par des ajouts numériques de couleur. Les images monochromes résultantes – des verts et des bleus – sont d'une beauté envoûtante et inquiétante, leur aspect semblable à un décor apte à recevoir un récit. Stylistiquement, elles s'inscrivent dans la suite de la série *Twisted Roots* par leur linéarité : une image composée de motifs de lignes entortillées qui rappellent le dessin. King note que les arbres semblent pousser « à la fois vers le haut et vers

8. Amitav Ghosh, *Le pays des marées*, trad. de l'anglais par Christiane Besse, Paris, 10/18, coll. « Domaine étranger », 2008, p. 181.
9. Gary Michael Dault, « Eerie photographs play like drawings », *The The Globe and Mail*, 27 février 2010, R15. [traduction libre.]

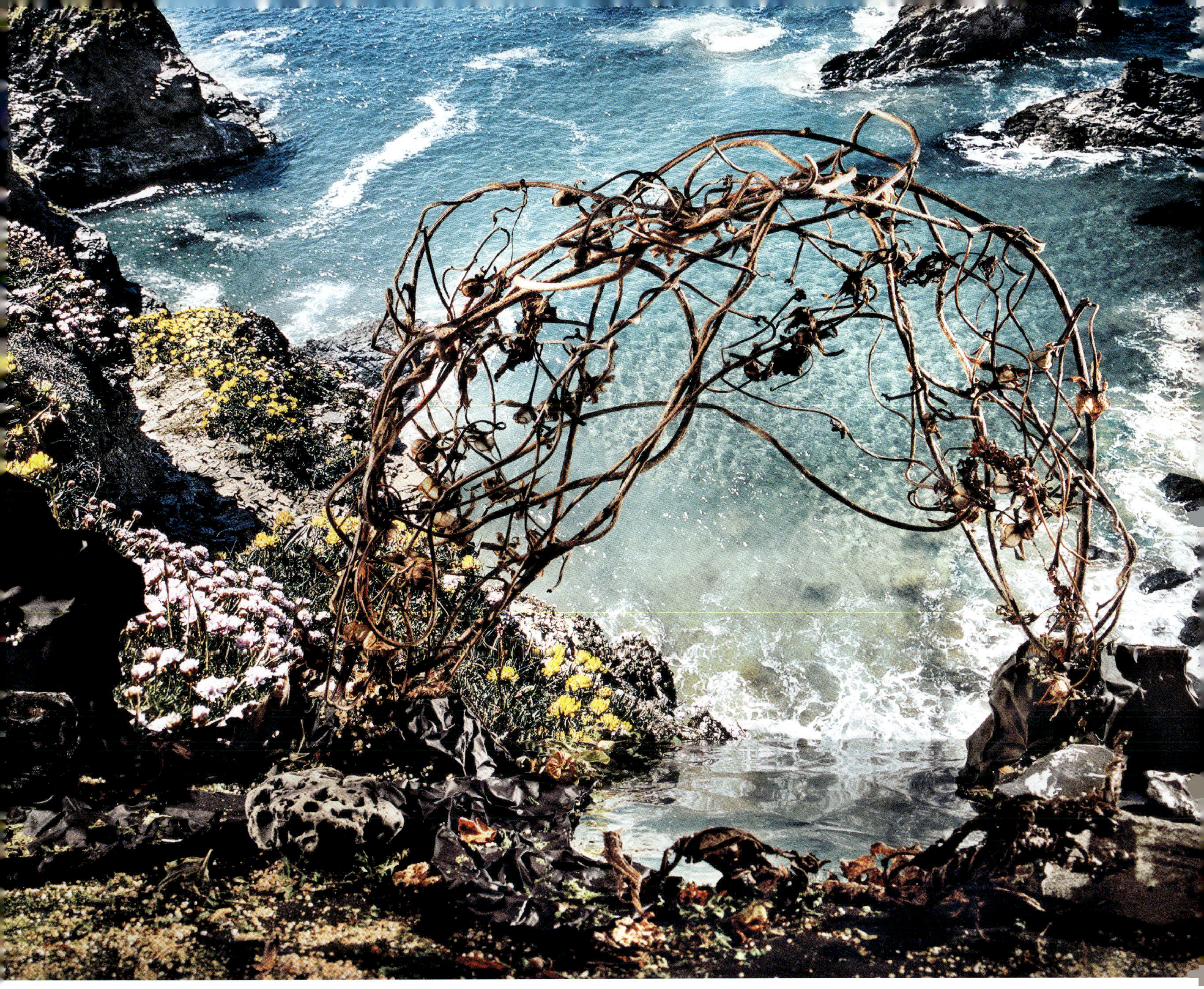

le bas[9] » et c'est cela, combiné avec l'étrangeté de la couleur et avec l'enchevêtrement des racines, qui crée des images sombres, troublantes, quoique terriblement belles.

L'échelle des images chez King est un aspect important de sa pratique. Si les décors servant à créer des œuvres, comme pour sa série *Twisted Roots*, sont plutôt petits, les épreuves qui en sont tirées sont de grande échelle. Le spectateur et la spectatrice, comme devant les abstractions de Barnett Newman, se perdent dans la dimension de l'œuvre, dans la monumentalité de l'image. Comme le dit King : « Le grand format des photographies permet de se projeter dans ces espaces imaginaires[10]. » La transformation d'échelle constitue en partie le sujet de l'œuvre : la contradiction entre le miniature et le monumental.

La série *Grand Canyon : Unseen* devait suivre l'exemple de la série des *Mangroves* et donc être tournée sur place et s'inspirer de la Hudson River School, une école de peintres américains, dans son entreprise de création du sublime face à la grandeur de la nature. L'inspiration initiale de la série est un documentaire du cinéaste américain Ken Burns (*The National Parks: America's Best Ideas*), où il est question de l'importance du système des parcs nationaux et de la manière dont les paysages constituent « une force incroyablement puissante[11]». L'ironie est que la bordure du canyon, cet endroit où devait se révéler le paysage sublime, était inaccessible lors de la visite de King en raison d'une tempête de neige imprévue, puisque hors saison. La tempête a créé un monde en noir et blanc que King a trouvé intéressant, et c'est ainsi que la série *Grand Canyon* s'est avérée un retour au noir et blanc. Sur le fait d'avoir raté ce point de vue sur la bordure du canyon, King écrit : « Le regardeur doit imaginer le paysage accidenté qui est visible au-delà du bord de l'abîme[12]. » Avec cette série, c'est la première fois que King combine l'utilisation de véritables photographies avec des détails à l'avant-plan fabriqués en atelier. En plaçant une diapositive de 30 par 40 centimètres derrière son « décor » artisanal de roches et de petites branches représentant des arbres, et de plans d'eau en mylar sur lesquels elle a réalisé des dessins à l'encre, elle a créé une tension entre réalité et artifice. Elle met au défi notre compréhension de l'image : l'arrière-plan embrumé versus les contours définis de reflets et de cailloux tracés à la main qui ressemblent à de gros blocs de pierre. Toujours dans la série *Grand Canyon*, Pathway to an Illusion et *Reflections Tantalize* sont des exemples qui témoignent de cette dichotomie de lectures : l'éclairage irréel de l'atelier, le point de vue vertigineux qui ramène le paysage à l'avant-plan, puis la belle et nébuleuse image en arrière-plan qui enveloppe de mystère

10. Texte de démarche de l'artiste, mai 2015. [Notre traduction.]
11. http://www.pbs.org/kenburns/films/the-national-parks, consulté le 14 août 2015.
12. Texte de démarche de l'artiste, mai 2015.

toute l'image photographique. L'idée n'est pas de tromper; en fait, les photographies finales rappellent les premiers films de science-fiction et les décors de télévision, à la fois bancals et créateurs d'ambiance, qui nourrissent l'imagination juste assez pour qu'on s'y accroche.

La série *English Cliffs* réunit les plus récentes photographies de King. Ici, l'artiste revient à la couleur et continue d'allier des photographies de paysages à des images construites. Les grandes falaises qu'elle a photographiées à Cornwall et à Essex, en Angleterre (elle avait en tête des falaises précises, soit en granite, basalte, craie et ardoise), ont évoqué pour elle sa pratique en atelier, parce que les reliefs sous les falaises semblaient miniaturisés, lui rappelant ses propres décors. En se tenant sur le bord de la falaise, King dit s'être sentie « dans le paysage, mais sans pouvoir le revendiquer ». « J'étais consciente… que j'en faisais à la fois l'expérience et que je m'en séparais – une distinction importante[13]. » King a fabriqué le feuillage à l'avant de l'image, et lui a donné un cadre dans le style Art Nouveau, avec des motifs de branches et de feuilles. Malgré la réalité de la photographie en arrière-plan, quand on regarde les images résultantes, on a toujours l'impression d'un décor construit. Et c'est le cas. Les couleurs de Chalk Shoreline sont profondément saturées : l'eau turquoise, la plage grise et les falaises aux tons multiples semblent construites sous le bleu du ciel. L'avant-plan est parsemé de petits cailloux qui imitent la plage, mais qui ne sont que des grains de sel. Le vaste paysage et la courbe infinie des falaises, de l'eau, sont incroyablement beaux, tel le décor d'un grand et mystérieux récit. *Basalt Cliff* et *Crowned Seascape* nous entraînent au bord de la falaise, dangereusement proche du précipice, et donnent l'impression que ces scènes sont simultanément terribles et spectaculaires. Les fragments de paysage ajoutés par King semblent surréels dans le contexte majestueux des photographies originales : des branches, arbres et buissons singuliers qui sont le fruit de son imagination. Elle prend un peu de recul pour *Tree and Field*, un paysage à la composition traditionnelle avec un avant-plan, un plan moyen et un arrière-plan, et les falaises au loin. Les éléments de l'avant-plan, confectionnés par King, sont dans l'ombre, soulignant ainsi la saturation des couleurs de l'image originale. Les photographies de cette série donnent l'impression d'un film rematricé : des couleurs ajoutées des décennies plus tard pour séduire un nouveau public. Finalement, ce n'est pas seulement les éléments à l'avant-plan qui semblent fabriqués, mais la scène au complet. Une vision aussi sublime est peut-être trop majestueuse pour être vraie.

13. Texte de démarche de l'artiste, mai 2015.

Viewing Box, 2015
bois, métal, paysage miniature, DEL / wood, metal and miniature 3d landscape, LED lights
46 x 32 x 92 cm

King ne vise pas à nous tromper avec ses paysages construits, et ses décors sont jusqu'à maintenant restés dans son atelier. Dans la présente exposition, elle a inclus deux boîtes à visionnement : deux cabinets élégamment conçus dans lesquels on peut voir un paysage construit à l'aide d'une perspective forcée. Ses « pierres »et ses « arbres » méticuleusement rendus s'offrent au regard, hors du contexte des photographies agrandies. La boîte devient un espace personnel pour nous, un lieu de contemplation. L'artiste note qu'avec cette structure, elle espère « construire un espace poétique en partie crédible[14]».

Holly King a dit de son travail qu'il était une « recherche de silence profond[15]». Revenons à l'affirmation de Pseudo-Longin : « [Le sublime] ne persuade pas proprement, mais il ravit, il transporte. » À la fois issues d'une construction et du réel, les photographies de King nous permettent, par la grandeur de leur échelle, par la profondeur de leurs couleurs et par la richesse des noirs des œuvres monochromes, de jouir de la beauté et de savourer le silence face au sublime.

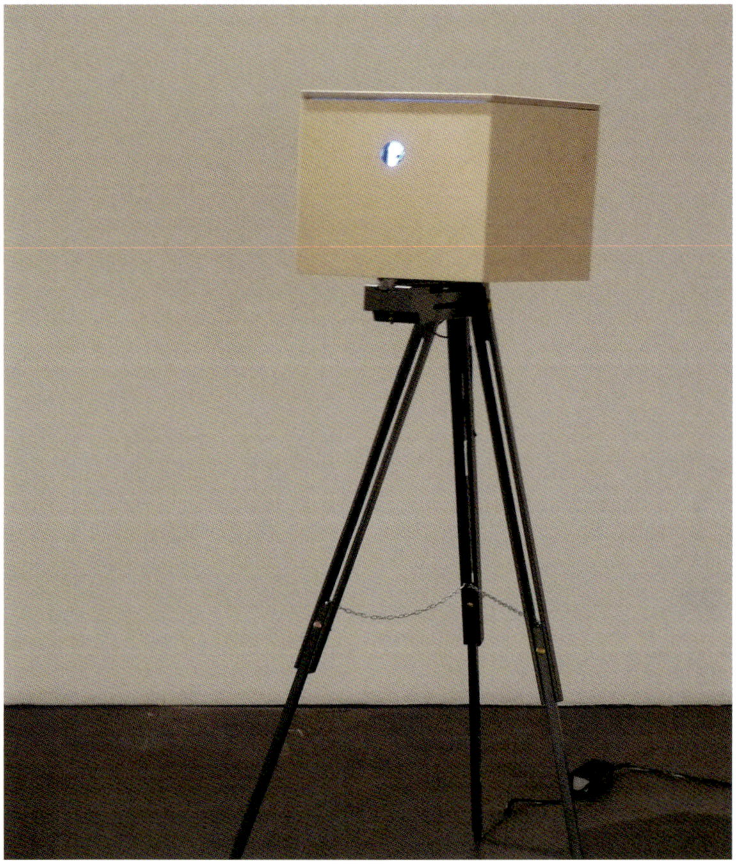

14. Texte de démarche de l'artiste, mai 2015.
15. Conversation entre l'artiste et l'auteure, 22 avril 2015, Montréal.

PORTFOLIO II

TWISTED ROOTS

MANGROVES : FLOATING BETWEEN TWO WORLDS

GRAND CANYON : UNSEEN

ENGLISH CLIFF SERIES

TWISTED ROOTS

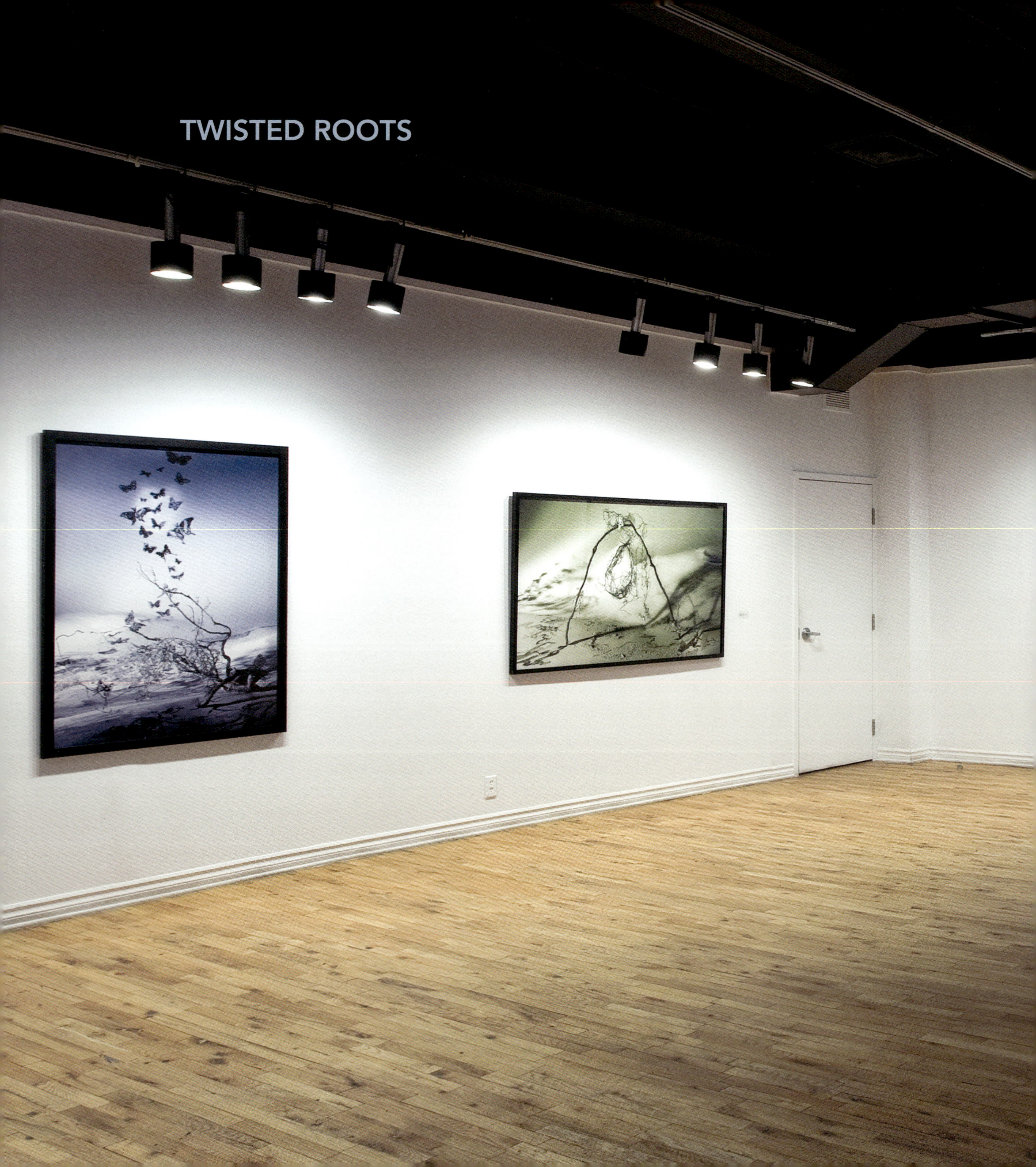

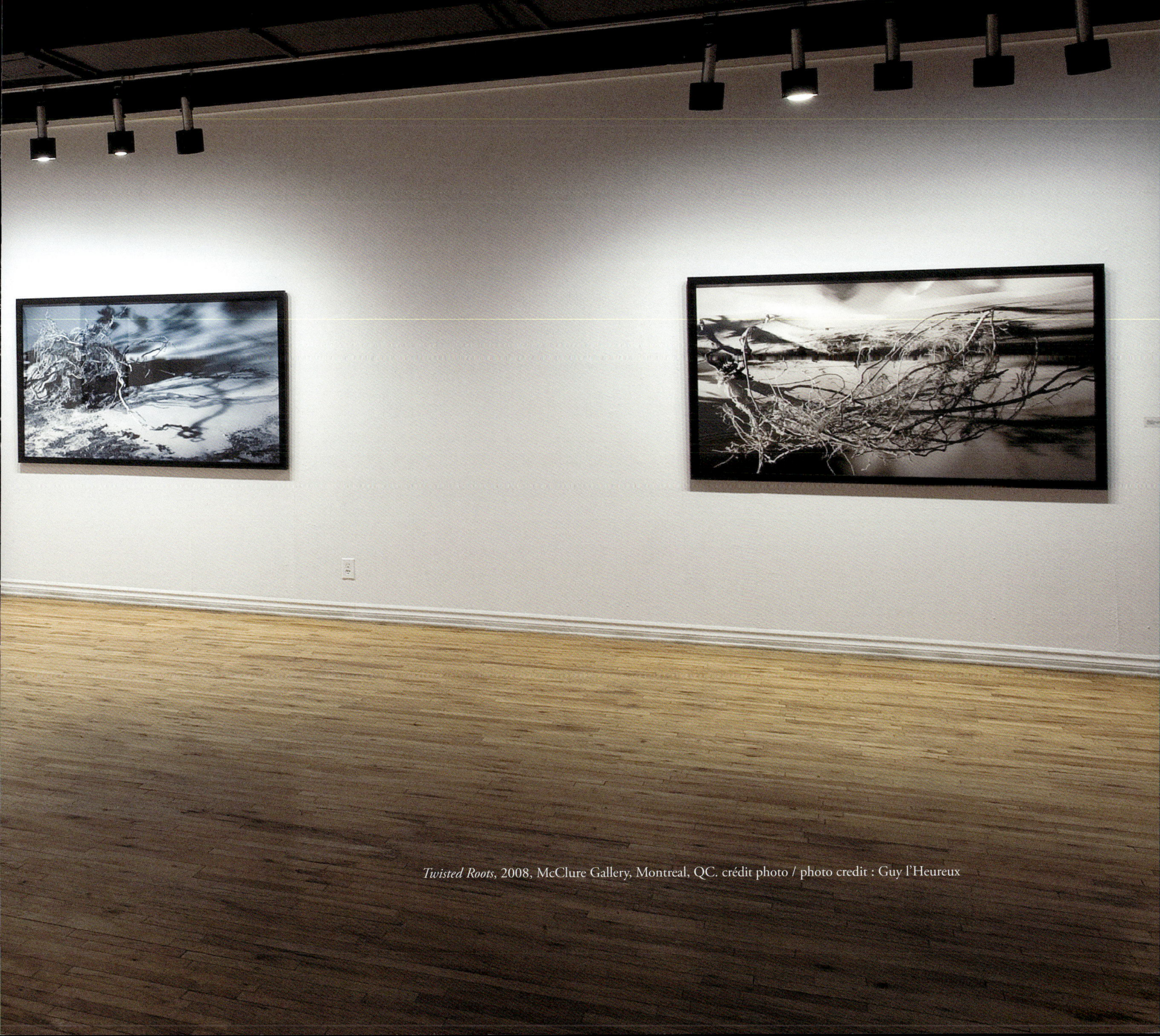

Twisted Roots, 2008, McClure Gallery, Montreal, QC. crédit photo / photo credit : Guy l'Heureux

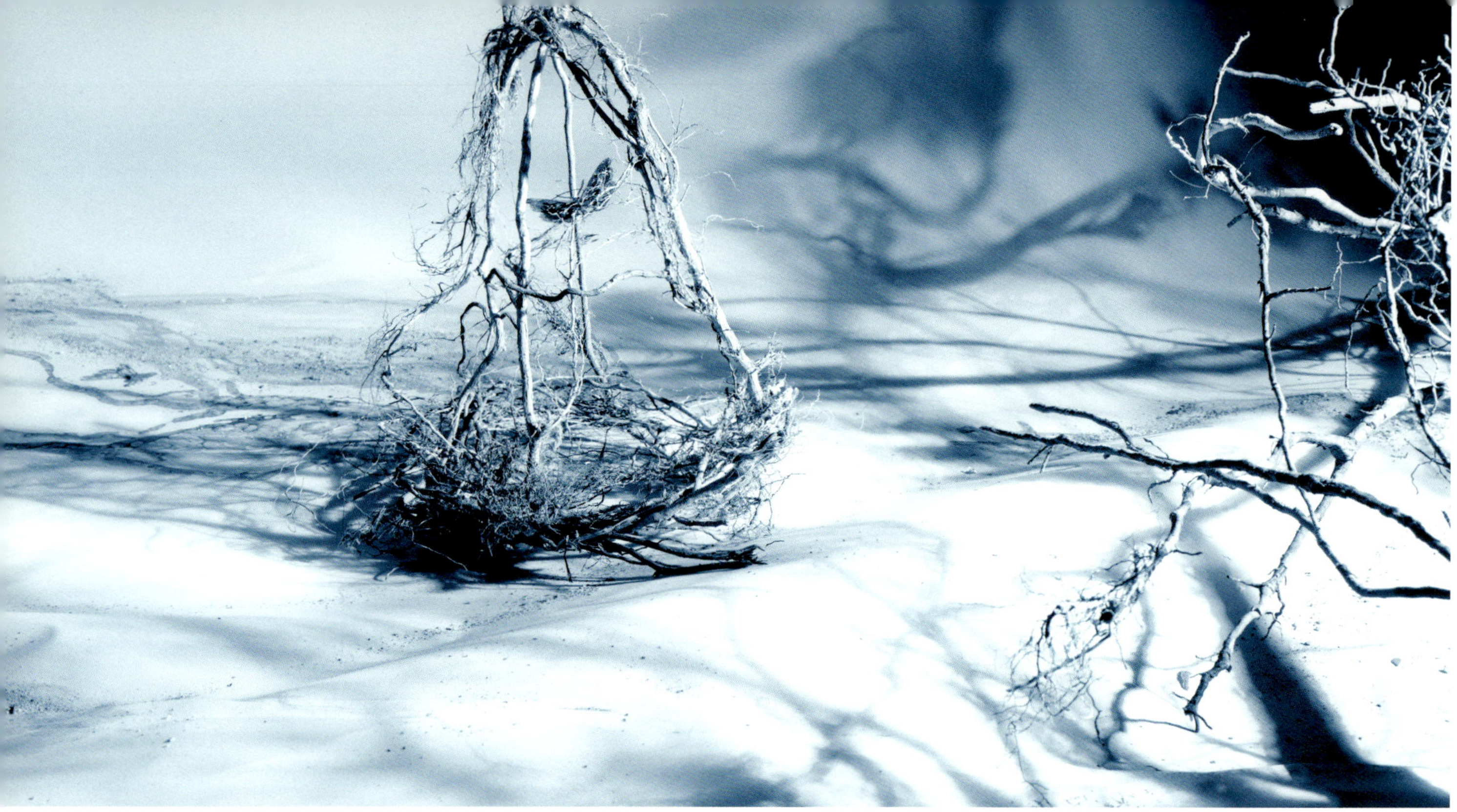

Prevailing Shadows, 2006
épreuve à jet d'encre sur papier Hahnemuhle /
ink jet print on Hahnemuhle paper
132 x 99 cm

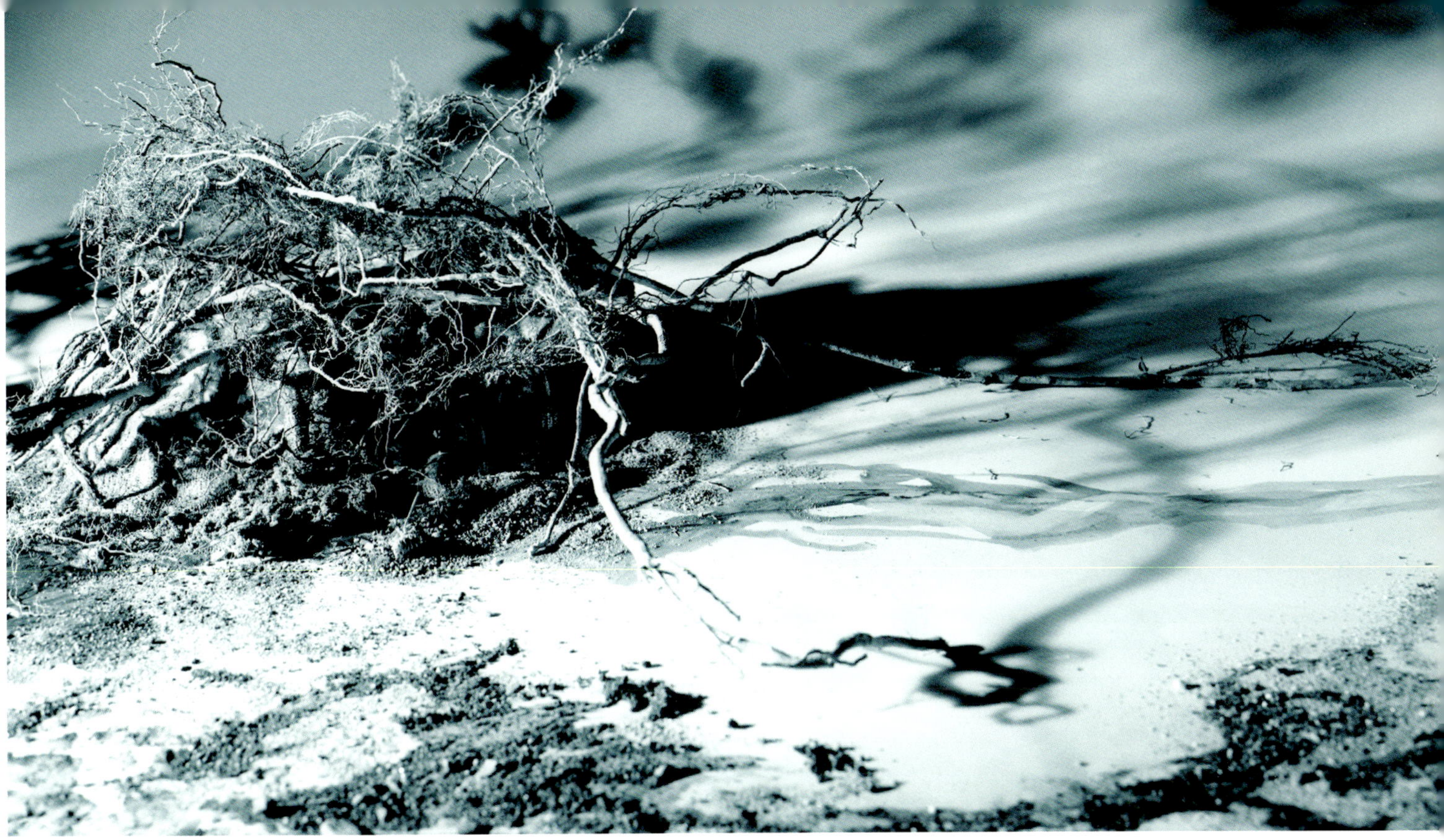

Windblown Tangle, 2006
épreuve à jet d'encre sur papier Hahnemuhle /
ink jet print on Hahnemuhle paper
132 x 99 cm

MANGROVES : FLOATING BETWEEN TWO WORLDS

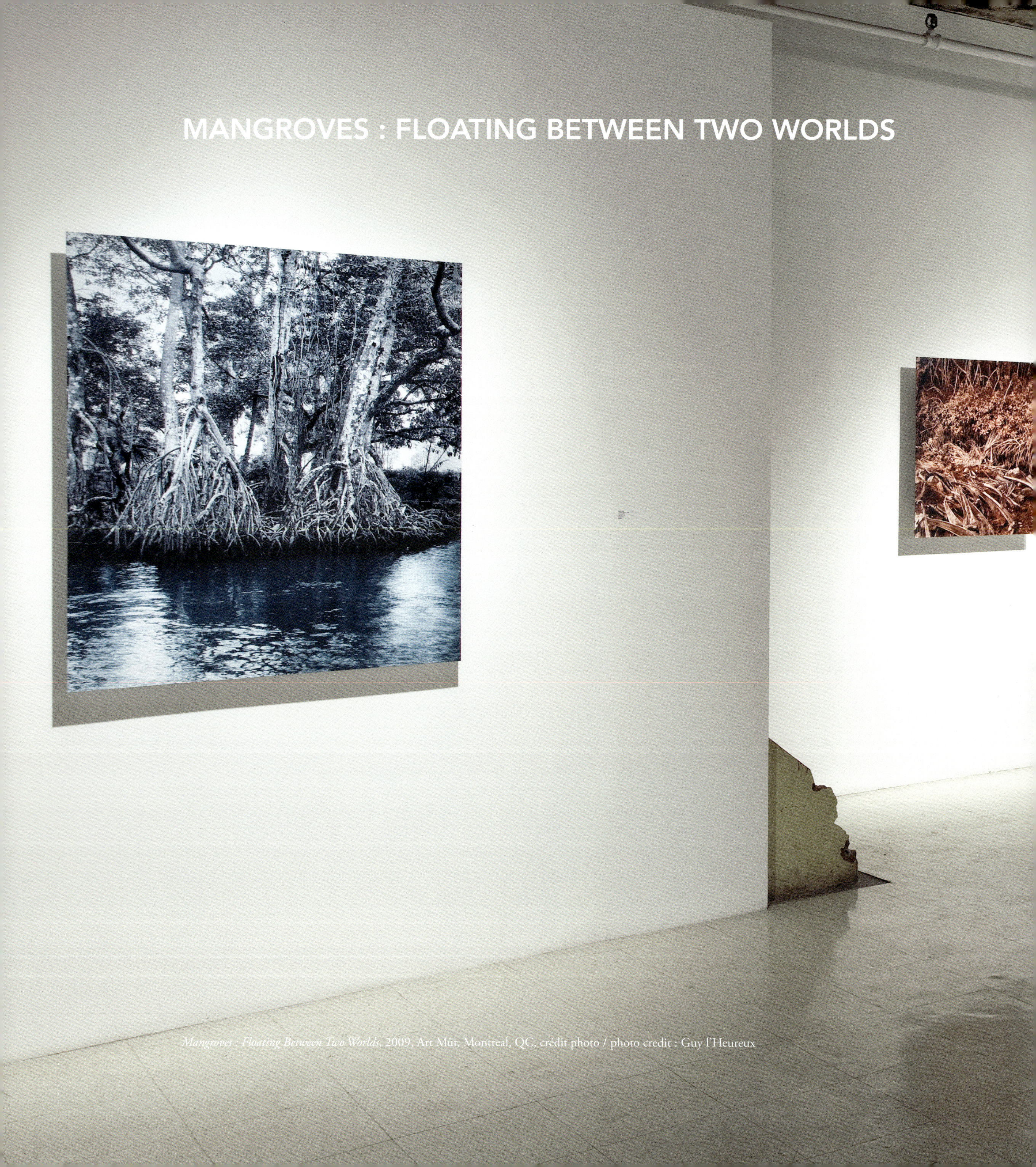

Mangroves : Floating Between Two Worlds, 2009, Art Mûr, Montreal, QC, crédit photo / photo credit : Guy l'Heureux

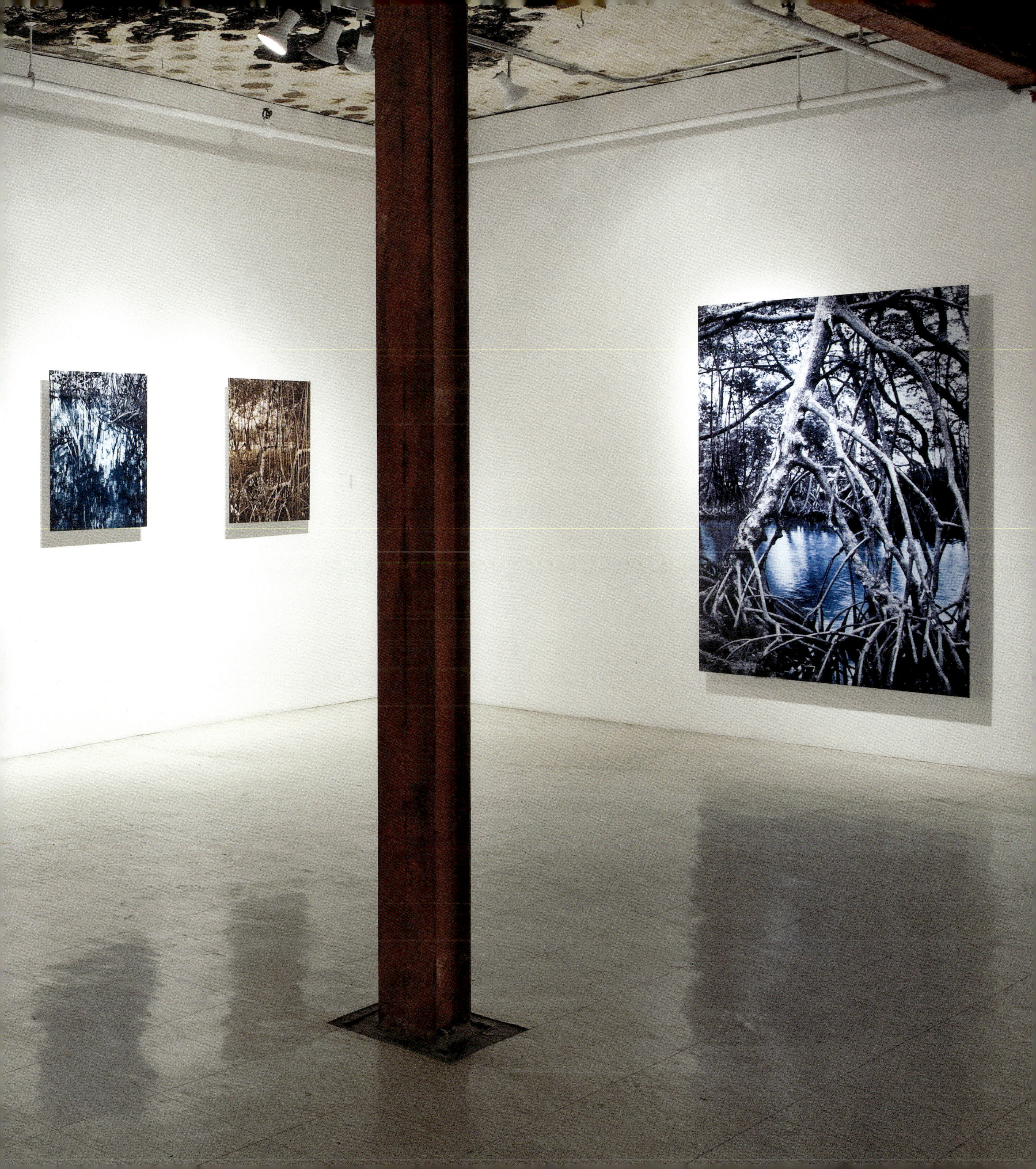

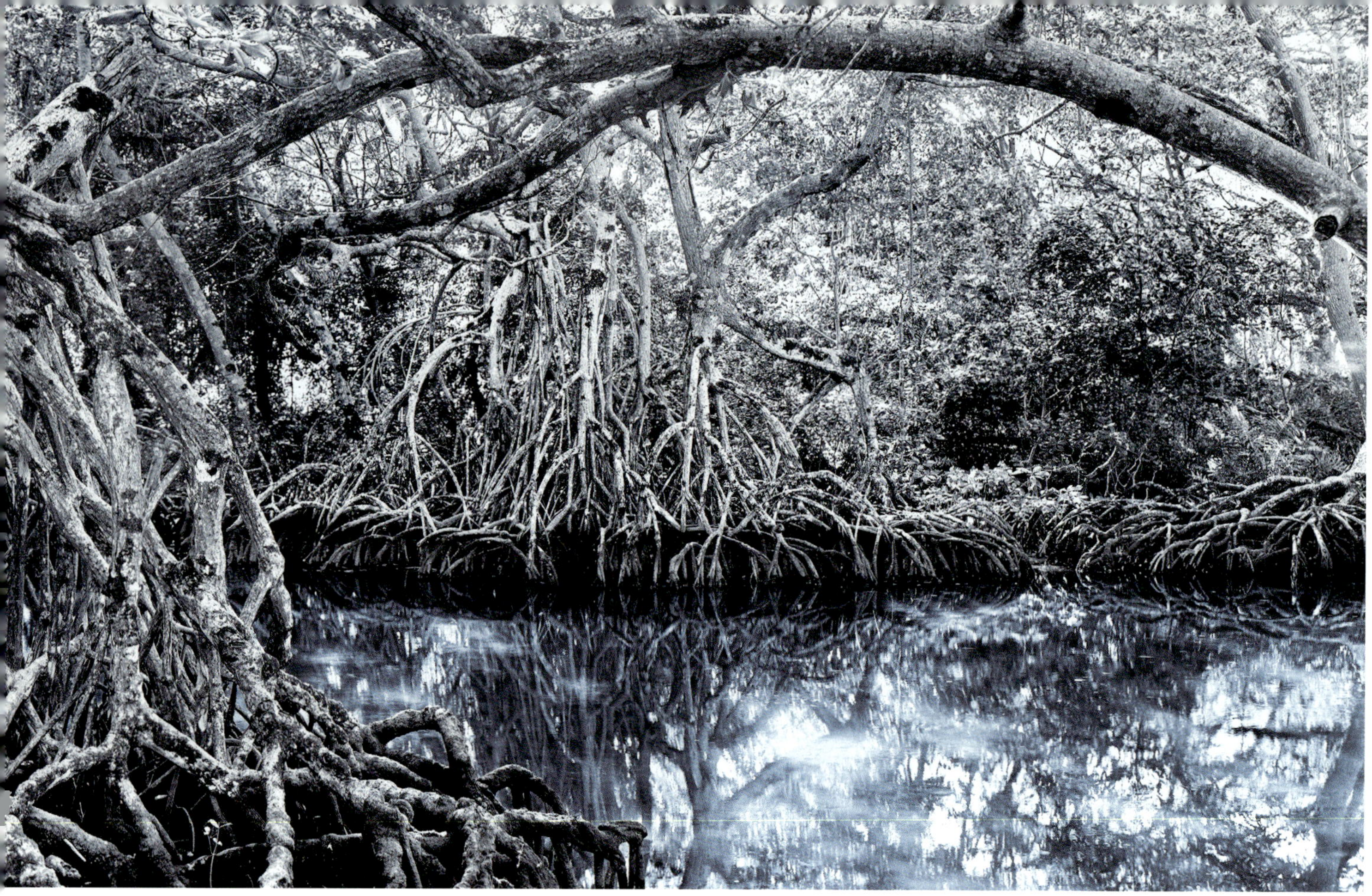

Heavenly Invitation, 2009
épreuve à développement chromogène /
chromogenic print
122 x 183 cm

Image : p. 91
Arching and Majestic, 2009
épreuve à développement chromogène /
chromogenic print
182 x 122 cm

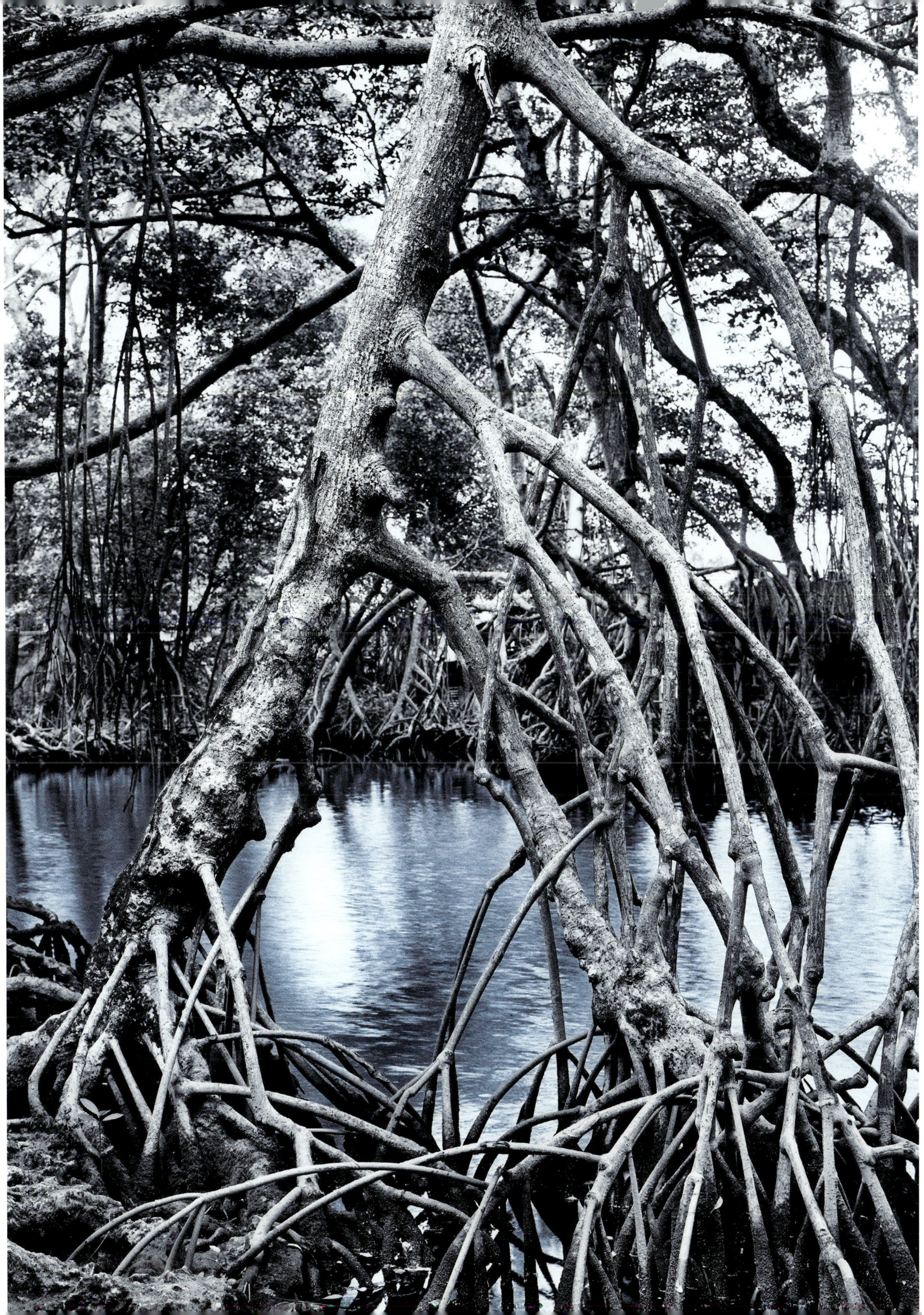

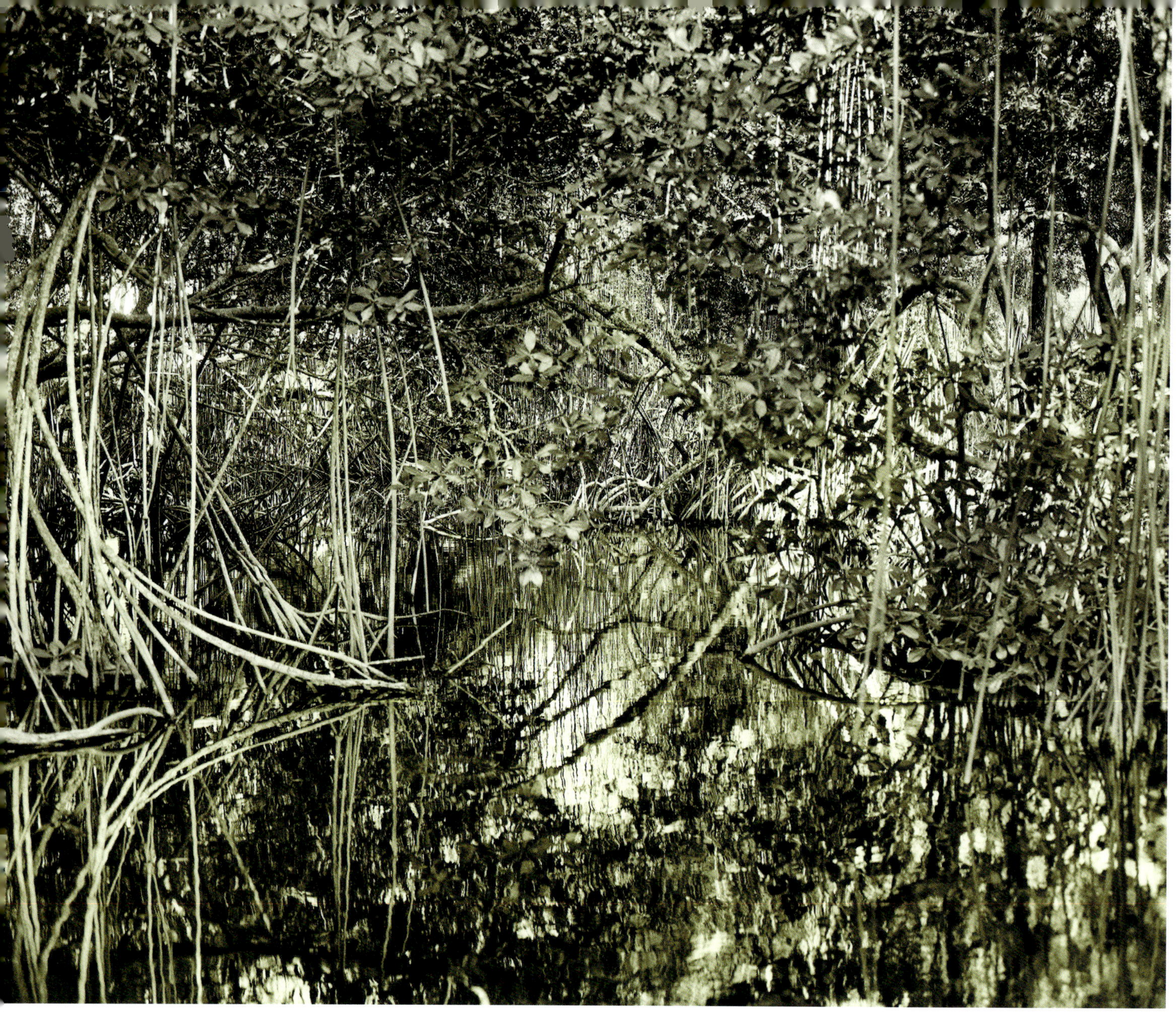

Tapestry, 2009
épreuve à développement chromogène /
chromogenic print
122 x 152.5 cm

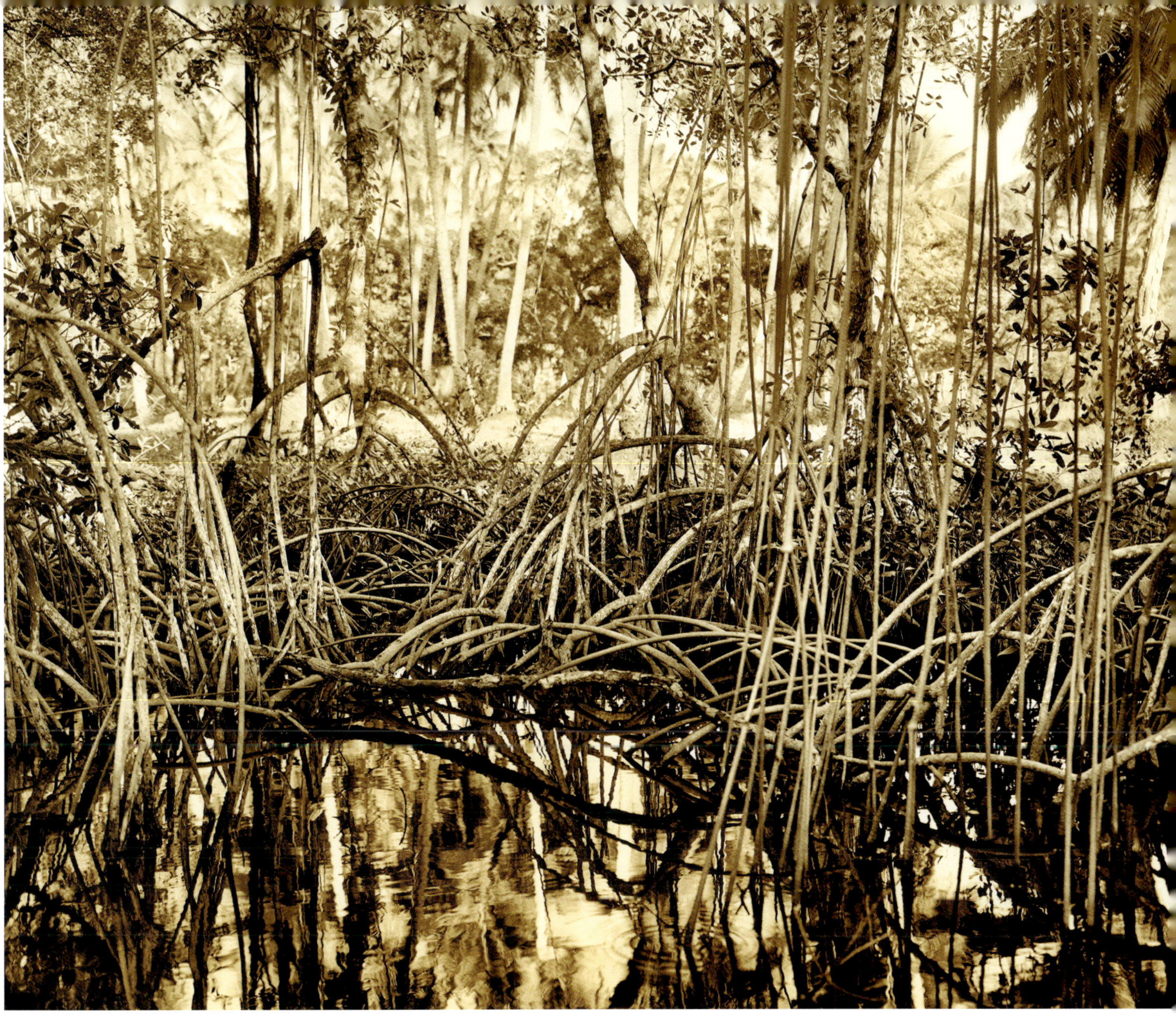

Luminous, 2009
épreuve à développement chromogène /
chromogenic print
122 x 155 cm

GRAND CANYON : UNSEEN

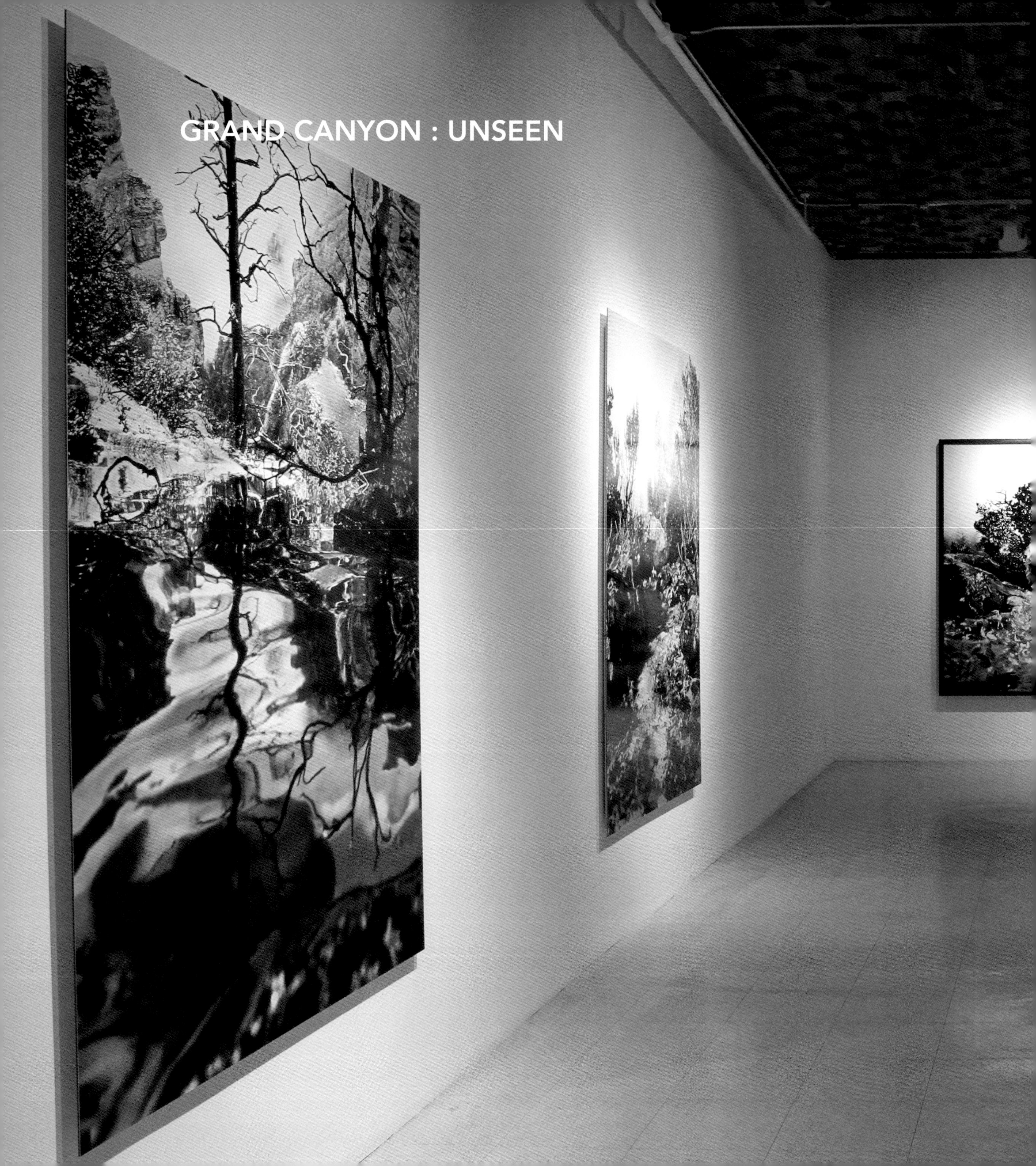

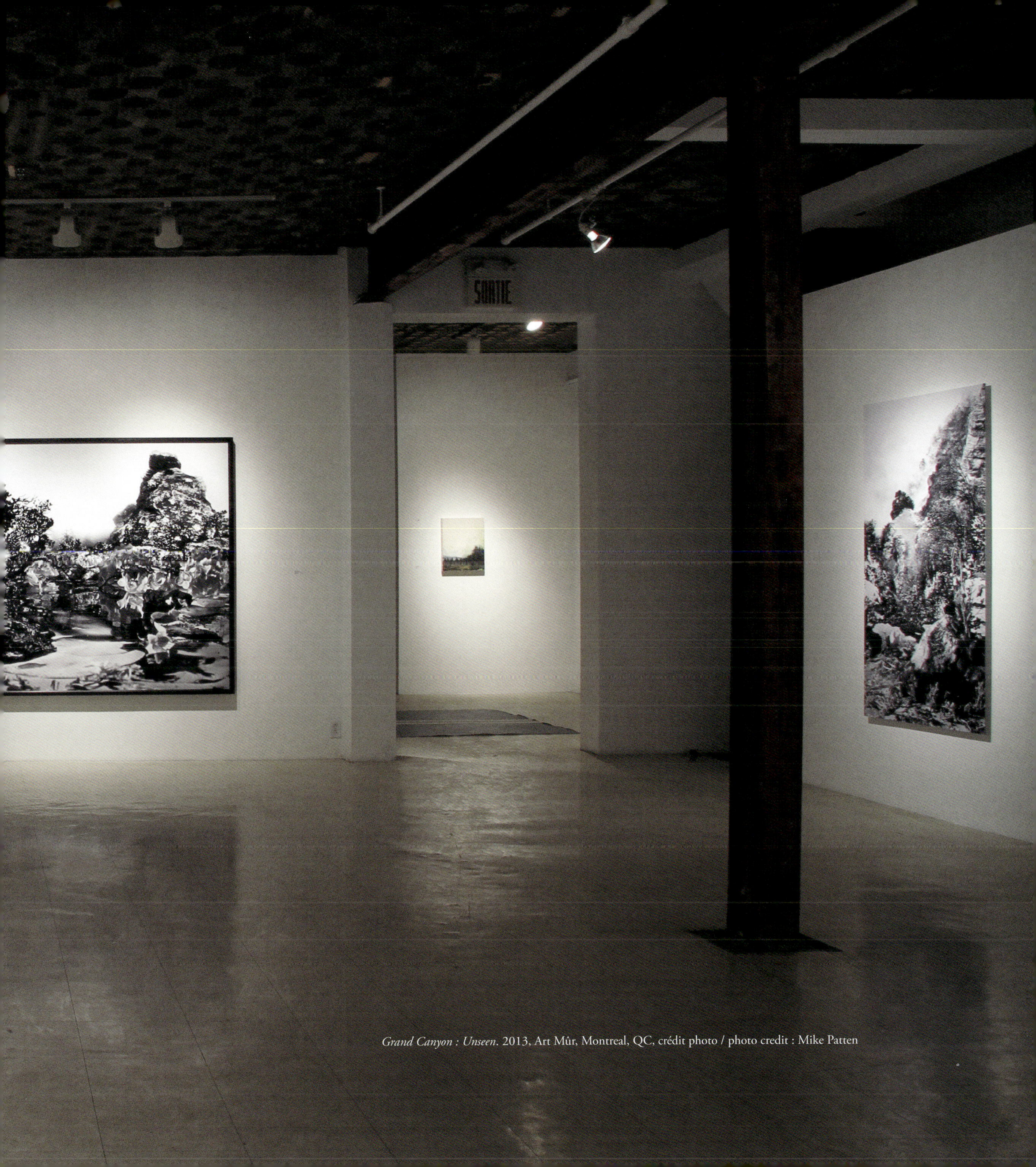

Grand Canyon : Unseen. 2013, Art Mûr, Montreal, QC, crédit photo / photo credit : Mike Patten

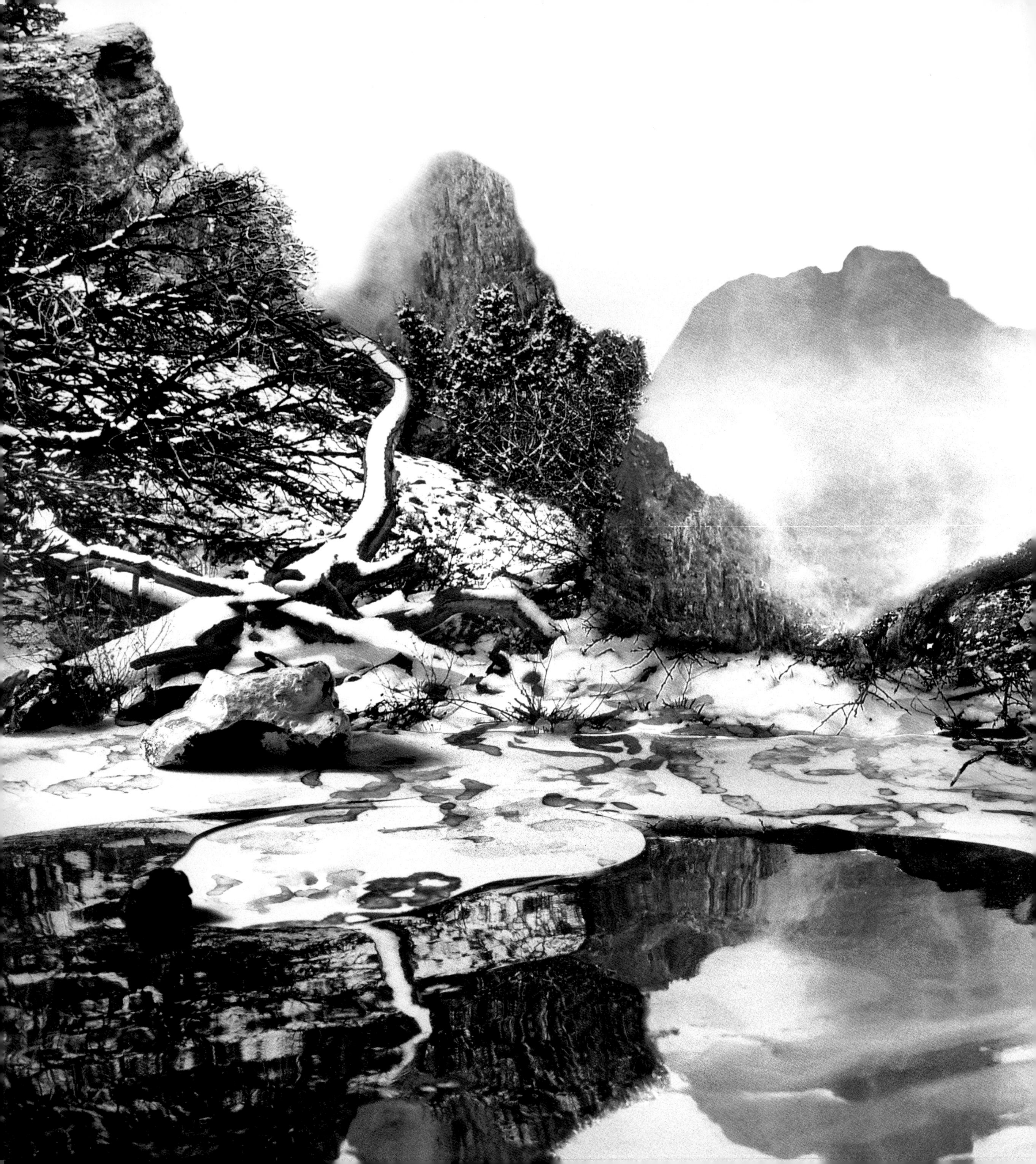

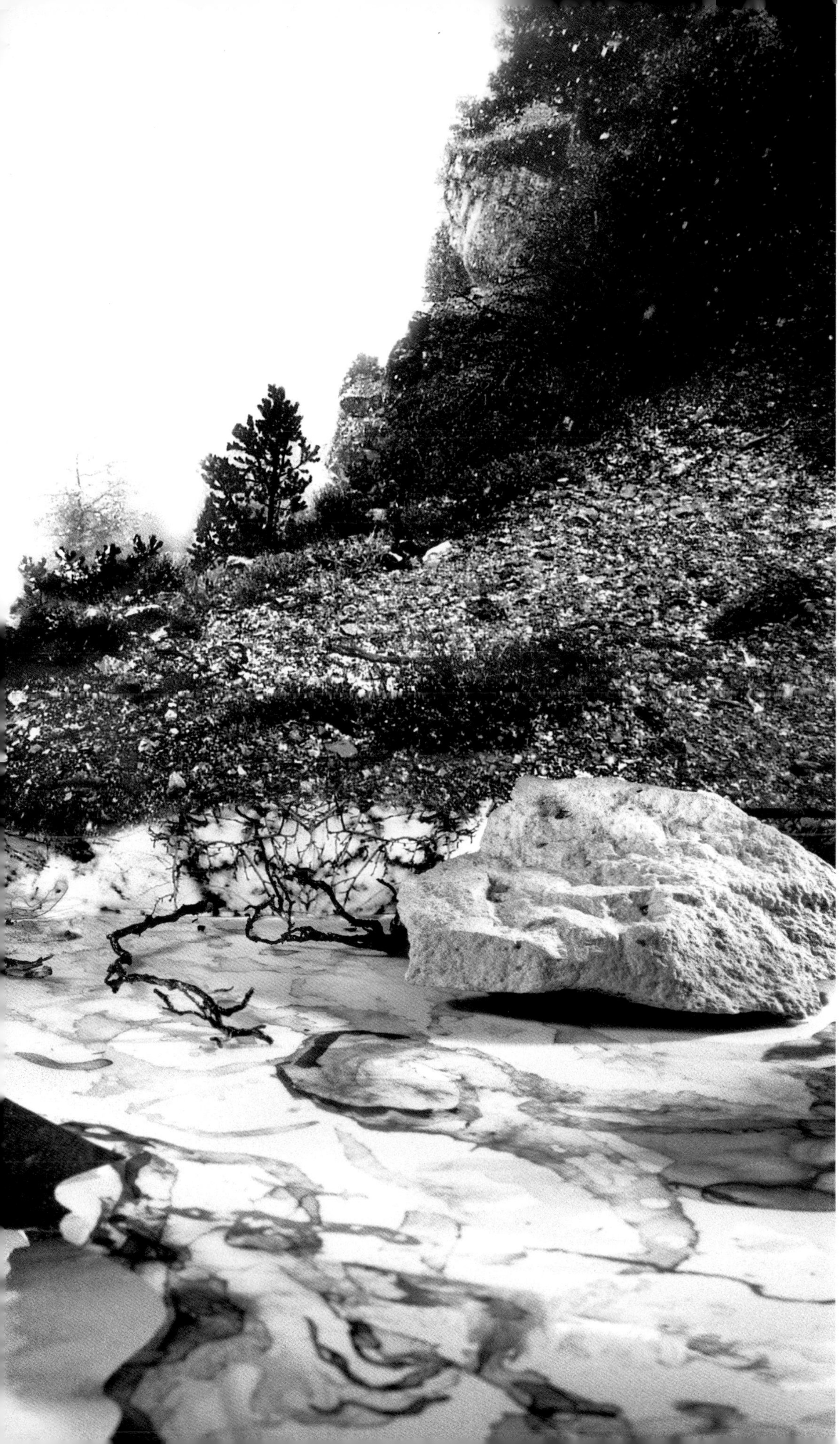

Into the Mist, 2012
photographie en noir et blanc
/ black and white photograph
122 x 183 cm

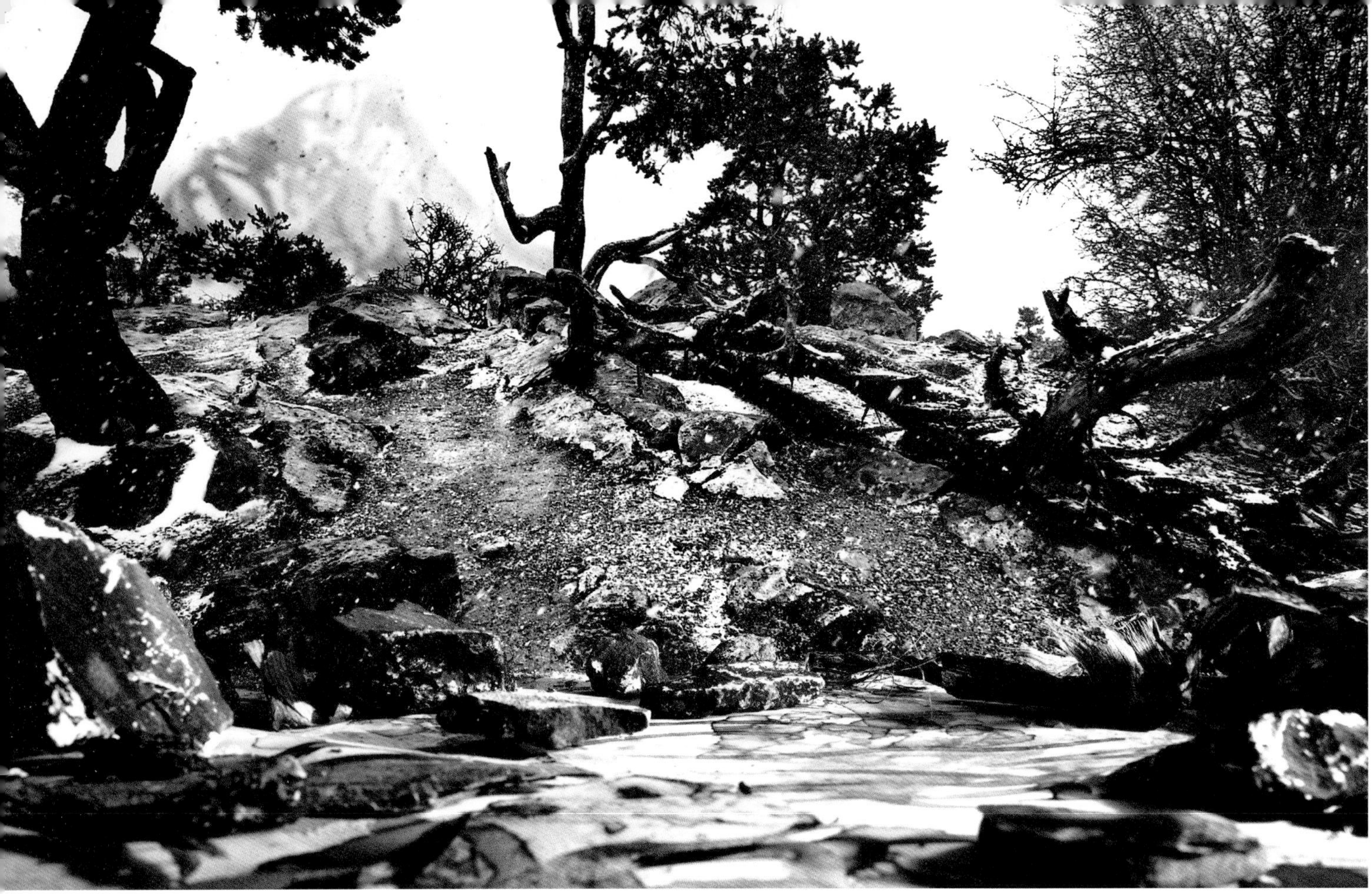

Scenic Delirium, 2012
photographie en noir et blanc /
black and white photograph
122 x 183 cm

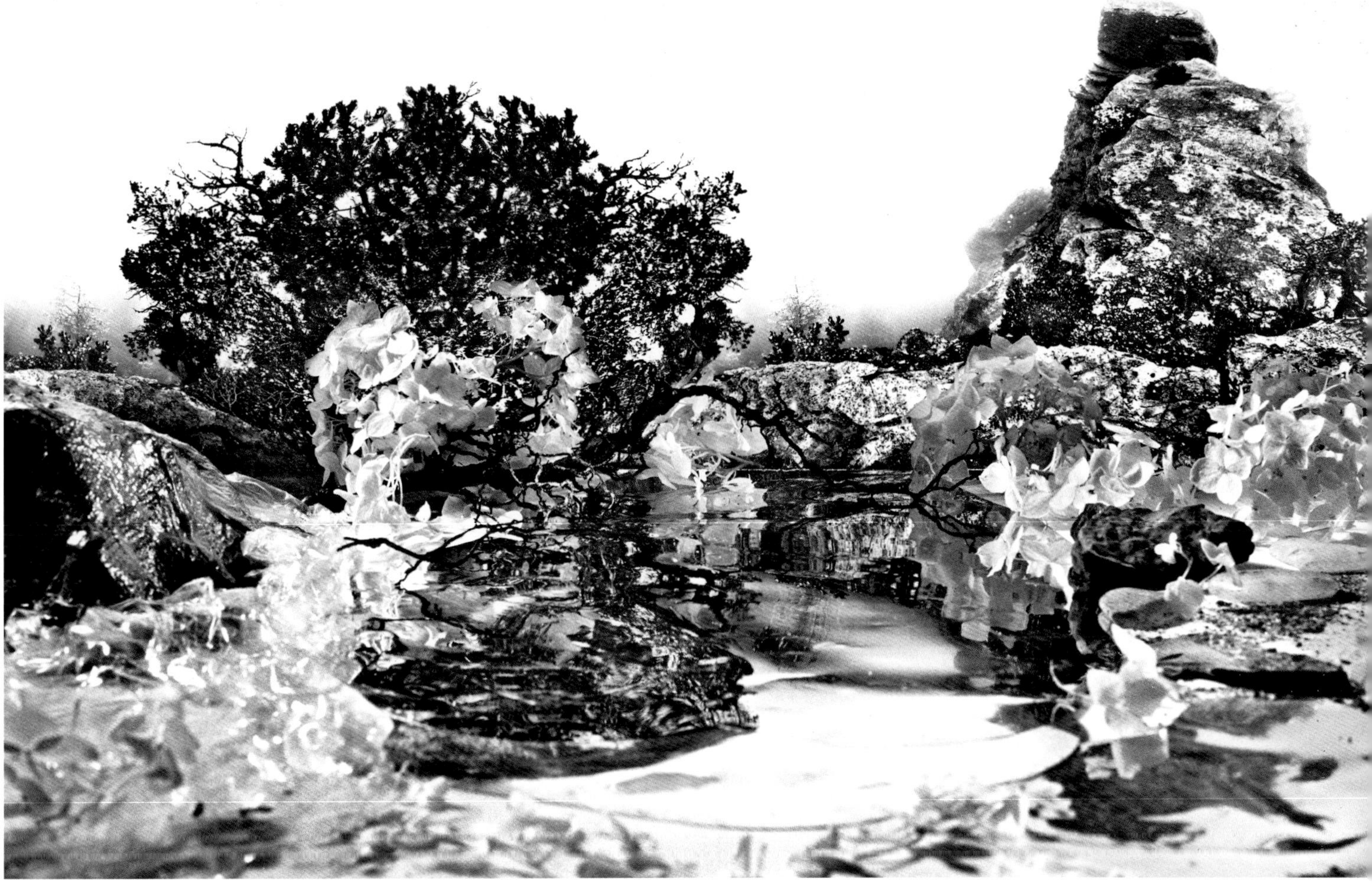

Almost Paradise, 2012
photographie en noir et blanc /
black and white photograph
163 x 244 cm

ENGLISH CLIFF SERIES

Tree and Fields, 2013
épreuve à développement chromogène /
chromogenic print
122 x 152 cm

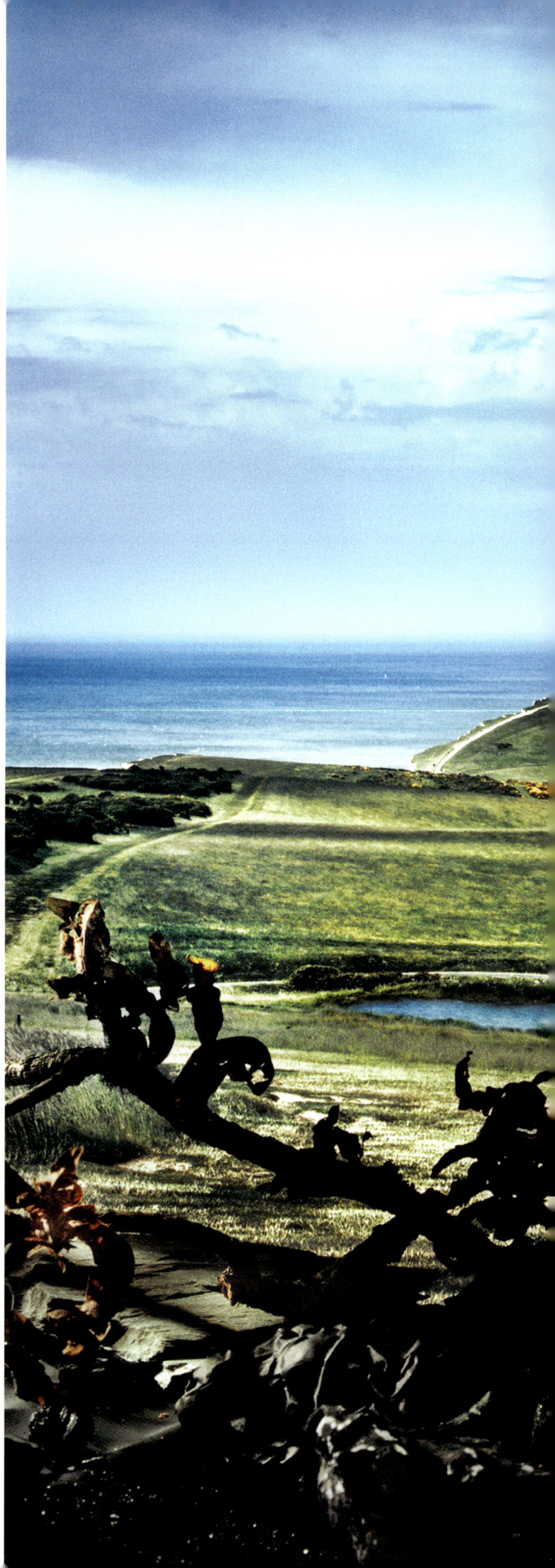

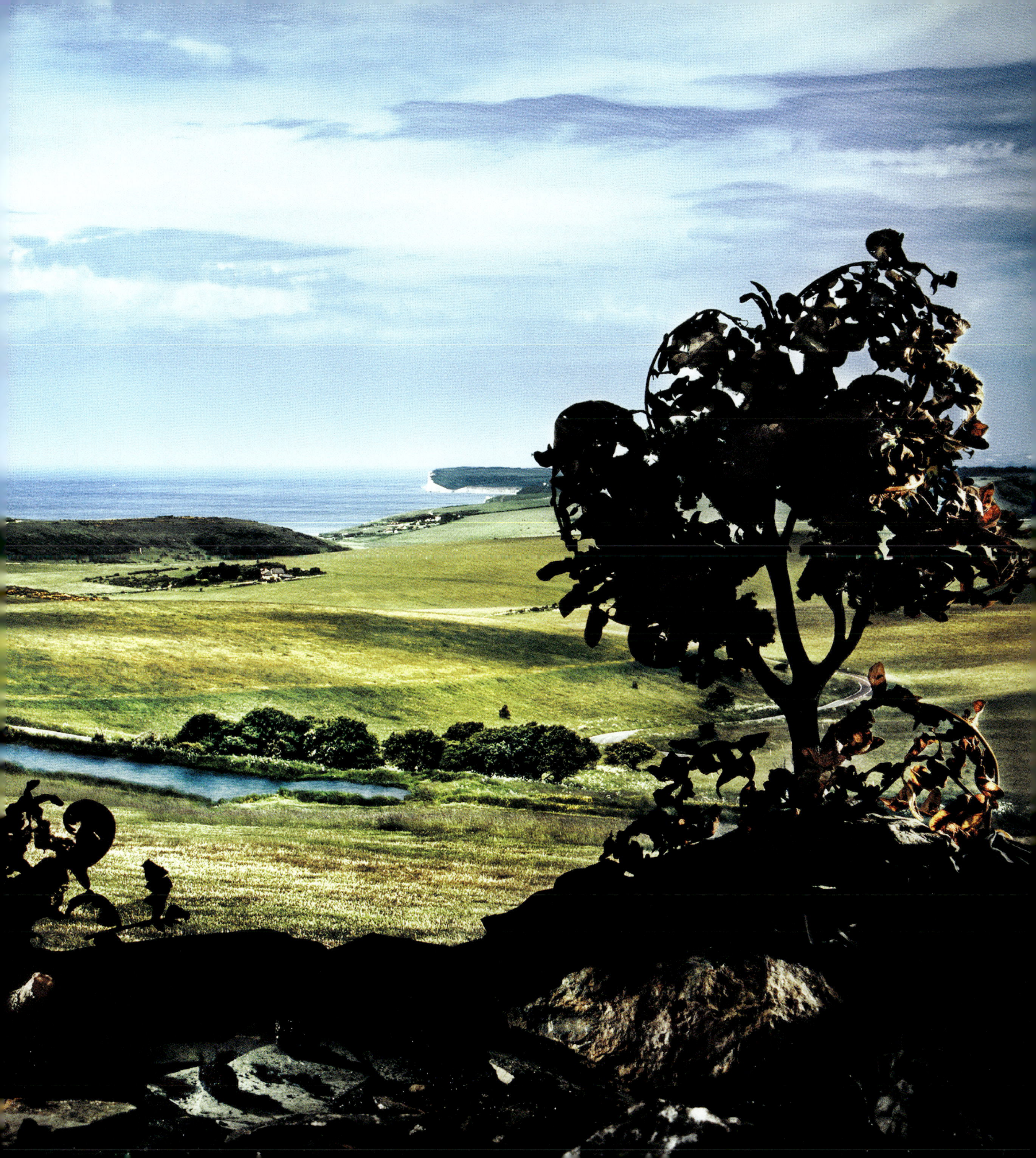

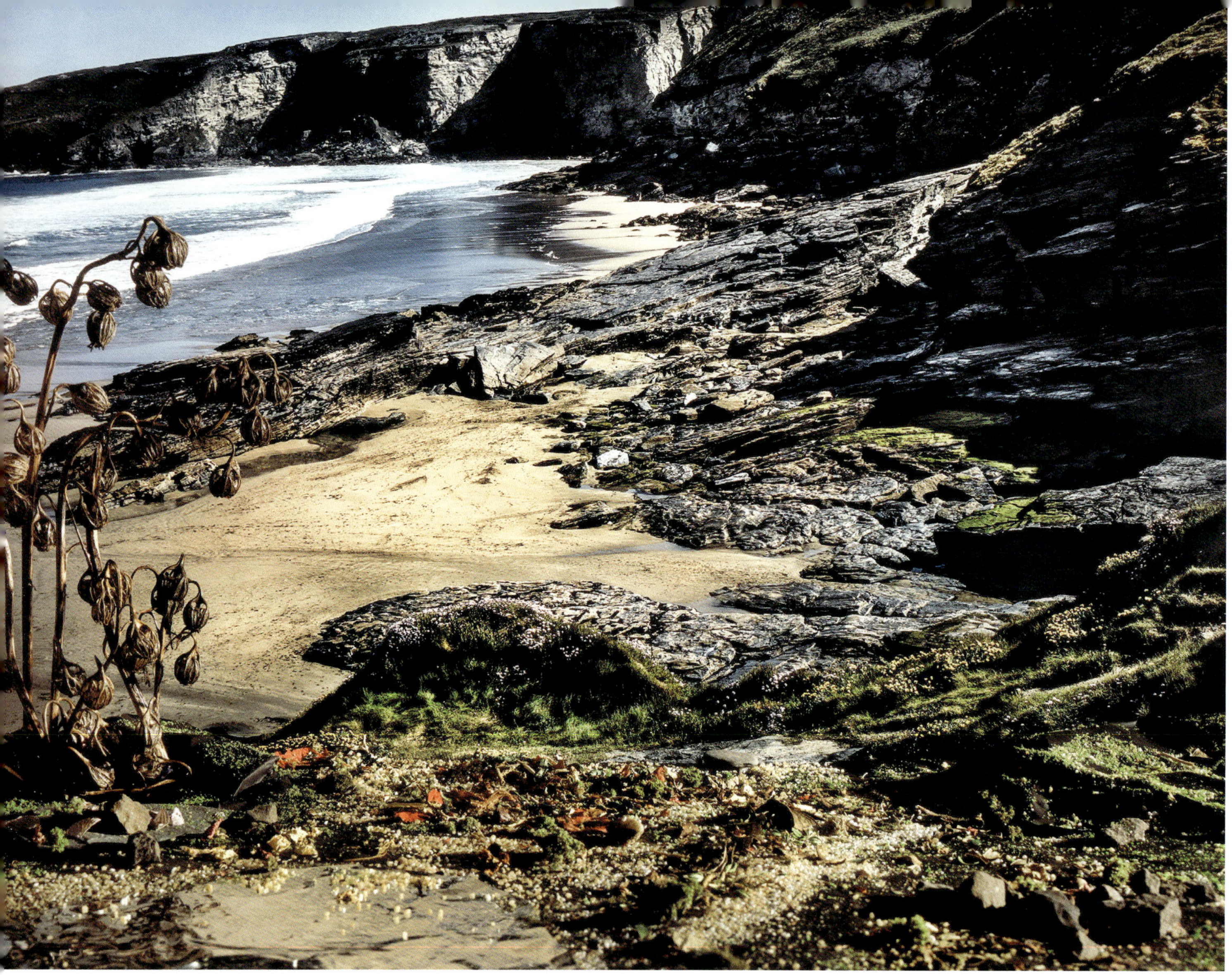

Beach and Cliffside, 2014
épreuve à développement chromogène /
chromogenic print
122 x 152 cm

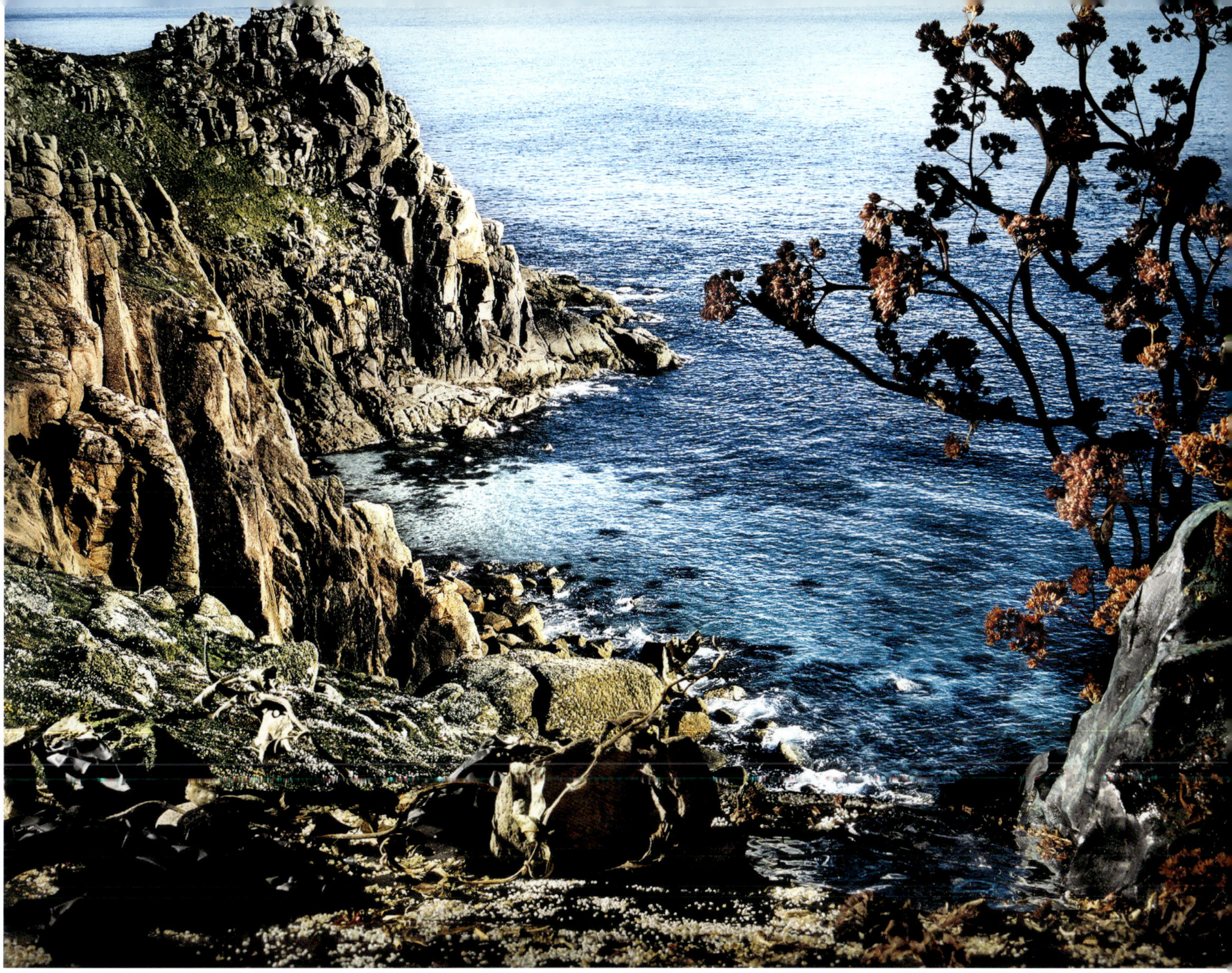

Basalt Cliff, 2015
épreuve à développement chromogène /
chromogenic print
122 x 152 cm

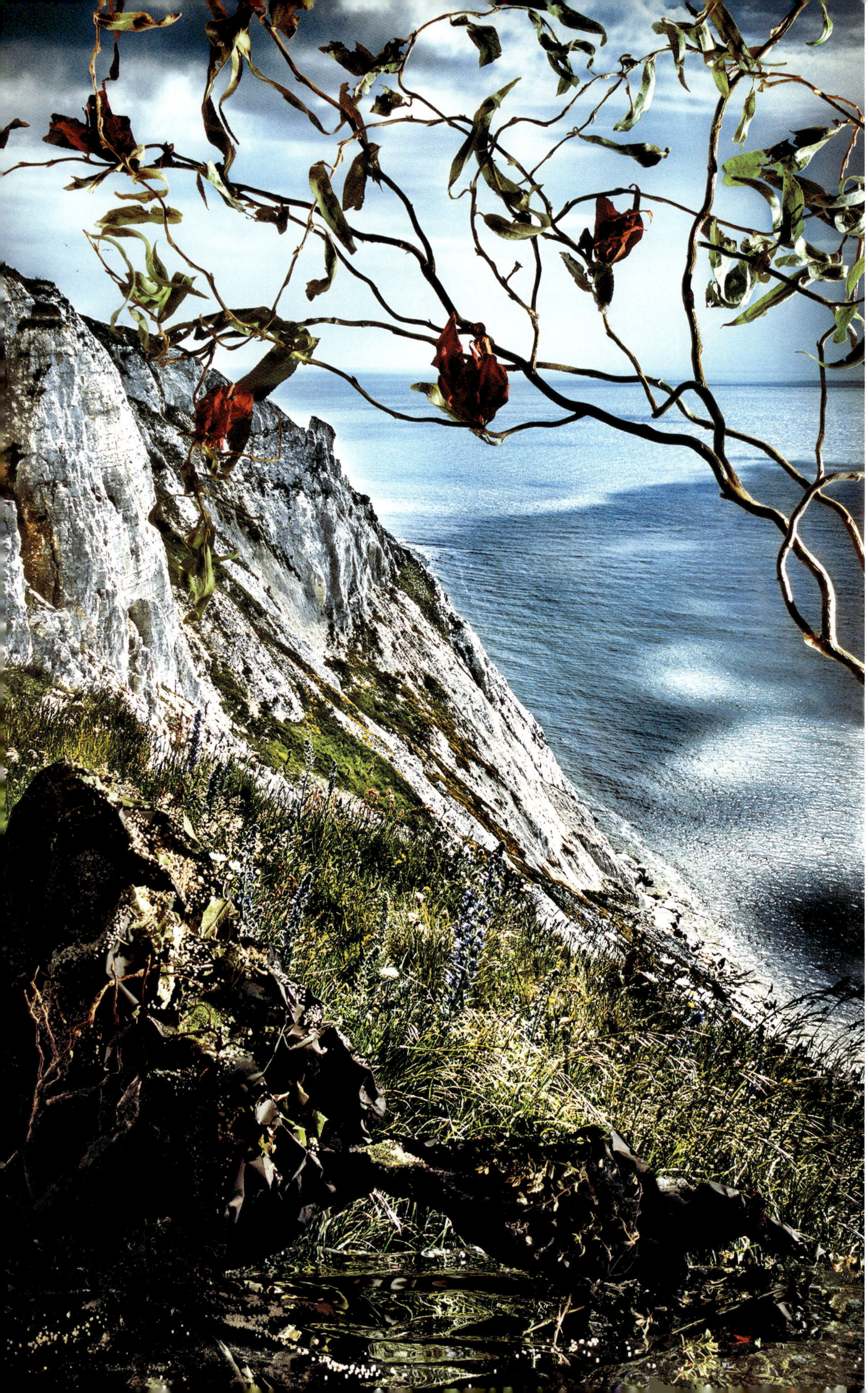

Cliff with Vines, 2015
épreuve à développement chromogène /
chromogenic print
152 x 93 cm

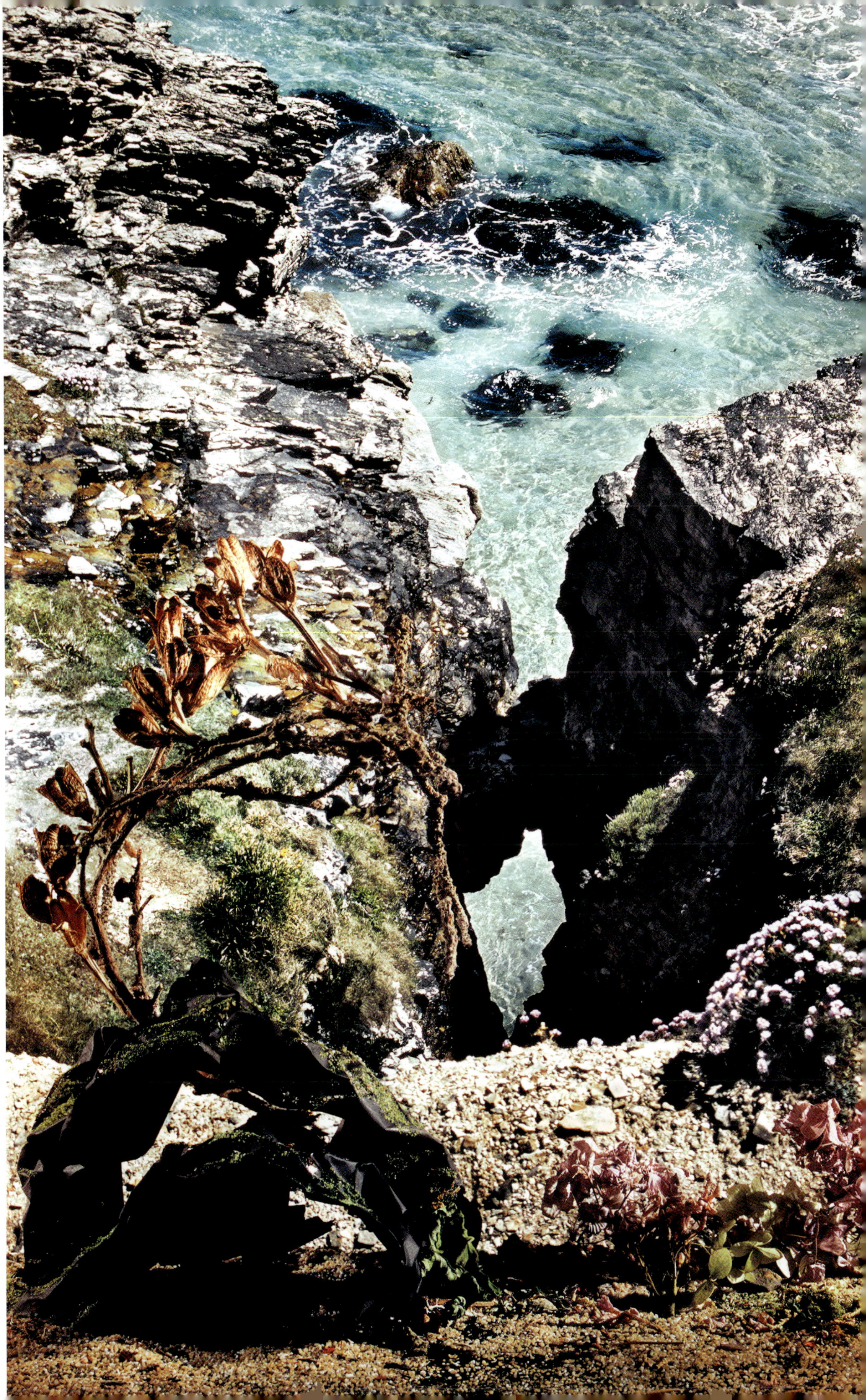

Crowned Seascape, 2015
épreuve à développement chromogène /
chromogenic print
152 x 93 cm

LISTE DES ŒUVRES DE L'EXPOSITION / LIST OF WORKS IN THE EXHIBITION

Heightened Release, 2006
épreuve à jet d'encre sur papier Hahnemuhle / ink jet print on Hahnemuhle paper
132 x 99 cm

Impossible Sanctuary, 2006
épreuve à jet d'encre sur papier Hahnemuhle / ink jet print on Hahnemuhle paper
132 x 99 cm

Tender Cradle, 2007
épreuve à jet d'encre sur papier Hahnemuhle / ink jet print on Hahnemuhle paper
99 x 168 cm

Heavenly Invitation, 2009
épreuve à développement chromogène / chromogenic print
122 x 183 cm

World Beyond the Water, 2009
épreuve à développement chromogène / chromogenic print
122 x 183 cm

Tapestry, 2009
épreuve à développement chromogène / chromogenic print
122 x 152.5 cm

Almost Paradise, 2012
photographie en noir et blanc / black and white photograph
163 x 244 cm

Pathway to an Illusion, 2011
photographie en noir et blanc / black and white photograph
183 x 122 cm

Reflections Tantalize, 2011
photographie en noir et blanc / black and white photograph
183 x 122 cm

Into the Mist, 2012
photographie en noir et blanc / black and white photograph
122 x 183 cm

Scenic Delirium, 2012
photographie en noir et blanc / black and white photograph
122 x 183 cm

Chalk Shoreline, 2013
épreuve à développement chromogène / chromogenic print
122 x 152 cm

Tree and Fields, 2013
épreuve à développement chromogène / chromogenic print
122 x 152 cm

Beach and Cliffside, 2014
épreuve à développement chromogène / chromogenic print
122 x 152 cm

Basalt Cliff, 2015
épreuve à développement chromogène / chromogenic print
122 x 152 cm

Cliff with Vines, 2015
épreuve à développement chromogène / chromogenic print
152 x 93 cm

Crowned Seascape, 2015
épreuve à développement chromogène / chromogenic print
152 x 93 cm

Viewing Box #1, #2, 2015
bois, métal, paysage miniature, DEL / wood, metal and miniature 3d landscape, LED lights
46 x 32 x 92 cm

CURRICULUM VITÆ

EDUCATION

1979–81	York University, Toronto, MFA, Studio Art
1976–79	Université Laval, Quebec, BFA, Visual Arts
1974–76	Dawson College, Montreal DEC, Fine Art

WORK HISTORY

2009–14	Visual art specialist, Intégration aux arts à l'architecture
1983–present	Concordia University, Instructor, Department of Painting and Drawing
2012–13	Champlain College, Lennoxville, Fine Arts Department
2006–09	The Art Institute of Boston, MFA Mentor-Advisor
1984–94	Dawson CEGEP, Instructor, Fine Arts Department
1980–81	York University, Instructor, Fine Arts Department

LECTURES

Dawson College, Montreal (2009, 2011, 2014, 2015), Concordia University (1998), Champlain College, Montreal (1998, 2006, 2014), Montreal Museum of Fine Arts (2006, 1998), Passe-Partout (TV5 2006), Ontario College of Art (2000), Alberta College of Art (1987, 2001), Lethbridge University (1987, 2001, 2004).

JURIES

Jury chair, Prix Borduas (2007), Prix Borduas (2006), Canada Council B Grants (2000, 1997, 1988); CALQ (1994, 1991); MFA Concordia jury(1999), Dazibao Gallery, Montreal (1996–88).

SOLO EXHIBITIONS

2017	*Edging Towards the Mysterious*, le Musée du Bas-St-Laurent, Rivière-du-Loup, QC
2017	*Edging Towards the Mysterious*, Art Mûr, Montreal, QC
2016	*Edging Towards the Mysterious*, le Musée des beaux-arts de Sherbrooke, QC
2016	*Edging Towards the Mysterious*, Thames Art Gallery, Chatham, ON
2016	*Edging Towards the Mysterious*, The Robert McLaughlin Gallery, Oshawa, ON
2014	*Territoires d'émotions*, Agora de la danse, Montreal, QC
2013	*Grand Canyon : Unseen*, Art Mûr, Montreal, QC
2010	*Return to the Silt Lands*, Leo Kamen Gallery, Toronto, ON
2009	*Mangroves : Floating Between Two Worlds*, Art Mûr, Montreal, QC
2008	*Holly King*, Bibliothèque Eleanor London, Montreal, QC
2008	*Twisted Roots*, Galerie McClure, Montreal, QC
2006	*Twisted Roots*, Galerie d'art de l'Université de Sherbrooke, Sherbrooke, QC
2005	*The Transcendent Sublime*, Mois de la Photo, Art Mûr, Montreal, QC
2004	*Vistas*, Art Mûr, Montreal, QC
2004	*Coming into View*, Trépanier-Baer Gallery, Calgary, AB

2003 *Coming into View*, Leo Kamen Gallery, Toronto, ON
2002 *Selected Recent Works*, Galerie 418, Montreal, QC
2002 *Landscapes of the Imagination*, Yellowknife Art Gallery, Yellowknife, NWT
2001 *Mirages* Extended, Trépanier-Baer Gallery, Calgary, AB
2001 *Mois de la Photo*, Stewart Hall Art Gallery, Montreal, QC
2001 *Holly King*, Galerie de Bellefeuille, Montreal, QC
2001 *Mirage*, Leo Kamen Gallery, Toronto, ON
2001 *Landscapes of the Imagination*, Art Gallery of Mississauga, ON
2000 *Mirage*, Expression: Centre d'exposition de St-Hyacinthe, St-Hyacinthe, QC
2000 *Holly King*, Galerie d'art de l'Université de Sherbrooke, Sherbrooke, QC
2000 *The Forest of Enchantment*, Leo Kamen Gallery, Toronto, ON
1999 *Landscapes of the Imagination*, Montreal Museum of Fine Arts, Montreal, QC
1998 *Landscapes of the Imagination*, Canadian Museum of Contemporary Photography, Ottawa, ON
1998 *The Forest of Enchantment*, Galerie Parallèle, Montreal, QC; Galerie Verticale, Laval, QC
1995 *Imprisoned in the Viewless Winds,* Costin & Klintworth Gallery, Toronto, ON
1993 *The Mining Project*, Costin & Klintworth Gallery, Toronto, ON
1993 *Holly King*, Galerie Ville de Grasse, Nice, France
1993 *Oeuvres choisis 1983–1993*, Musée de Joliette, Joliette, QC
1991 *The Gardens*, Brenda Wallace Gallery, Montreal, QC
1990 *The Gardens*, Costin & Klintworth Gallery, Toronto, ON
1990 *Holly King*, Galerie Bob Van Orsouw, Zurich, Switzerland
1989 *Holly King*, YYZ, Toronto, ON
1989 *Holly King*, VU, Centre d'animation et de diffusion de la photographie, Quebec City, QC
1989 *Holly King*, Galerie Dazibao, Montreal, QC
1988 *The Realms of Night*, Galerie d'art de l'Université de Sherbrooke, Sherbrooke, QC
1987 *The Realms of Night*, Southern Alberta Art Gallery, Lethbridge, AB
1987 Galerie des arts visuels, Laval University, Quebec City, QC
1987 Stride Gallery, Calgary, AB
1986 *The River of Hades*, John A. Schweitzer Gallery, Montreal, QC
1985 *The Waters*, Galerie Dazibao, Montreal, QC
1985 *Holly King*, Galerie Articule, Quebec City, QC
1981 *Holly King*, Galerie Articule, Quebec City, QC
1980 *Holly King*, La chambre blanche, Quebec City, QC
1979 *Holly King*, La chambre blanche, Quebec City, QC

GROUP EXHIBITIONS

2016 *Must Art be Appealing?* Art Souterrain, Montreal, QC
2015 *Masterworks Now*, Beaverbrook Art Gallery, Fredericton, NB
2015 *Landscape x 7*, Newzones Gallery, Calgary, AB
2015 *Correspondances*, Musée du Bas-St-Laurent, Rivière-du-Loup, QC
2014 *Montréal Créative*, ARTV Studio, Place des Arts, Montreal, QC
2013 *Objects May Be Closer Than They Appear*, The Robert McLaughlin Gallery, Oshawa, ON
2011 *The Photography of Holly King, Dyan Marie and Diana Thorneycroft*, Glenbow Museum, Calgary, AB
2011 *The Last Frontier*, Art Gallery of Nova Scotia, Halifax, NS
2010 *The Earth Is Blue Like an Orange*, Montreal Museum of Fine Arts, Montreal, QC

2010 *Léclatement des frontières: 1960–2000*, Musée national des beaux-arts du Québec, QC
2009 *Le salon du printemps*, Musée des beaux-arts de Sherbrooke, Sherbrooke, QC
2009 *Into the Wild*, Art Gallery of Nova Scotia, Yarmouth, NS
2008 *Eastern Township Artists*, Galerie Arts Sutton, Sutton, QC
2008 *La Galerie d'art Stewart Hall*, Pointe-Claire, QC
2008 *Graphzines et autres publications d'artistes*, La Grande Bibliothèque, Montreal, QC
2008 *The Big Gift and Through the Looking Glass*, Glenbow Museum, Calgary, AB
2008 *Abracadabra*, Edward Day Gallery, Toronto, ON
2007 *Correspondence*, St. Thomas Elgin Art Centre, St. Thomas, ON
2006 *Art Fiction*, Art Mûr, Montreal, QC
2006 *The Perm Show*, Museum of Contemporary Canadian Art, Toronto, ON
2006 *Illumination Escapade*, Foreman Art Gallery, Bishop's University, Lennoxville, QC
2005 *Variations on the Picturesque*, Kitchener-Waterloo Art Gallery, Kitchener, ON
2005 *Le paysage invisible*, Galerie d'art de l'Université de Sherbrooke, Sherbrooke, QC
2005 *National Gallery of Canada*, Ottawa, ON
2005 *Esplanade Art Gallery*, Medicine Hat, AB
2004 *Gallery Artists*, Esthésio art contemporain, Quebec City, QC
2004 *Signatures photographiques*, Maison des arts de Laval, QC
2004 *Small Surprises*, Verge Gallery, Vancouver, BC
2003 *L'école des femmes*, Musée de Joliette, QC
2003 *Air, Clouds, Trees, Moon and Uncertain Light*, Open Space Gallery, Victoria, BC
2002 *Photoworks from MOCCA* (Toronto), Art Gallery of Windsor, ON
2002 *Cool Stuff*, Leo Kamen Gallery, Toronto, ON
2001 *Le cadre*, la scène, et le site, El centro de la imagen, Mexico City, Mexico
2001 *Hitchcock and Art: Fatal Coincidences*, Centre Georges Pompidou, Paris, France
2001 *Photosynkria*, Macedonian Museum of Contemporary Art, Thessaloniki, Greece
2001 *Gallery Artist's*, Trépanier-Baer Gallery, Calgary, AB
2000 *Le cadre, la scène, et le site*, Occurrence Espace d'art et d'essai contemporains, Montreal, QC
2000 *Hitchcock and Art: Fatal Coincidences*, Montreal Museum of Fine Arts, Montreal, QC
2000 *Architexture*, Archive Gallery, Toronto, ON
1999 *Redefining the Still Life: Selections from the Permanent Collection*, Leonard & Bina Ellen Art Gallery, Montreal, QC
1998 *True North: Contemporary Canadian Landscape*, Kaoshsiung Museum of Fine Arts, Taiwan
1998 *Passages(s)*, Centre international d'art contemporain, Montreal, QC
1998 *Temps composés*, Musée de Joliette, Joliette, QC
1997 *Fifth Anniversary Exhibition*, Leonard & Bina Ellen Art Gallery, Concordia University, Montreal, QC
1995 *Staging: The Prefabricated Image/L'image préfabriquée*, Saidye Bronfman Centre, Montreal, QC
1995 Herron Gallery, Indiana University, IN
1995 California State College, San Bernardino, CA
1994 *Hidden Values*, Musée d'art contemporain de Montréal, Montreal, QC
1994 *La performance au Quebec/Tour d'horizon*, Université Laval, Quebec City, QC
1993 *De la perspective…dans l'art contemporain*, Centre d'exposition du Vieux Palais, St.Jerôme, QC
1993 *Bestiaire*, Parachute, Montreal, QC
1993 *Reflecting Paradise*, Expo 1993, Taejon, Korea
1992 *Beau*, Canadian Museum of Contemporary Photography, Ottawa, ON
1992 *Diagonales*, Centre International Art Contemporain, Les Cents Jours, Montreal, QC
1992 *Gallery Artists*, Galerie Brenda Wallace, Montreal, QC

1992 *Dialogues*, Centre international d'art contemporain de Montréal, Montreal, QC
1991 *Festival des films de femmes*, Cinémathèque québécoise, Montreal, QC
1990 *Recent Acquisitions*, Montreal Museum of Fine Arts, Montreal, QC
1990 *Lointain de l'imaginaire*, Galerie Latitude, Nice, France
1990 *Constructed Spaces*, Photographic Resource Centre, Boston, MA
1990 *Expressions Plurielles*, Musée du Québec, Quebec City, QC
1989 *Art Jonction Internationale*, Galerie Latitude, Nice, France
1989 *La réalité reconstruite*, Université de Montréal Galerie d'art, Montreal, QC
1989 *Babel—Tentative d'une orientation*, Basel International Fair, Basel, Switzerland
1988 *Québec 88*, Art Gallery of Ontario, Toronto, ON
1988 *Paysages*, Contemporary Art Gallery, Vancouver, BC
1988 *Paysages*, Centre Eye, Calgary, AB
1988 *Paysages*, YYZ, Toronto, ON
1987 *10th Anniversary Exhibition*, La Chambre Blanche, Quebec City, QC
1987 *Summer at Costin & Klintworth Gallery*, Costin & Klintworth Gallery, Toronto, ON
1986 *Lumières-Perception/Projection*, Les Cents jours d'art contemporain de Montréal, QC
1986 *La magie de l'image*, Musée d'art contemporain de Montréal, Montreal, QC
1986 *La magie de l'image*, Walter Phillips Gallery, Banff, AB
1986 *La magie de l'image*, Musée du Bas-St-Laurent, Rivière-du-Loup, QC
1985 *Narrativité/Perfomativité*, Optica Gallery, international exhibition
1985 *Recent Acquistions*, Musée du Québec, Quebec City, QC
1984 *Situational Photography*, San Diego State University Art Gallery, San Diego, CA
1984 Herron Gallery, Indiana University, IN
1984 California State College, San Bernardino, CA
1984 *Fragments: La photographie actuelle au Québec*, Centre VU, Quebec City, QC
1984 *New Image Contemporary Quebec Photography*, 49th Parallel Gallery, New York, NY
1983 *Recent Acquisitions*, Musée du Québec, Quebec City, QC
1983 *Quebec Photography Invitational*, Saidye Bronfman Centre, Montreal, QC
1983 Department of External Affairs, Spain, France, Romania, England, India, Brazil and other countries

PERFORMANCES

1981 *Two Characters II*, Grange Arts and Performance, Toronto, ON
1980 *Two Characters*, Véhicule Gallery, Montreal, QC
1980 *Two Characters*, La chambre blanche, Quebec City, QC
1980 *Two Characters*, International Sculpture Festival, Chicoutimi, QC
1979 *Dialogue vers un obscurcissement*, with Cyril Reade, Musée d'art contemporain de Montréal, QC
1979 *Photo-réalisme, La chambre blanche*, Festival l'objet fugitif, Quebec City, QC
1979 *Behind the Mask I Am Invisible*, La chambre blanche, Quebec City, QC
1978 *Variation sur blanche et sienne*, with Cyril Reade, La chambre blanche, Quebec City, QC
1978 *Variation sur blanche et sienne II*, with Cyril Reade, La chambre blanche, Quebec City, QC

COLLECTIONS

Art Gallery of Nova Scotia, Halifax, NS, Art Gallery of Ontario, Toronto, ON, Canada Council Art Bank, Ottawa, ON, Department of External Affairs, Ottawa, ON, Glenbow Museum, Calgary, AB, Hydro Québec, Leonard & Bina Ellen Art Gallery, Montreal, QC, Montreal Museum of Fine Arts, Montreal, QC, Musée d'art contemporain de Montréal, Montreal, QC, Musée de Joliette, Joliette, QC, Musée du Bas-St-Laurent, Rivière du Loup, QC, Musée national des beaux-arts du Québec, QC, Museum of Contemporary Canadian Art, Toronto, ON, National Gallery of Canada, Ottawa, ON, Peel Art Gallery, Museum and Archives, Brampton, ON, The Robert McLaughlin Gallery, Oshawa, ON

University of Lethbridge Art Gallery, Lethbridge AB, Air Canada, Culinar, Guaranty Trust, London Life, McCarthy-Tetrault, Nissan, Pepsi, Steelcase, Sunlife, Private collections in Canada, the United States, France and Switzerland

PUBLIC ART COMMISSIONS

2009	École primaire J. A. Bélanger, St-Jean-sur-Richelieu, QC
2008	Séminaire de Sherbrooke, Sherbrooke, QC
2007	CHSLD de l'Amiante, Thetford QC
2007	L'édifice l'Albert Dumouchel, Ahuntsic, QC
2006	École St. Pie, Centre Culturel (Sacré-Coeur), St. Pie, QC
2005	Concordia University, Fine Art and Computer Science, Montreal, QC
2004	École primaire St-Jean-sur-Richelieu, St-Jean-sur-Richelieu, QC

BIBLIOGRAPHY: BOOKS AND CATALOGUES

Linda Jansma and Francine Paul. *Edging Towards the Mysterious*. Oshawa: The Robert McLaughlin Gallery, 2016.

David Diviney. *The Last Frontier*. Halifax: Art Gallery of Nova Scotia, 2010.

L'éclatement des frontières: 1965–2000 de la collection permanante. Quebec: Musée national des beaux-arts du Québec, 2010.

Esther Trépanier. *Femmes Artistes du XXiéme siècle au Québec*. Quebec: Musée national des beaux-arts du Québec, 2010.

Sylvain Campeau. *Oikios: Habitable Places*. Montreal: SBC Galerie d'art contemporain, 2008.

Sylvie Alix. *Graphzines et autres publications d'artistes*. Montreal: Bibliothèque et Archives nationales du Québec, 2007.

Johanne Brouillet. *Holly King Twisted Roots*. Sherbrooke: Galerie d'art de l'Université de Sherbrooke, 2006.

Meridith Carruthers. *Illumination Escapade*. Lennoxville: Bishop's University Foreman Art Gallery, 2006.

Johanne Brouillette. *Twisted Roots*. Sherbrooke: Galerie d'art de l'Université de Sherbrooke, 2006.

Karen Love and Karen Henry. *Variations on the Picturesque*. Kitchener: Kitchener-Waterloo Art Gallery, 2006.

Martha Langford. *Image and Imagination*. Montreal: McGill-Queen's University Press, 2005.

Penny Cousineau-Levine. *Faking Death*. Montreal: McGill-Queen's University Press, 2003.

A Vindication of Tlon: Photography and the Fantastic. Thessaloniki, Greece: Thessaloniki Museum of Photography, 2001.

Guy Cogeval, et al. *Hitchcock and Art: Fatal Coincidences*. Montreal: Montreal Museum of Fine Arts, 2000.

Le cadre, le site, la scène. Montreal: Galerie Occurance, 2000.

John K. Grande. *Holly King. Mirage*. Saint-Hyacinthe: Expression Centre d'exposition de Saint-Hyacinthe, 2000.

Passages. Montreal: Centre internationale d'art contemporain, 1998.

Pierre Dessureault. *Landscapes of the Imagination*. Ottawa: Canadian Museum of Contemporary Photography, 1998.

Gary Michael Dault. "Holly King." *CV Photo 44* (fall 1998).

Sylvain Campeau and Melanie Blais. "Holly King." *PhotoVision* (Barcelona) 27: 1995

Sylvain Campeau. *Chambres obscures-photographie installation*. Laval: Éditions Trois, 1995.

Staging. Montreal: Saidye Bronfman Centre, 1995.

Pierre Boogaert, et al. *De la perspective dans l'art contemporain*. St-Jerome, QC: Centre du Vieux Palais, 1993.
Sylvain Campeau. *Plaques sensibles*. Montreal: Herbes Rouges, 1992.
Martha Langford. *BEAU: A Reflection on the Nature of Beauty in Photography*. Ottawa: Canadian Museum of Contemporary Photography/ National Gallery of Canada, 1992.
Diagonales: Montreal, 10 monographies. Montreal: Parachute, 1992.
Clive Robertson. *Performance in Canada 1970–1990*. Quebec City: Éditions intervention, 1991.
La réalité reconstruite. Montreal: Le Vidéographe, Université de Montréal, 1989.
Serge Bérard. *Paysages*. Montreal: Galerie Dazibao, 1987.
Don Corman. *Holly King: Realms of Night*. Lethbridge and Calgary: Southern Alberta Art Gallery and Stride Gallery, 1987.
Lumières: Perceptions, Projections. Montreal: Centre internationale d'art contemporain, 1986.
Richard Baillargeon. *Fragments: La photographie actuelle au Québec*. Quebec City: Centre VU, 1985.
Chantal Boulanger. *Scenarios*. Montreal: Galerie Chantal Boulanger, 1985.
Paulette Gagnon. *La magie de l'image*. Montreal: Musée d'art contemporain de Montréal, 1984.
Catherine Lutz-Walthard. *Babel 2. Bauetappe*. Basel, Switzerland: Basel Art Fair, 1984.
Situational Photography. San Diego: University Art Gallery, San Diego State University, 1984.
Quebec Photography Invitational. Montreal: Saidye Bronfman Centre, 1983.
Robert Stacey, Barbara Volkmann and Rose-France Raddatz, eds. *OKanada*. Berlin: Akademie der Künste, 1982.
Performances: Festival l'objet fugitif. Quebec City: La chambre blanche, 1980.

SELECTED BIBLIOGRAPHY: REVIEWS

Jérôme Delgado. "Paysages Personnels et cartographies imaginaires." *Le Devoir*, February 16, 2013.
François Escalmel. "Holly King: Le Vertige à distance." *Vie des Arts*, February 8, 2013 (web).
John Pohl. "Holly King." *The Gazette*, January 19, 2013.
Will Burgess. "Where the Wild Things Are." *McGill Tribune*, January 14, 2013.
Gary Michael Dault. "Eerie Photographs Play Like Drawings." *The Globe and Mail*, February 27, 2010.
Jérôme Delgado. "Et après la mi-carrière?" *Le Devoir*, Decembre 6, 2009.
Anna Carlevaris. "Mois de la Photo #70." *CV Photo* (2005).
"Holly King, Art Mûr." *Parachute* (Spring 2005).
Gary Michael Dault. "Holly King." *The Globe and Mail*, May 30, 2001.
Lyne Crevier. "Holly King." *Vie des Arts* (fall 2001).
Georges Bogardi. "Holly King." *Canadian Art* (spring 2000).
Ray Conologue. "A Postmodern Romantic." *The Globe and Mail*, March 18, 2000.
Gillian MacKay. "Gallery Going." *The Globe and Mail*, March 11, 2000.
"Primer: The New Document." *Canadian Art* (summer 2000).
Blake Gopnik. "Romantic Fake Landscapes Implicate Viewer in Illusion." *The Globe and Mail*, November, 1999.
Bernard Lamarche. "L'éloge de l'ombre." *Le Devoir*, October 10, 1999.
Henry Lehmann. "Eerie Landscapes Conjure Fantasies." *The Gazette*, October 2, 1999.
Julia Apostle. "Holly King blurs the lines of reality." *McGill Daily*, September 1999.
Gary Michael Dault. "Loss Leaders." *Canadian Art* (summer 1999).
Gary Michael Dault. "Holly King." *CV Photo* (winter 1999).
Michael Molter. "Holly King: Landscapes of the Imagination." *Vie des Arts* (fall 1998).
Francine Dagenais. "Holly King." *Parachute 92* (fall 1998).
Gary Michael Dault. "Holly King." *Canadian Art* (summer 1996), "50th Anniversary Project," *Parachute*
Johanne Lamoureux. "Bestiaire." Parachute 73 (1994).
John Bentley Mays. "Hidden Value." *The Globe and Mail*, November 26, 1994.

Bernard Lamarche. "La nuit, théatre et arts visuels songent ensembles." *Le Devoir*, July 23, 1994.
Francois Escamel. "Holly King: Lieux Proches et Lointoins." *Vie des Arts* (winter 1994).
M. E. Vetrocq. "Report from Montreal." *Art in America* (November 1991).
Marie-Michèle Cron. "Plaidoyers pour la vie humaine." *Le Devoir*, May 18, 1991.
Marie-Michèle Cron. "Leçon d'observation sur l'univers." *Le Devoir*, May 18, 1991.
Jennifer Fischer. "Holly King." *Parachute 57* (1990).
"Paysages." Canadian Art (winter 1989).
Francine Dagenais. "Focus: Holly King." *Canadian Art* (December 1989).
John Bentley Mays. "Paysages." *The Globe and Mail*, July 9, 1988.
Arni Runar Haraldsson. "Paysages." *C Magazine*, June 1988.
René Payant. "Holly King." *Parachute 24* (1987).
Lesley Johnstone. "Paysages." *Vanguard* (November 1987).
Gilles Daigneault. "Paysages." *Le Devoir*, May 1987.
Isabelle Lelarge. "Holly King." *Vie des Arts* (March 1987).
Nancy Tousley. "Holly King." *Calgary Herald*, February 12, 1987.
Michel Denée. "Paysages." *Vie des Arts* (winter 1987).
Cyril Reade. "Holly King." *Parachute 45* (1986).
David Bate. "La magie de l'image." *Parachute 45* (1986).
Charles Hagan. "Lumières: Perception/projection." *Artforum* (November 1986).
P. Evans-Clark. "Lumières: Perception/projection." *Art Presse* (November 1986).
Gilles Daigneault. "Holly King." *Le Devoir*, October 18, 1986.
Cheryl Simon. "Holly King." *Vanguard* (April 1985).
Gilles Daigneault. "Holly King." *Le Devoir*, February 16, 1985.
Gilles Daigneault. "Narrativité/Performativité." *Le Devoir*, January 12, 1985.
Paul Tiffet. "Holly King." *Parachute 36* (1984).
Paul Tiffet. "Aspects of Theatre and Artifice." *Parachute 36* (1984).
David Lewison. "Photos Show Contrast in Art." *San Diego Union*, March 22, 1984.
Chantal Boulanger. "Art as Ellipse." *Vanguard* (February 1984).
Gilles Daigenault. "Fictions et réalités." *Le Devoir*, January 22, 1983.
Jean Tourangeau. "Québec: Déroutés." *Vie des Arts 12* (1981).

BIOGRAPHIES

Francine Paul

Historienne de l'art, Francine Paul travaille dans le domaine des arts visuels depuis plus d'une trentaine d'années. Diplômée en science politique et en études des arts de l'UQAM, ses recherches personnelles ancrées théoriquement dans la sémiologie du langage visuel, portent principalement, depuis ses études doctorales, sur les rencontres entre les arts visuels, le paysage et la nature dans la création contemporaine. Commissaire d'expositions, critique d'art contemporain et membre de nombreux jurys, elle fut également chargée de cours en histoire de l'art. Elle occupa de 1989 à 2000 le poste de conservatrice de la Collection d'œuvres d'art de la Banque nationale du Canada. De 2000 à 2014, à titre de chargée de projet au ministère de la Culture et des Communications du gouvernement du Québec, elle a coordonné quelques 300 projets d'intégration d'œuvres d'art à l'architecture et à l'environnement. Depuis 2015, elle est la directrice artistique invitée de la revue Le Sabord.

Linda Jansma

Linda Jansma est commissaire à la Robert McLaughlin Gallery depuis 1994 et a été promue au poste de commissaire-en-chef en 2012. Avant de rejoindre la RMG, Jansma a travaillé dans une galerie privée et fut commissaire pour un collectionneur de Toronto. Elle est titulaire d'un baccalauréat spécialisé de l'université Queen's et d'une maîtrise de l'université d'East Anglia, tous deux en Histoire de l'art. Elle a assuré le commissariat de maintes expositions ayant voyagé au niveau national et international, dont *The Collaborationists: Jennifer Marman and Daniel Borins, Shelagh Keeley, Gordon Monahan: Seeing Sound; Simone Jones: All That Is Solid; Walter Tandy Murch: The Spirit of Things et Kazuo Nakamura: The Nature of Things*. Elle a agi en tant que co-commissaire de l'exposition Jock Macdonald: Evolving Form, organisée en collaboration avec la Vancouver Art Gallery et l'Art Gallery of Greater Victoria en 2014-2015. Jansma a signé plusieurs textes pour des catalogues portant sur de l'art historique et contemporain. Elle préside le comité d'art et d'histoire de la ville d'Oshawa, siège sur le comité consultatif du programme de beaux-arts du Durham College et est membre du comité consultatif en art public de la ville d'Oshawa.

BIOGRAPHIES

Francine Paul

As an Art Historian, Francine Paul has been actively involved in the art world for over thirty years. With a Political Science and Art Studies' degree from UQAM, she based her research on theories related to the semiology of visual language. Following her doctoral studies, she began to concentrate more specifically on the intersection of visual arts, landscape and nature in contemporary art productions. She worked as a curator and an art critic, has sat on numerous juries, and was also an Art History class lecturer. She worked as the curator of the National Bank of Canada's art collection between 1989 and 2000. Between 2000 and 2014, she coordinated over 300 projects under Quebec's Program of Art Integration within the Architecture, better known as the "1%". Since 2015, she has been Le Sabord's guest artistic director.

Linda Jansma

Linda Jansma has been the Curator of The Robert McLaughlin Gallery since 1994 and was promoted to Senior Curator in 2012. Prior to the RMG, Jansma worked in a commercial gallery and as Curator for a Toronto-based collector. She completed an Honours BA at Queen's University and a MA at the University of East Anglia, both in art history. She has curated and produced numerous exhibitions that have travelled nationally including *The Collaborationists: Jennifer Marman and Daniel Borins, Shelagh Keeley, Gordon Monahan: Seeing Sound; Simone Jones: All That Is Solid; Walter Tandy Murch: The Spirit of Things and Kazuo Nakamura: The Nature of Things*. She co-curated the 2014-15 exhibition *Jock Macdonald: Evolving Form* which was organized in collaboration with the Vancouver Art Gallery and Art Gallery of Greater Victoria. Jansma has written essays for catalogues dealing with both historical and contemporary art. She is the Chair of the City of Oshawa's Art and History Committee, as well as the Chair of the Advisory committee of Durham College's Fine Art programme and is a member of the City of Oshawa's Public Art Advisory Committee.

REMERCIEMENTS | ACKNOWLEDGEMENTS

J'aimerais remercier Linda Jansma d'avoir proposé ce projet d'exposition et d'y avoir travaillé avec autant d'enthousiasme. Aussi, de la galerie Art Mûr, j'aimerais remercier Rhéal Lanthier et François St-Jacques pour leur soutien au fil des ans ainsi que Mike Patten pour son dévouement dans la production d'un si beau catalogue. Ce fut un plaisir de travailler avec Francine Paul sur son texte éclairant, et avec Linda Jansma dont le texte définit avec passion mes récents travaux. Je remercie également Don, Clea et Devon Corman d'être auprès de moi avec tout leur amour, affection et sagesse. Finalement, un merci tout spécial à l'unité de gestion de la douleur Alan-Edwards de l'université McGill à Montréal de m'avoir redonné vie.

Je remercie aussi la Robert McLaughlin Gallery, Thames Art Gallery, le Musée des beaux-arts de Sherbooke, Art Mûr, le Musée du Bas-Saint-Laurent, le Conseil des arts du Canada, le Conseil des arts de l'Ontario, le Ministère de la Culture et des Communications du Québec, et la Société de développement des entreprises culturelles du Québec pour leur appui financier.

Holly King

I would like to thank Linda Jansma for initiating this exhibition and working toward it with such enthusiasm. Also, from Art Mûr gallery, I wish to thank directors Rhéal Lanthier and François St-Jacques for their many years of support, and Mike Patten for his dedicated work in producing such a beautiful catalogue. It was a pleasure to work with Francine Paul on her illuminating text, and with Linda Jansma, whose passionate text defines my recent work. Many thanks, as well, to Don, Clea and Devon Corman for being there with much love, affection and wisdom. Finally, special thanks go to the Alan Edwards Pain Management Unit, at McGill University in Montreal, for giving me my life back.

I would also like to thank the Robert McLaughlin Gallery, Thames Art Gallery, Musée des beaux-arts de Sherbooke, Art Mûr, and the Musée du Bas-Saint-Laurent as well as the Canada Council for the Arts, the Ontario Arts Council, the Ministère de la Culture et des Communications du Québec, and la Société de développement des entreprises culturelles du Québec for their financial support.

Holly King

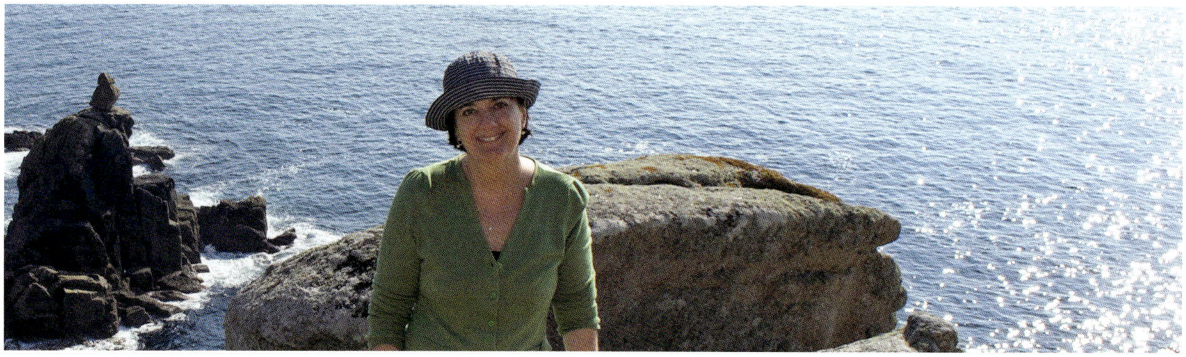

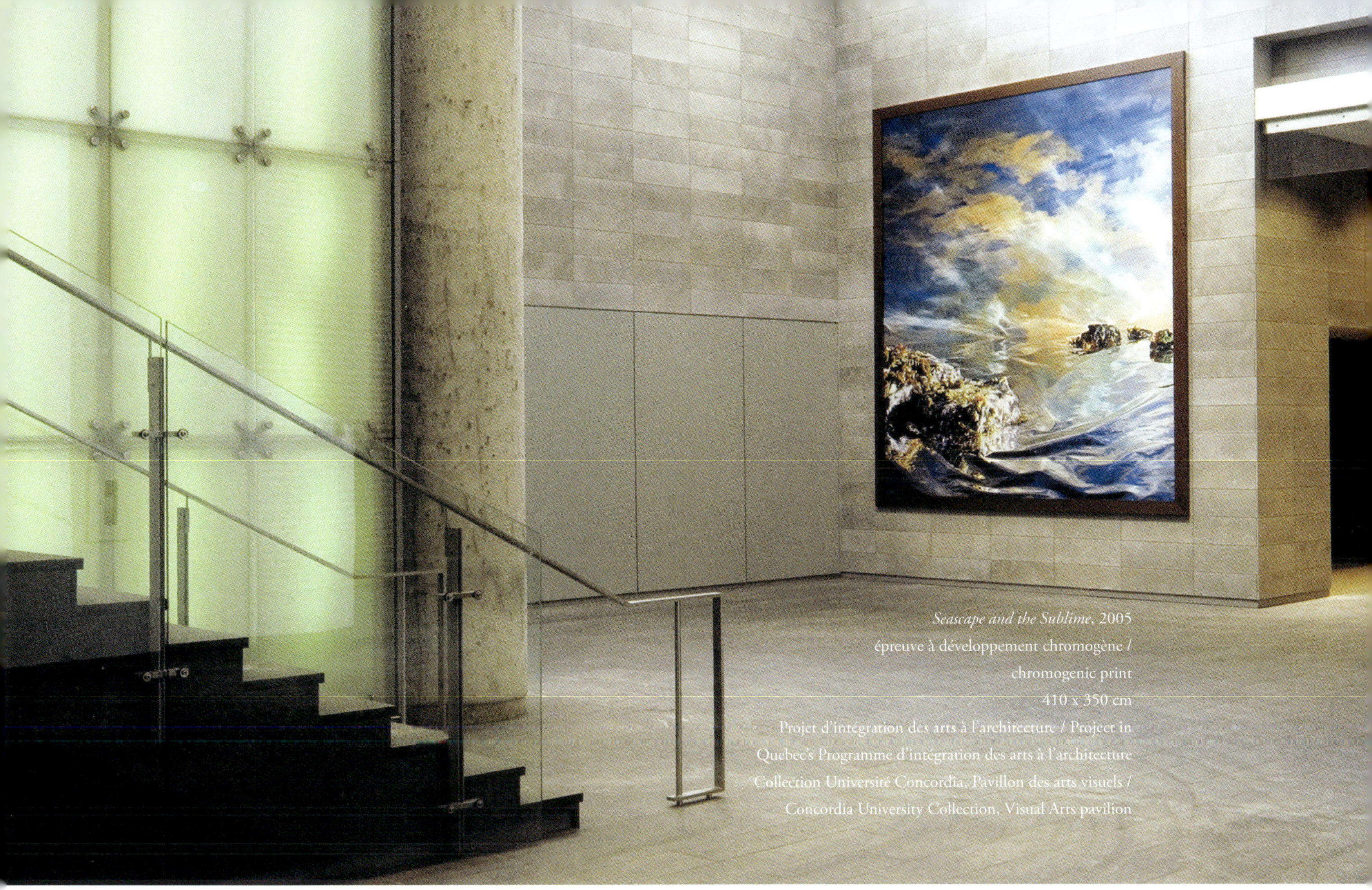

Seascape and the Sublime, 2005
épreuve à développement chromogène / chromogenic print
410 x 350 cm
Projet d'intégration des arts à l'architecture / Project in Quebec's Programme d'intégration des arts à l'architecture
Collection Université Concordia, Pavillon des arts visuels / Concordia University Collection, Visual Arts pavilion

SODEC Québec

Conseil des Arts du Canada
Canada Council for the Arts

Conseil des arts et des lettres Québec

CUPFA

ONTARIO ARTS COUNCIL
CONSEIL DES ARTS DE L'ONTARIO
an Ontario government agency
un organisme du gouvernement de l'Ontario

The Robert McLaughlin Gallery

thamesartgallery

MUSÉE DES BEAUX-ARTS DE SHERBROOKE

Art Mûr

MUSÉE DU BAS-SAINT-LAURENT